Self-Defense

STEPS TO SURVIVAL

Katy Mattingly

Human Kinetics

Library of Congress Cataloging-in-Publication Data

Mattingly, Katy.
  Self-defense : steps to survival / Katy Mattingly.
      p.   cm.
  Includes bibliographical references.
  ISBN-13: 978-0-7360-6689-1 (soft cover)
  ISBN-10: 0-7360-6689-6 (soft cover)
  1. Self-defense.   2. Hand-to-hand fighting.   3. Crime prevention.   4. Survival skills.
I. Title.
  GV1111.M383   2007
  613.6'6--dc22   2007016326

ISBN-10: 0-7360-6689-6
ISBN-13: 978-0-7360-6689-1

Copyright © 2007 by Human Kinetics, Inc.

The Web addresses cited in this text were current as of June 2007, unless otherwise noted.

Acquisitions Editor: Jana Hunter; **Developmental Editor:** Cynthia McEntire; **Assistant Editor:** Scott Hawkins; **Copyeditor:** Susan Campanini; **Proofreader:** Jim Burns; **Graphic Designer:** Nancy Rasmus; **Graphic Artist:** Sandra Meier; **Cover Designer:** Keith Blomberg; **Photographer (cover):** Human Kinetics; **Photographer (interior):** Neil Bernstein; **Photo Asset Manager:** Laura Fitch; **Visual Production Assistant:** Joyce Brumfield; **Photo Office Assistant:** Jason Allen; **Printer:** Versa Press

Human Kinetics books are available at special discounts for bulk purchase. Special editions or book excerpts can also be created to specification. For details, contact the Special Sales Manager at Human Kinetics.

Printed in the United States of America

10   9   8   7   6   5   4   3   2   1

Human Kinetics
Web site: www.HumanKinetics.com

United States: Human Kinetics
P.O. Box 5076, Champaign, IL 61825-5076
800-747-4457
e-mail: humank@hkusa.com

Canada: Human Kinetics
475 Devonshire Road Unit 100, Windsor, ON N8Y 2L5
800-465-7301 (in Canada only)
e-mail: orders@hkcanada.com

Europe: Human Kinetics
107 Bradford Road, Stanningley, Leeds LS28 6AT, United Kingdom
+44 (0) 113 255 5665
e-mail: hk@hkeurope.com

Australia: Human Kinetics
57A Price Avenue, Lower Mitcham, South Australia 5062
08 8372 0999
e-mail: info@hkaustralia.com

New Zealand: Human Kinetics
Division of Sports Distributors NZ Ltd.
P.O. Box 300 226 Albany, North Shore City, Auckland
0064 9 448 1207
e-mail: info@humankinetics.co.nz

This book is dedicated to everyone who was ever violated and *didn't* fight back—because you didn't know how, you were scared, you feared you'd be hurt worse, or you thought it was your fault. It wasn't your fault. It's important that you survived. And it's safe to learn how to resist now.

◧ Contents

◨ Climbing the Steps to Survival

In almost every self-defense course I've taught, my students have confessed to me at some point that they were surprised by the content of the program. Many come to a study of self-defense looking for a couple of "moves" and maybe a handout of safety tips. Instead, they find the topic much richer and far-reaching than initially expected! The truth is, if someone could guarantee you personal safety by spending a half hour showing you how to punch, we would all have been safe a long time ago. Instead, *Self-Defense: Steps to Survival* promises you much more than advice and tips. You now have the chance to follow a simple, progressive, professional course in self-defense and personal safety, one that will help you become safer, stronger, and more secure in the knowledge that you can protect yourself and your family.

Throughout the book, you will read the stories of others who have survived violence and learned to defend themselves. Unless otherwise noted, the student voices and success stories in this book are composites based on the actual experiences of my students and others from around the world. I have removed or changed personally identifying characteristics and sometimes other details such as location or context. Some stories mesh elements from several survivors I've worked with. The bravery, creativity, and commitment of the women and men who survived remain intact and all their own.

I look forward to the day when surviving a sexual assault or escaping an abusive relationship carries no more stigma than surviving a car accident. However you survived, you did the right thing. We're so glad you made it! My thanks to all the brave women and men who chose to share their stories with me and with their classmates.

Four basic obstacles prevent people from defending themselves. Care to guess what they might be? Being small isn't one of them—the average 8-year-old is quite capable of breaking an attacker's kneecap. Being female isn't either—women can and do defend themselves every day, even against much taller and heavier perpetrators. Nor do disability, previous victimization, age, or degree of fitness prevent you from effectively using self-defense techniques. The four obstacles are 1) never having been taught, 2) lack of confidence, 3) overconfidence, and 4) believing myths about violence and safety. Sometimes all four obstacles can be present in one student!

Despite an incredibly high rate of violent victimizations in the world, most people have never received training of any kind in self-defense. Just because you're female doesn't mean that you've been given access to rape prevention information. Just because you're male doesn't mean that you were born knowing how to throw or dodge a punch! In fact, lack of training may describe your situation even if you've studied martial arts or taken kickboxing at the YMCA. Your teachers may have never addressed the real-life, "off the mat" scenarios that most of us fear. The good news is that self-defense can be studied, practiced, and learned. Professionals around the world have studied actual perpetrators, survivors, and victims; you can learn what they know.

The second obstacle is lack of confidence. A lot of cultural messages out there are simply lies: "*Women could never defend themselves against men*"; "*There's nothing you can do if he has a gun.*" The weight of these false messages encourages many to give up before they've even started. Of course, there are no guarantees that you will be safe in every situation or that a particular strategy will work against a particular perpetrator. But choosing not to study self-defense out of fear of the unknown only robs you of the possibility of safety. Each of us has our own ability to defend ourselves, and training will improve that ability.

The third obstacle to training is overconfidence. Some of my students have been getting by for years on a combination of bravado and naïveté. Maybe you've been so confident that you never bothered to train at all, thinking "*Rape would never happen to someone like me*" or "*I'm sure I could handle somebody if I really had to, I used to wrestle with my brothers.*" The truth is that none of us are impervious to violence. It's a great asset to feel strong and proud, but if you haven't practiced shouting "Don't touch me!" in a crowded public place or used your physical skills even when you're scared or surprised, how do you know what you're capable of? By following the steps to survival, you'll have the benefit of professional training from an instructor who specializes in personal safety.

The final obstacle to being able to defend ourselves is being taught wrong information. All of us have internalized some false information about who to fear, where we're at risk, what successful self-defense looks like, and what works and what doesn't. For example, most women I meet have been told to never walk alone at night and, if they do, to talk on their cell phones. Although I'm sure the advice was well intentioned, talking on your phone when you're feeling threatened or unsure is one of the *least* helpful things you can do. It's a far better idea to walk confidently at night, looking around, hands free, and fully focused on what's in front of you. Still this myth lives on.

Whether one or more of the four common obstacles show up in your own life or not, whether you've had little to no training or are physically skilled, whether you're confident or doubtful about your abilities, whether you've been given accurate information about assault or been exposed to a lot of myths, this book has something to offer you.

Start at the beginning. You will begin with the most basic skills and progressively build to more difficult techniques and strategies. Allow yourself to master each chapter before stepping up to the next one. Advance at your own pace.

Follow the same sequence in each step:

1. Read the explanation of what the step covers. One step may cover a physical skill, another a psychological technique, another a strategy for facing one type of attacker. Many steps will combine elements of all of these. Study the featured myth and fact for each step. Memorizing the myths and facts about assault, as well as writing about them and discussing them, will assist you in your learning process, because you will undo any incorrect information you've already internalized about self-defense.

2. Follow the photos. The photos will show you precisely how to position your body to perform each skill correctly. Some photos also include context information about different attack and defense scenarios. For example, you'll be invited to practice using some techniques in seated, standing, and lying-down positions.

3. Review the missteps, which note common errors and corrections.

4. Read the instructions and *perform* the drills. Don't just think about them! Drills appear near the skill instruction so that you can easily refer to the instructions if you have trouble.

5. If you so choose, have a qualified observer, friend, or study partner evaluate your basic skills after each drill. She or he can use the missteps and success checks to evaluate your execution. A friend can help you see details of positioning, encourage you if you get discouraged, and point out your successes—all essential supports for learning a new skill.

The time to begin is now. You can be more motivated to protect yourself than any attacker can be motivated to harm you. And motivation is more than half the battle.

At the end of your study, you will be safer. You're going to have greater confidence, a deepened commitment to your own safety, and a sense of pride that you're doing what you need to do to take care of yourself. Having the physical skills necessary to stop someone from hurting you may result in a ripple effect throughout your life. You can become free to choose different relationships, stand up for yourself at work, and recover on a deeper level from past experiences of violence.

With *Self-Defense: Steps to Survival*, you can be safer, right now. Let's get started!

◨ Acknowledgments

A great number of people have made this book possible. First and foremost, thank you to all of the members of the IMPACT style self-defense community—instructors, staff, donors, and graduate assistants. Thank you for bringing joy and creativity to a job that not many people could do. It was only in a community of men and women who were passionate about ending violence that I was able to realize my own strength. My special thanks to Hailey and Cori, who nurtured my hope that I too could become an instructor.

I also warmly thank Joan Nelson, who published the first self-defense book for Human Kinetics, and everyone who came before us—those who started the first shelters for battered women, support groups for survivors of sexual assault, and martial arts schools. Thank you to all those who dared to suggest that we *could* do something to stop violence.

Finally, thank you from the bottom of my heart to my students. By sharing your stories of survival and your immense courage, you remind me every day that we are worth fighting for. Together we are building a safer world, one person at a time.

◨ Self-Defense Today

In all of my years of teaching, I have been repeatedly amazed by the truth that self-defense is both incredibly simple and incredibly difficult to practice. As in any other intensive sport or physical endeavor, it's often the psychological edge that defines a successful performance. Last year, one of my students may have saved her own life with a very simple technique. She was accosted in a parking lot by two young men, one of whom grabbed her by the wrist and began yanking her off balance toward the dark area behind the shopping mall. She swiftly turned toward him, held up her free hand with a flat palm, and yelled as loudly as she could, "Let go of me!" Both men looked startled and ran away. How simple!

But, up until that point, these young men had followed her around a public shopping area for over an hour, assessing her as a target and trying to engage her in conversation. Although she felt threatened, she at first ignored her own sense of unease, didn't ask anyone in the crowded stores for help, and failed to face the men or tell them to stop. She pretended to talk on her phone, smiling uncomfortably while turning her back on them and generally wishing they would go away. Eventually, she told a store employee what was happening. He didn't know how to help her, and she felt disappointed and left the store.

Why was it so hard for her to practice self-defense in the hour leading up to the parking lot assault? Training. Each and every one of us has been trained at some level to distrust our natural instincts. To practice effective self-defense, we must reawaken both the ability to trust our own instincts and the willingness to act on that knowledge.

Most of us, however, would rather not honestly and openly think about the possibility of being the victim of a violent, unprovoked attack, and so we don't, thus missing out on the opportunity to prepare for our own defense. Congratulations! By choosing *Self-Defense: Steps to Survival*, you are courageously refusing to remain in denial. By beginning to read about the reality of violence, you become safer.

Myth   Violent attacks are rare and not a major problem in my community. Violence mostly happens to people who make bad choices. I'm smart enough to avoid it.

Fact   Violence is incredibly common. People of all ages, genders, ethnicities, sexual orientations, and walks of life are victimized, and it's not their fault.

Consider these statistics:

- An American is sexually assaulted every 2.5 minutes (Rape, Abuse, and Incest National Network, no year).
- In 2005, law enforcement agencies throughout the United States reported an increase in the number of most violent crimes: murder, manslaughter, robbery, and aggravated assault (Federal Bureau of Investigation, 2005).
- Every year, 1.2 million women are forcibly raped by their current or former male partners, some more than once (National Organization for Women, no year).

- Males experience higher victimization rates than females for all types of violent crime except rape. According to the FBI Uniform Crime Reports, 78 percent of murder victims were male in 2003 (Federal Bureau of Investigation, 2005). Men were twice as likely as women to be the victim of a carjacking (U.S. Department of Justice, no year).

- In the United States, a woman is beaten every 18 minutes. Domestic violence is the number one cause of injury to women of reproductive age; in fact, 22 to 35 percent of women in an emergency room are there because of injuries sustained in a violent attack by their partner. (United Nations Department of Public Information, no year).

- Children, teens, and young people are especially vulnerable. One study found that 83 percent of sexual assault survivors were under 25 years of age when they were first raped (Tjaden and Thoennes, 1998). In 2003, 12 percent of male students and 6 percent of female students reported experiencing a threat or injury at school (U.S. Department of Justice, no year).

- Although some studies indicate that reported sexual assault declined 64 percent from 1995 to 2004, one in six American women has been the victim of an attempted or completed rape (Rape, Abuse, and Incest National Network, no year).

Furthermore, personal, sexual violence is widely considered to be one of the most underreported crimes. According to the Criminal Victimization survey of 2004 by the U.S. Bureau of Justice Statistics, only 50 percent of all violent crimes are reported (U.S. Department of Justice, 2005). Most experts believe that this percentage is even lower for sexual assault.

Contrary to the myth that violence is rare and avoidable, violence is endemic to our society—street, sexual, domestic violence, entertainment, criminal, and political violence. It affects each and every one of us. Even if you yourself are not a survivor of violent behavior, the truth is that you know someone who is. And many of us make daily choices based on a conscious or unconscious fear of experiencing violence in the future.

Self-Awareness Drill 1. *How Does Violence Affect You?*

Read the examples below. For each example, fill in the blank with an "A" for always, an "F" for frequently, an "S" for sometimes, or an "N" for never.

Do you ever make one of these choices because you are worried about your safety?

___S___ Choose to skip something you want to do to avoid going out alone.

___A___ Leave the house only at certain times of day or if accompanied.

___N___ Get into a fight when challenged, even when you don't want to.

___N___ Consider quitting a job because you're afraid of clients, patients, coworkers, or customers.

___N___ Allow "protectors" to make decisions for you—where to go, whom to see, what to wear.

___S___ Wonder after the fact if you did something risky or unwise through overconfidence.

___S___ Refuse to allow your children to do something that may or may not be safe.

___S___ Avoid certain streets, neighborhoods, cities, or countries that you'd like to visit.

___A___ Turn down jobs for which you'd have to travel, be alone, or work late.

_____ Get angry at loved ones when you fear you can't protect them.

___N___ Get angry at yourself for being afraid.

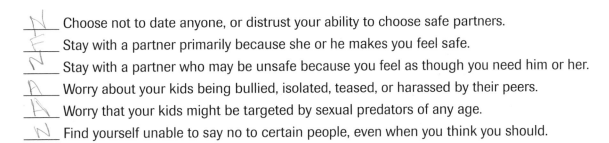

___N___ Choose not to date anyone, or distrust your ability to choose safe partners.

___F___ Stay with a partner primarily because she or he makes you feel safe.

___N___ Stay with a partner who may be unsafe because you feel as though you need him or her.

___A___ Worry about your kids being bullied, isolated, teased, or harassed by their peers.

___A___ Worry that your kids might be targeted by sexual predators of any age.

___N___ Find yourself unable to say no to certain people, even when you think you should.

Success Check

Simply completing this drill is a success. There is no "correct" or optimal number of responses of always, frequently, sometimes, or never. Notice if there are any changes you'd like to make or any answers that you wish were different.

Score Your Success

Complete the drill = 10 points

Complete the drill and discuss it with another person = 20 points

---

When asked how violence affects their choices, many people report that they feel confusion, fear, and ambivalence on a regular basis. At least half of the women I know have told me that they regularly skip activities they love because they're worried that they are not safe. Many people enjoying walking in the woods, exploring a new city, or jogging in the evening, but they don't allow themselves to do it. Or they go anyway, but feel fear and self-doubt the whole time. Some people never go out at night, or can't allow their kids to sleep over at a friend's house.

Some feel controlled by a member of their family, feeling that they can never say no to that person even when they want to. Many women feel unsafe about dating but are unsure how to address the issue without locking the doors and staying home alone.

Although the solution is not always simple, learning effective and realistic self-defense can give you the skills you need to live confidently in the world, neither avoiding life nor assuming unnecessary risks. You're not alone. And you do not have to continue to live a life ruled by fear.

REAL SKILLS FOR REAL PEOPLE

Here's the good news: according to a U.S. government study, intended rape victims are four times more likely to escape from an assault if they physically defend themselves than if they don't (U.S. Department of Justice, 1985). In many communities in the recent past, self-defense skills were considered specialized knowledge, necessary only for members of the military, police officers, and perhaps boxers or wrestlers. Today, these skills are being made available to novices, athletes, experts, and couch potatoes alike. But compared to the number of people who learn other life skills, such as driving, swimming, or balancing a checkbook, the number who choose to study self-defense is still astonishingly low. According to U.S. Department of Justice statistics, five out of six people

can expect to experience violence during their lifetimes. Imagine if five out of six people were expected to be in a car accident, and yet almost no one took driving lessons!

This book teaches you real skills that work for real people. You don't have to study martial arts for 20 years in order to master these moves, and you don't have to lift weights all summer before you can successfully defend your personal boundaries. The tactics, strategies, and scenarios in this book are based on years of research into the lives of survivors and perpetrators of assault. The physical techniques offered within are effective, realistic, and easy to learn. They don't require any particular balance, grace, or strength. Some techniques are, of course, enhanced by strong muscle tone, and some may appear more graceful if you have been practicing yoga. But these skills are inherently adaptable to a variety of bodies and situations.

Because this book is not based solely on one martial art modality or one type of assault, its tools are accessible to a broad range of readers. Many people can benefit from this book for self-defense training, including the following:

- Women who have never been assaulted but are aware of the possibility and want to know what to do
- Parents of teenagers who are hoping to pass on safety skills to their kids

- Martial arts instructors who are looking for new ways to present life skills to their students
- Survivors of violence who want to be able to protect themselves in the future
- Men and women who are brand-new to thinking about self-defense and personal safety
- Physical education teachers who are eager to add elements of self-defense training to their coursework
- Skilled athletes who would like to apply their training in a personal safety context

FULL FORCE TRAINING

It is essential that you practice the skills in this book full force. When you are using a technique the first few times, feel free to practice in slow motion to the air. As your comfort increases, each drill coaches you to strike, hit, and kick a target *as hard as you can*. This ensures that your body learns the skills accurately in the most effective and realistic way. Full force also means incorporating your voice with each technique (more on voice in step 2, Defining Your Space). Complete each drill fully, in order, throughout the book. Please don't just read or think about the skills—practice them! After all, your body, not just your brain, will be called on to react in an attempted assault. Your body needs to practice.

Whenever possible, use kick pads and training mats for your physical techniques. If you don't have access to professional pads, consider purchasing some at a martial arts supply store. I also suggest household alternatives, such as car seats, couches, and pillows. Or consider using this book in conjunction with a class in which the instructors wear protective padding. Padded at-

tacker courses allow students to hit and kick with full power. It can be tremendously reassuring to experience the truth that you have the power to stop someone who is trying to hurt you.

An important caveat—do not act out these techniques using friends or family as false targets. When you do so, you inevitably hold back. Because we are unwilling to hurt our loved ones, we perform the techniques ineffectively, whether consciously or unconsciously. We struggle, we can't figure out how it's supposed to work, and we wind up feeling overpowered, weak, and ashamed. Because you are practicing brand-new skills, you need to have the freedom to hit, bite, scream, and kick *as hard as you can*. If you have people in your life who want to know more about what you're learning, show them this book or invite them to join you in your studies. But let them know that you will not tolerate taunts such as "How would you get out of *this*?". That type of challenge puts your loved ones at risk of injury and puts you at risk of interfering with your own learning process.

ISSUES FOR MEN AND WOMEN

Although most assailants are men, both men and women are targeted as victims. It is essential to understand that perpetrators assault men differently than they assault women. No single approach matches all attacks, but you can

study some commonalities in order to choose the responses that are best calculated to ensure your safety.

In general, men who are assaulting other men stand and throw punches. They expect their intended victims to fight back. They may attempt to goad the targeted victim into a verbal fight or into throwing the first punch. Intimidation, humiliation, and power over the victim are usually the goals of the assailant, and intended male victims can successfully end many attempted assaults by backing down and by choosing not to be forced into a fight despite the perpetrator's wishes.

Men assaulting women generally do not stand and throw punches. They attempt to surround the woman physically from the front or behind and force the victim to the ground. In fact, most sexual assaults either begin in or progress to a ground position. Men assaulting women generally do not expect resistance and often have a prescripted scenario in their heads in which their victim is passive. Intimidation, humiliation, and power over the victim are usually the goals of the assailant. Female intended victims can successfully end many attempted assaults by showing forceful, immediate resistance of any kind.

People who are perceived as somehow violating social norms of gender expression are probably targeted more frequently for violence, and perpetrators increase the severity of the violence they choose to use in these assaults. People who identify as transgender, women whom society labels as overly masculine, men who crossdress, or anyone perceived as homosexual are at risk of being targeted by these types of attackers. These assailants also seek to intimidate, humiliate, and dominate the victim. People who live outside of gender expectations may want to consider first how they are generally perceived by their culture when deciding which gender-specific self-defense techniques will serve them best.

In addition to the expectations of the perpetrators, your own socialization, culture, and upbringing has a huge effect on your ability to defend yourself. The following generalizations will never apply to all people of all cultures, but they do give a starting point for assessing your risk.

A great number of women learning self-defense have to practice being louder, more aggressive, less friendly, and more "masculine" in order to break off an assault. Women who were raised in cultures that place a high value on being nice or good girls are particularly urged to look deeply at their early training. If you find that you generally have a hard time saying no to friends or family, that you've been trained to smile even when you feel uncomfortable, or if you were not given opportunities as a child to be loud and physically raucous, you will probably benefit from increasing both your assertiveness and your aggressiveness as you follow the steps in this book.

Women have also grown up in a world with no realistic depictions of females successfully defending themselves. We are bombarded daily with images of women shrieking ineffectively, twisting their ankles, falling down, or waiting for a man to rescue them. In my lifetime of media consumption, I've seen only one minor improvement. Now, perhaps one time out of a thousand, we also get to see a woman fly through the air performing a cartoonish kung fu kick. The absence of realistic images of strong, effective women has deeply damaged real women's abilities to defend themselves. Imagine trying to drive a car if you'd seen 5 million images of women causing car crashes but never witnessed a single female, known or unknown, actually driving safely. Sadly, for most of the world this is the state of affairs for women learning self-defense today.

A great number of men learning self-defense have to practice being willing to not fight, being willing to be perceived as weak, and refusing to be forced into a fight against their will. Men are often safest when choosing to assertively de-escalate a violent situation. For many men, the challenge of allowing themselves to be judged as passive or feminine by refusing to fight back is difficult. Some men are also challenged in a different way; they may have internalized the idea that they were somehow, genetically, supposed to know how to fight already. Never having been taught how to defend themselves, men may experience shame or fear about their inability to do so. For some men, the biggest challenge in learning self-defense is the willingness to be a beginner and wholeheartedly admit that you do not yet understand how best to defend yourself. If that is a challenge for you, congratulations for picking up this book!

ISSUES FOR PEOPLE WITH DISABILITIES

People who are perceived to have a disability are probably targeted more often for physical and sexual assault than others. Perpetrators falsely assume that disabled people cannot or will not fight back or do not have the social support to get help or report an assault. These cowards cannot stop you from defending yourself. If a particular chapter or technique is not right for your body, move on to the next one. Select the techniques that work best for you. Ask your instructors and supporters for whatever modifications you need to successfully execute a strike.

In fact, I encourage you from the beginning to reframe your concept of "disability" and consider it instead from the point of view of "differing ability." For example, having good vision could be a disability if you are attacked in the dark. You may be overly panicked or confused if you're unable to see the assailant. Being large or overweight could be an advantage when using one of the techniques involving weight transfer. I've also noticed that my larger students are much less likely to exhaust themselves by flailing

ineffectively. They tend to be experts at landing a blow with maximal efficiency.

We don't usually think of children as disabled, but they clearly have a set of abilities that are different from those of adults. Have you ever tried to hold an 18-month-old who was determined to get down? Most kids are faster, slipperier, and more willing to scream than adults. They may have smaller muscles and a shorter reach than most adults, but they are also less likely to be inhibited by social judgments about making a scene and preserving their dignity. Kids are formidable opponents!

People who use wheelchairs are far better at judging distance and correctly interpreting the body language of others than those who don't use wheelchairs. Most so-called able-bodied people would be exhausted by an hour of wheeling through a normal day in a nonmotorized chair. People who use wheelchairs also profit more from the element of surprise than other defenders. Attackers are even more shocked by your spirited defense than if they were attacking someone they judged as not disabled.

Self-Awareness Drill 2. Personal Safety Assessment

The following exercise is designed to help you look at your own personal risk factors and any barriers that could inhibit you from effectively defending yourself. You will be asked to consider your history, community, habitual responses to the world, and society's expectations of you.

This drill is, first and foremost, for you—not for a grade. I suggest that you find a notebook specifically for your study of self-defense. Many of the drills in this book invite you to record your thoughts, feelings, questions, and reactions in a Practice Journal.

Because you will be asked questions about your past, your fears, and your activities, you may find that this drill brings up some feelings. Before you begin, please consider the following questions (I've included some typical responses from students):

- How long do I want to write? *I should probably limit myself to 15 minutes. I'd rather just get this over with and do the whole thing.*

But I know that's what I usually do with new projects. Then I get overwhelmed and quit. I'll do 15 minutes now, and then I'll ask Cathy tonight if she wants to do the Personal Safety Assessment too.

- What will I do if I get overwhelmed? *I'll stop writing, make a cup of tea, and then call someone to talk.*

A. Skills

1. Have you ever taken a self-defense class before? What kind?

2. Did you feel safer afterward? Why or why not?

3. How much regular physical activity have you engaged in over the past 2 years?

4. Have you ever regularly participated in a physical sport or club (soccer, dancing, yoga, baseball, football, kayaking, or others)?

5. If you drive, can you change a tire?

B. Assets

1. Is your car in good shape? Do you get regular maintenance checkups?

2. Are you currently able to support yourself and your dependents financially?

3. If you had to unexpectedly move, could you support yourself for 3 months?

4. Is your home adequately secured? Working locks on all doors and windows? Deadbolt locks and chains on doors? Peepholes in doors?

5. Do you have a working phone at home and a cell phone? Do you keep them accessible and fully charged?

6. Do you feel safe calling the police for help?

C. Others' Perceptions of You

1. What is your gender?

2. What is your ethnicity?

3. Do others sometimes react to you as if you violate their gender expectations? Or do you identify as gay, lesbian, bisexual, or transgender?

4. Are you a "people pleaser"? Is it hard for you to say no to others, even when you want to?

5. Are you physically or mentally different in terms of your abilities? Do others perceive you as disabled?

6. Have you ever gotten into a physical fight with a stranger?

7. Do you feel as though tough guys regularly single you out to pick on?

8. If male, are you shorter or smaller than average in your community?

D. History

1. Have you experienced panic or shock when you or another person was injured?

2. Have you ever made a big scene in public despite the negative reactions of others?

3. Did you witness violence as a child?

4. Have you been the victim of emotional abuse?

5. Have you been the victim of sexual assault or abuse?

6. Have you been the victim of physical violence?

7. If you answered yes to questions 3, 4, 5, or 6, did anyone in your life offer you support, counseling, or help to recover? Have you ever sought ongoing help from a professional or nonprofessional support system (therapy, counseling, self-help groups, spiritual advisors, survivors' groups, domestic violence shelters, etc.)?

8. Is there anyone in your life you feel uncomfortable or unsafe around?

9. Do you have contact of any kind with someone who has already abused you? With someone who has abused other people or animals? If yes, does this person live with you?

10. Do members of your current or former family assume that parental or spousal violence is normal, to be expected, or caused by the person getting hit?

E. Risk Assessment

1. Do you hitchhike?

2. Do you date?

3. Do you ever go out on a date without enough money to take a cab home?

4. List as many ways as you can that you've taken care of yourself in the past 30 days, not just ways you avoided sexual assault, but all kinds of self-care.

5. Are you or any friends or family members engaged in illegal or semilegal behavior (insider trading; compulsive gambling; illegal drug sales or use; gang membership; illegal weapons possession or sales; corporate embezzlement; identity theft; production, sale, or use of pornography)?

6. Have you ever met face-to-face with someone that you first got to know online?

7. Do you or friends or family that you live with frequent online chat rooms, dating sites, or pornographic sites where users share personal information about themselves?

8. Do you have a gun in the house? Do you suspect someone else has brought a gun into the house?

9. Do you drink alcohol or use mood-altering drugs in public? If yes, do you ever leave your drink unattended? Do you ever accept a glass or open drink from someone else?

10. Do you work in the service or sex industries (waitresses, convenience store or gas station clerks, prostitutes, strippers, dancers, bartenders, club bouncers, etc.)?

11. Do you work in public safety (police officers, security guards, social workers who do home visits, fire and rescue workers)?

F. Your Community

1. Do you know your neighbors by name?

2. Have you asked neighbors or coworkers for personal help in the past?

3. Who has access to your home (landlord, repairmen, friends, family, ex-partners, chil-dren's friends)? Do you feel safe with each of these people? Have any of them ever abused your trust?

4. What kind of support system do you have?

5. How many people do you ask for help in a typical month?

To Decrease Difficulty

• Complete the Personal Safety Assessment with a friend or a group for support.

• Write for short periods, 5 or 10 minutes, and take lots of breaks.

• Don't judge yourself! This is a fact-finding mission, not a measure of your worth.

Score Your Success

Complete the Personal Safety Assessment = 100 points

Complete the Personal Safety Assessment *after* answering the two self-care questions = 125 points

Interpreting the Personal Safety Assessment

The following guide for interpreting your Personal Safety Assessment is just that, a guide, not a test or a fortune teller. Please keep in mind that the person with 20 areas of concern may never experience violence and the person with only one risk factor could still be assaulted. This guide is not a guaranteed predictor of safety or danger; it's a tool for you to use to get safer.

A. Skills

1 and 2. Your physical skills and previous training are one piece of your safety. Many people have taken self-defense training but felt a complete disconnect from the ability to actually apply the skills they learned. If you didn't feel any safer afterward, or if you don't remember the content of the course, you may not have benefited.

3 and 4. In general, being in good physical condition and having a routine workout can be helpful. Any strength, conditioning, body awareness, and flexibility that you bring to your study of self-defense benefits you. It's not, however, strictly required.

5. It's a good idea to be familiar with simple repairs to your car, bike, or wheelchair. Having the physical ability to get where you need to go protects you from the need to hitchhike or rely on people you don't trust for help.

B. Assets

1. Being able to afford and maintain a safe car is a great asset.

2 and 3. Being unable to take care of yourself and your dependants physically and financially places you at higher risk of assault. When you feel unable to meet your own needs, you are more likely to rely on others, even if you sense that they are a danger to you. This may be as simple as accepting a ride from a stranger when your car breaks down on the highway, to staying in an abusive relationship because your kids

only have health insurance through your husband. Your physical safety is benefited by developing a prudent financial reserve of at least 3 months of living expenses.

4. Having the financial ability and taking the time to ensure that your house is adequately secure also benefits your safety.

5. Using a phone to call for help is not usually the first line of defense when you are being assaulted, but it is an important asset if you need to get help, from ending a date to reporting a break-in.

6. Many people do not feel safe calling the police. You or your friends may have experienced violence at the hands of the police, or you may live in a neighborhood with a slow response rate. Maybe you have been married to an abusive officer who still works for the force, or you may have fears about your immigration status that prevent you from asking for help. Feeling protected by law enforcement is an asset that you may or may not have in your current community.

C. Others' Perceptions of You

1. Your number one risk factor for being sexually assaulted or for being attacked or murdered by someone you know is being female. Males, especially young males, experience higher rates of violent victimization other than sexual assault and higher rates of violence by strangers.

2. Young African-American men have the highest rate of violent victimization in the United States, significantly higher than other age, gender, or ethnic groups.

3. Perpetrators regularly target those they perceive as gay, lesbian, transgendered, or violating cultural gender expectations in any way. These attacks are frequently particularly violent. You may or may not be able to control others' perceptions of your gender expression.

4. Because the majority of violent perpetrators are someone you know, those who are perceived as unable to say no, people pleasers, or pushovers have a higher risk factor as well. Even perpetrators who are strangers search for victims who have trouble setting limits and saying no.

5. People perceived as mentally or physically disabled have a higher rate of violent victimization. Many of these individuals are targeted by their caregivers.

6 and 7. If you have a habit of getting into fights with strangers, you may suffer from being "unable to say no" to being goaded into a fight. The perception that you're easy to anger, especially for men, may also increase the likelihood that a perpetrator will attempt to assault you.

8. Many men are targeted who are considered smaller or weaker than the perpetrators.

D. History

1 and 2. Having already experienced panic or shock in response to injury is an asset to your self-defense, as is having previously made a big scene in public. You have direct experience of what the adrenaline response feels like and how it may affect you in the future.

3, 4, 5, and 6. Currently there is no completely clear-cut information about the effects of having witnessed or experienced violence as a child. Many people feel that childhood victims are more likely to become either future perpetrators (especially boys) or future victims (especially girls). But that probably doesn't take into account the enormous number of survivors who do not repeat any patterns of violence.

7. If those exposed to violence as children are promptly given good help, they will more easily be able to protect themselves in the future. Good help includes a safe place to recover, a nonjudgmental person to talk to about their experiences and feelings, and an opportunity to learn that it wasn't their fault. If instead violence was normalized in your family, it will affect your ability to respond appropriately to violence as an adult.

8 and 9. The questions in this section about current relationships are extremely significant to your safety and will be examined in depth in the drill that follows.

10. If your family of origin or your current community expects and accepts violence or blames the victims of violence, you are more in danger than if they don't. This normalization increases the difficulty of your being aware of violence, getting help, and getting to safety.

E. Risk Assessment

1, 2, and 3. People who hitchhike and people who date are regularly targeted by assailants. You can choose to abstain from either of these activities. You can also increase your safety by always having a backup plan and a safe way to get yourself home. In terms of dating, this plan may include meeting at an event; always driving your own car; and carrying extra money, a phone, and numbers for cabs, buses, or friends. You should be able to get to safety at any point, which may include choosing not to enter someone else's car or home.

4. Did you easily think of 20 or more examples of ways that you regularly take care of yourself? If not, you should know that ongoing self-neglect puts you at risk of being targeted for abuse by others. Failing to get enough sleep, feed yourself properly, allow yourself to have fun, take breaks, and otherwise take good care of yourself may be signs that you have difficulty setting boundaries. Perpetrators can read these signs and attach themselves to people who do not value themselves.

5. If you or your friends regularly break the law, you are likely to be exposing yourself to the threat of future violence from others without recourse to law enforcement, violence from law enforcement itself, or violence within the prison system.

6 and 7. Web sites related to online dating, socializing, pornography, and sex add an element of danger to personal relationships in that they enhance a perpetrator's ability to lie, obscure his or her identity, and mislead the target. If you or those you live with socialize in this way and, particularly, if you feel drawn to meet someone you've talked to online in a face-to-face situation, you will be exposed to higher risks than those associated with other types of dating.

8. Having a gun in the house *increases* the chance of a gun being fired in your house. Every accidental death (usually children shooting other children) occurs in a household in which the residents were certain it wouldn't happen to them.

9. Alcohol and "date rape drugs" are everywhere. Using any mood-altering drug can lower your inhibitions and your reaction time. It can be more difficult to spot the effects of being drugged against your will if you have already purposefully ingested other drugs or alcohol. Perpetrators of sexual assault in particular engage in drug-facilitated rape anywhere that drugs and alcohol are used.

10 and 11. People who work in service industry jobs or those for which they must enter people's homes are more often targeted for violence.

F. Your Community

1 and 2. Knowing your neighbors and feeling able to ask them for help can be a great resource for your personal safety. People are much more likely to respond to yelling, cries for help, or phone calls if they know you by face, name, and location. If your neighbors know that you are single or that your ex-husband doesn't live with you anymore, they may be more suspicious if they see a man enter your house when you're at work.

3. If anyone with access to your home or car has abused your trust, threatened you, or refused to respect your boundaries, you have a right to change your locks and get safe. Depending on tenant law in your community, your landlord may pay for the changes. Many tenants have a legally protected right to privacy and can establish limits on who comes into the home and when. You may refuse entry to anyone who makes you feel uncomfortable or unsafe. Ask to see identification from repair and utility workers and your landlord before opening your door.

4. Having a working support system is extremely helpful to your safety. Friends and

family who respect your boundaries, keep confidences, and follow through on offers of support contribute enormously to your ability to defend yourself.

5. Asking for help is an excellent self-defense skill. It's normal to need help!

Self-Awareness Drill 3. *Sharing Your Personal Safety Assessment*

If you're comfortable doing so, it can be incredibly helpful to discuss your Personal Safety Assessment with another person, maybe your partner, your therapist, or a friend who is also working through *Self-Defense: Steps to Survival*. Too often, we assume that our histories are unique. It's important to realize that many of us share common backgrounds and risk factors. You may choose to share just one or two sections of your Personal Safety Assessment or you may want to go through every question with someone. First ask yourself the following questions:

- Who is one safe support person I could share this information with? When?

- Is there someone who will also complete a Personal Safety Assessment and share theirs with me? Can I ask?

I've been using the Personal Safety Assessment for years in my classes. I tell my students that I, myself, am a survivor of childhood sexual abuse, was raped by strangers when I was a teen, escaped an emotionally abusive relationship as an adult, and had a stranger point a gun at me in traffic. Generally, their eyes widen in shock and the air goes still. Although awareness of violence has increased a great deal, most of us still live in communities in which no one ever says, "It happened to me." In most classes, more than one of my students says I'm the first person she has ever heard say out loud that she is an assault survivor.

When my students hand in their Personal Safety Assessments, I tally the results in percentages. Usually only about 20 to 30 percent of my students are able to answer no, they have never been verbally, emotionally, physically, or sexually abused. That means 70 to 80 percent of my students answer yes to at least one of those questions. In every class I have ever taught, 30 percent or more of the students have been previously sexually abused or sexually assaulted. Invariably, up to the moment when I share the percentages, most of the survivors in the room think that they and I are the only two.

Score Your Success

Share at least part of the Personal Safety Assessment with another person = 50 points

Self-Awareness Drill 4. *Taking Action on the Personal Safety Assessment*

Answer the following questions about your own Personal Safety Assessment. You might want to use a highlighter as you compare your responses to the interpretation section (see page xvi). Table 1 has some typical student responses for you to use as a guide.

1. What do I feel are the top three areas of concern on my Personal Safety Assessment?

2. If I could change any one thing about my Personal Safety Assessment, what would it be?

3. What three specific actions would I like to take first to increase my safety?

4. What is a realistic timeline for me to accomplish each action?

After you have identified your own personal areas of concerns and three actions you would like to take first to address these areas, set a timeline for each one. It's usually easier to commit to actions that take 15 minutes or less. "Ask at the bank if they're hiring this month" is probably a lot more manageable than "Change careers and double my income." If you like, share your action plan with a friend or support person to help keep you accountable.

To Decrease Difficulty

- Focus on just one section of the Personal Safety Assessment and identify just one action.
- Allow yourself enough time. No one can transform a life overnight.
- Start with a manageable task. Ask for a small favor or make a small change for the better.

Success Check

- Identify three areas of concern.
- Identify three specific actions you would like to take.
- Create a timeline for completing those three actions.

Score Your Success

Highlight the three areas of your Personal Safety Assessment of most concern to you = 30 points

Choose three actions you'd like to take to address those concerns = 50 points

Table 1   Personal Safety Assessment Sample Responses

Student	If I could change one thing	Three areas of concern	Three specific actions	Timeline
Ken	Being beaten up so much as a kid by my dad	1. That I might freeze up if I get scared or if someone threatens me 2. That I'll stop studying this book if I get overwhelmed 3. That I'm too small to hurt a big guy	1. Ask my wife for that therapist's name 2. Call Gary to ask if he'll study this book with me 3. Start going to the gym again	1. Tonight 2. This weekend 3. After the holiday
Marissa	Having enough money to get the car fixed and to change the locks now that Anthony's moved out	1. Hitchhiking 2. Being able to take care of myself financially 3. Not knowing how to hit somebody	1. Tell Shelly I don't want to hitchhike to work anymore 2. Go to the hardware store and find out how much new locks would cost 3. Ask at the bank if they're hiring this month	1. Before my next shift 2. Wednesday afternoon 3. After work today
Denise	I would have left Chris the first time he hit me	1. History of picking abusive guys 2. Being out of shape physically 3. Not knowing anyone in this neighborhood	1. Call the shelter and ask about a restraining order 2. Take a 30-day break from dating 3. Introduce myself to the woman across the hall	1. The next time I'm at my sister's place 2. Starting now! 3. Next time I see her at the playground
Martin	I wish I started studying Tae Kwan Do when I was younger	1. Being a bartender 2. Being gay-bashed after leaving work late 3. Not being good at asking for help	1. Ask work to staff two of us to close on weekends 2. Show this book to a friend I work with 3. Buy pepper spray	1. At the staff meeting next week 2. Tonight 3. Online or at the hardware store Monday

Feeling Safe

Questions D8 and D9 of the Personal Safety Assessment ask whether there is currently anyone in your life with whom you feel uncomfortable or unsafe. When my students answer yes, I ask them what one action they wish they could take in response and what support they would need in order to take it. I tell them not to worry too much about whether the action is realistic, to be as outrageous as they like. Even impossible actions can help you to start thinking about possible actions.

One of my students told me, "I'm uncomfortable with several of the guys who come in to the restaurant where I work. They're always flirting and trying to look down my blouse and ask me out. As if! I wish I could quit or force my boss not to seat them in my section anymore. Can I request a million dollars? I guess the real support I'd need would be a better boss. Tim used to notice where he sat the creepy guys for me, but ever since Cheryl took over, she tells me 'too bad.' Maybe one of the guys would serve their tables for me. I could ask Allen when he's on shift."

"I do feel uncomfortable around my boyfriend sometimes," another student admitted. "He's a great guy. I'm really lucky to have him. But he wants me to do some stuff, sexual stuff, that I'm just not sure about. I can't really talk about it with anyone. If I could do anything, I'd tell him he's not allowed to ask me ever again, but maybe that's not fair. Anyway, I can't imagine saying that. I'd need every self-help book in the world to support me to say something like that!"

One of my male students noted, "My person is my ex-wife. I only have to see her when I pick up the kids or she comes in the store, but it's always uncomfortable, especially when she's drunk. The action I wish I had taken is to have divorced her a long time ago, when she started drinking again in 2002. But I didn't really have any support back then. Her family was worse than she was, and the boys were just babies. Maybe, if I'd been in Al-Anon, I could have gotten more support. I don't know what action I'd like to take now."

Another student said, "I don't feel safe when my uncle is here. He molested me when I was little, and I don't think anybody in the family believes me about that. He comes over at least a couple weekends a month to help my husband around the house. I wish I could send him to Siberia. But I guess I'd need Russia's support for that action. Barring that, I wish I could make a rule that he's not allowed to come in the house if I'm here or to spend time with our kids. I'd have to get my husband's support, I think. Maybe my cousins would back me up if I asked them to talk to him about it."

It is impossible to live a completely risk-free life. You are powerless over some areas of the Personal Safety Assessment. Perhaps you have been targeted because of your race or ethnicity, or you face greater risk of sexual assault because you are female or transgender. Other risk factors—such as learning to accept help from others, saving up enough money to make car repairs, or finding the safest way to leave a job with an abusive boss—take time to change. But there is also a great deal that you can control. By lowering the number of risks that you take, learning to assess dangerous situations accurately, and adding protective behaviors, you can increase your overall safety.

ESSENTIAL RULES OF SELF-DEFENSE

There are very few rules when practicing effective self-defense. In most cases, the correct response for one person in one situation could be completely inappropriate for another person or another situation. However, the following four rules apply to everyone. Take time to memorize each one and copy them into your Practice Journal.

1. **You do not deserve to be attacked.** Everyone of us—men, women, and children—has a right to live free from harm and a right to resist physical assault. Even if you feel you may have made poor choices in the past, even if you feel you have gotten yourself into a dangerous situation or should have known better, no one deserves to be hurt. You must believe that you are worth defending. An attack is not your fault.

2. **The size of your commitment is more important than the size of your muscles.** When survival is at stake, height, weight, and strength are not the deciding factors. You may have heard news reports of small women somehow accessing the strength to lift cars off of trapped children. When the human body is adrenalized and focused, even average bodies can achieve amazing power. The most important quality to bring to a study of self-defense is not Olympian strength or professional expertise, but an ability to tap into your own commitment. You can learn that ability.

3. **Trust your gut.** Most people who have survived violence report that, before the assault began, they had an internal feeling that something was wrong, that they were not safe. Studying self-defense allows you to heighten your sensitivity to that inner voice. Because every situation is different and there are no one-size-fits-all rules, your instinct is your strongest ally. Whenever you listen to your instinct, you gain more access to this precious resource.

4. **There are no rules.** An unprovoked assault is not a sport in which you are required to adhere to rules of fairness. Basic rules of humanity are violated when the assailant attacks you. Trust is broken. If you are assaulted, be prepared to break any so-called rules you may have been taught, such as "Hitting a man in the groin is out of bounds," "Biting or hair pulling is girly," "Never hit a woman," "Nice girls don't make ugly scenes," "Real men never back down from a fight," etc. Self-defense doesn't have to be fair or look good; it just has to work.

RESOURCES

Equipment

Decide what supplies you will use to practice your skills full force. Consider asking a local gym what they have or could loan you or check out a martial arts supply company online. You can use this book without purchasing any fancy equipment; many of the drills use items you have around the house. You'll want a large strike pad for kicking and a smaller one for hitting. You can find professional strike pads for $20 to $60 (extrafirm couch cushions work too). You may also want to practice with a body bag, a weighted medicine ball, and a full-length mirror to check your alignment. Regular, comfortable clothing and sturdy flat shoes are fine. Choose a notebook or something to write in for a Practice Journal.

Padded Attacker Courses

IMPACT Self-Defense and personal safety courses are taught throughout the United States and around the world. The IMPACT system of self-defense trains participants in awareness, deterrence, verbal boundaries, and full-force, full-contact self-defense. IMPACT courses are the best in the world for creating an environment of emotional safety for all students, including survivors of violence. Classes are generally small and specially designed to meet the needs of particular groups of students—men, women, adults, teens, and kids. IMPACT International is a group of independent organizations that are affiliated by philosophy and programming. IMPACT is offered throughout the United States, primarily in metropolitan areas, and in Israel, with other chapters being developed in England, Japan, and South Africa. To find an IMPACT course near you, contact one of the larger chapters, including IMPACT Bay Area (San Francisco, California) at www.impactbayarea.org or IMPACT Personal Safety in Columbus, Ohio, at www.impactsafety.org.

IMPACT has received a great deal of media coverage in the past several years. Highlights include spots on network morning news shows and the Oprah Winfrey Show; pieces in major newspapers such as the *Los Angeles Times*, *New York Post*, *New York Newsday*, and *New York Daily News*; magazine articles in *Fit*, *Cosmopolitan*, and *Seventeen*.

Kidpower Teenpower Fullpower International is a nonprofit organization with an outstanding track record in the field of violence prevention, personal safety, and self-defense for all ages and abilities. Founded in California in 1989, Kidpower is highly recommended by many experts for its positive and practical approach to teaching people from all walks of life to prevent and stop most bullying, molestation, assault, and abduction. This organization has brought training and education to over a million children, teenagers, and adults from many different cultures around the world. Visit the Web site at www. kidpower.org for free articles, publications, and DVDs, and a free monthly e-newsletter. Contact 831-426-4407 or safety@kidpower.org for more information.

Rape Aggression Defense, or RAD (www. rad-systems.com), is a padded attacker course available at many college campuses around the country. RAD classes are generally free or low cost to students and are taught by campus police or safety officers.

Suggested Reading

The Gift of Fear (1997, Little, Brown) and *Protecting the Gift: Keeping Children and Teenagers Safe* (1999, Dell, Random House), both by Gavin De Becker. De Becker is a survivor of violence and an expert in predicting violence and assessing threats. He recommends IMPACT-style self-defense training.

The Courage to Heal by Ellen Bass and Laura Davis (1994). This is a recovery guidebook for survivors of childhood sexual abuse. It includes information on the phases of healing, resources for survivors, and personal stories of surviving and thriving.

When Love Hurts: A Guide on Love, Respect, and Abuse in Relationships (www.dvirc.org. au/whenlove) is an award-winning Web site especially geared toward teenagers. It includes information about healthy and unhealthy relationships, how to get safe, and how to get help.

NCASA Guidelines for Choosing a Self-Defense Course. The National Coalition Against Sexual Assault created this document to assist potential students in choosing a safe, realistic, and effective self-defense training program. The guidelines can be found online in a variety of places, including www. karatevid.com/article-SDguidelines.html.

Support Organizations

The Rape, Abuse, and Incest National Network (www.rainn.org) maintains a National Sexual Assault Hotline at 1-800-656-HOPE, which connects you to agencies in your area with staff who can listen, provide referrals, and help survivors get safe.

The National Domestic Violence Clearing House (1-800-799-SAFE) staffs a 24/7 hotline with trained counselors who can provide crisis assistance and information about shelters, legal advocacy, health care centers, and counseling.

Success Stories

Her Wits About Her: Self-Defense Success Stories by Women edited by Denise Caignon and Gail Groves is an excellent compilation, including kids' success stories.

IMPACT Self-Defense Web sites often include links for program graduates to share success stories, including successful defenses against physical, verbal, and emotional attacks.

Women Against Domestic Violence publish success stories from survivors at wadv.org.

SUCCESS SUMMARY

Successful self-defense requires that you first come to understand your own personal strengths, risk factors, fears, and challenges. Using the Personal Safety Assessment and factoring in Issues for Men and Women and for People with Disabilities, you now have a sense of your own risk factors and areas of challenge. You have a plan in place for how you will use full force training in future drills. You have also identified a safe person with whom you can connect during your study. And you have identified three safety priorities and three actions you will take to move toward meeting those goals. You don't need to have completed the three actions before moving ahead in the steps, but be sure that you have identified them. You have memorized the four essential rules of self-defense, each of which you will make use of in future steps.

Before Taking the Next Step

Before moving on to step 1, Increasing Awareness of Your Surroundings, take time to reflect on what you have learned to this point. Answer the following questions honestly.

1. Have you completed the Personal Safety Assessment and interpreted your responses?

2. Have you memorized the four essential rules of self-defense?

3. Have you identified a safe person with whom you can connect during your study?

4. Have you identified three safety priorities and three actions you will take toward meeting those goals?

5. Have you started a Practice Journal?

If you answered yes to all five questions, you are ready to move on to step 1, Increasing Awareness of Your Surroundings.

Taking the Step Further.   *Homework Assignments*

Memorize the featured myth and fact and write about them in your Practice Journal. Share some of your thoughts and feelings about the myth and fact with at least one other person. What were you taught growing up about the kinds of people who are raped? Robbed? Attacked? Do you know many people who have survived violence? Given that violent assaults are so common, why do you think not many people talk about them?

If you answered yes to question D8 ("Is there anyone in your life you feel uncomfortable or unsafe around?") or D9 ("Do you have contact of any kind with someone who has already abused you?"), write in your Practice Journal what action you wish you could take and what support you'd need to take it. Be creative; list as many possible actions and sources of support as you can imagine. Is there one action on your list that you'd be willing to take now? One method of support that you can request? It's normal to need support to resolve these situations; you do not have to figure it all out on your own.

Increasing Awareness of Your Surroundings

Awareness is one type of self-defense that many people overlook. You may already be thinking about skipping this step to jump ahead to the page about the Knee to Groin strike, but I urge you not to. Learning physical self-defense is different in one key way from learning guitar, soccer, or archery. We have all been systemically taught a lot of misinformation about perpetrators and victims. Most of us who come to a study of self-defense are completely wrong about when, where, why, and from whom we are in danger.

To get a sense of how important awareness is to a study of self-defense, imagine that you are in charge of designing a summer-long Life Skills course for young people age 15 to 20. These teens have parents who are not involved in their lives, and they're relying on you to teach them how to care for themselves. What topics would you include? How long would you spend on each? Would certain topics be required and others be optional? If the course only lasted for 4 months, which would be the most important skills to include?

Now imagine that, of the 16 weeks available for the course, the first 15 weeks focused on how to escape from quicksand and the last week covered learning to drive, swim, balance a checkbook, defend yourself, cook a meal, date, have a successful marriage, and take care of children. Ridiculous, right? Sure, if you encounter quicksand, it's good to know what to do, but aren't all of those other skills even more likely to be useful, even essential? Awareness training in self-defense is typically shortchanged, like one of "those other skills." Complicated and rich in its study, awareness is a skill that you can use every day of your life, not just in quicksand.

Awareness has physical, psychological, intellectual, and emotional components. The information in this step will get you started on developing all four of those components. You need to develop awareness of your surroundings, of other people—including potential attackers—and of your own feelings, thoughts, and habitual actions and reactions.

PICTURE A RAPIST

You will need some time (10 to 15 minutes), a watch, your Practice Journal, and something to write with. Find a comfortable place where you can be uninterrupted. Now picture a rapist. Allow yourself 5 minutes to develop in your mind an image as general or as specific as comes to you. When you have your visualization in mind, write down in your Practice Journal everything you can remember about the picture. Include as many details as you can remember. Now read the following myths and facts and compare your image to each one.

> *Myth*   Rapists are strange men who hide in the bushes or in alleyways and look for women who are walking alone at night.
>
> *Fact*   Rapists are usually someone that we know, either intimately or casually. They may be men we used to go out with or that we are married to, someone in our fraternity, our old boss, our babysitter, or the nice guy we chat with after church.

The Stranger Myth

Was your image a stranger or someone you know? Was the rapist you pictured masked? Mysterious? Familiar? Hiding in the bushes?

This myth is particularly painful to confront. Who among us would like to believe that someone we know, maybe even someone we care about, is capable of assault? Assuming that assailants are strangers in the bushes serves as a coping mechanism to keep us functioning from day to day. If we all woke up tomorrow with a full understanding of the depth and breadth of violence in our communities, no one would be able to get out of bed. But the truth is that, in over half of reported rapes, the rapist and the victim know each other on a first-name basis. Statistics show that 22 percent of all murders are committed by family members (Durose et al., 2005). In 2002, 43 percent of murders of females were committed by family members (Durose et al., 2005). Teachers, neighbors, fathers, uncles, mothers, doctors, and other relatives and acquaintances have assaulted, raped, and killed men, women, and children.

Even when expanding the definition of violence to include all assaults, not just sexual assaults, a minimum of half of attackers are someone we know. In 2004, males were about as vulnerable to violence by strangers (50 percent of violence against males) as by nonstrangers (48 percent), whereas females were most often victimized by nonstrangers (64 percent) (Catalano, 2004). And 78 percent of murder victims knew the person who killed them (Catalano, 2004).

> *Myth*   The person who is most likely to rob me, jump me, or assault me is from that other ethnic group, the scary one that I don't talk to much. I know a few of them are all right, but you have to watch out for most of those people.
>
> *Fact*   The person who is most likely to assault you is the same race and ethnicity as you are. Many studies that presume to report on the race of criminals study only prison populations where data is skewed by long-term cultural racism that benefits white criminals. The U.S. Bureau of Justice Statistics, however, states that at least 80 to 90 percent of all violent crimes against women (not just sexual assault) are by someone of the same race or ethnicity (Bureau of Justice Statistics, 1994). Given the incredibly low rate of reporting of sexual assaults, particularly when the survivor knows the perpetrator, I suspect the actual statistic is even higher.

The Ethnicity Myth

How about your visualization? Was the rapist your own race or ethnicity? Did you notice his or her racial or ethnic identity?

The persistence of this particular myth is incredible. Every semester, I give my students a final exam with the following true/false item:

"African-American men commit more rapes than other racial groups." Every semester, at least five students get this item wrong. The answer is false. Most victims of all types of assault know their attackers, and most of us in the United States still live in racially segregated communities. Therefore, the vast majority of victims of rape are the same race or ethnicity as the perpetrator. Not only is the myth of the African-American rapist a lie, in those sexual assaults in which the victim and attacker have different racial or ethnic identities, it's slightly more common for white men to assault women who are Latina, African-American, American Indian, or members of other minority groups.

The persistence of this myth became clear in my own life one night in an airport parking lot. I had been out of town teaching a self-defense class, at which I criticized the myth of the African-American rapist quite passionately to my students. When I got back to my car, it wouldn't start. I was tired and uncomfortable; the airport was in a large city unfamiliar to me and completely deserted at that hour. And now I had to go back inside and find someone who could give my battery a jump. I had to wait a long time for the elevator. When the doors finally opened, I was surprised to see someone inside, and I gasped out loud. Students of anti-racism have probably already guessed that I'm white and that the man in the elevator was African-American.

I was devastated, ashamed, and resensitized to the power of this myth. My self-protective instinct failed me in that instant because I had been conditioned, like all white women to some extent, to fear the person I saw based on race. My conditioned "instinct" to trust white men is a danger to me as well. Both reactions dull my ability to notice accurately when I do have a bad gut feeling or protective reaction concerning someone male or female, young or old, white or not.

Myth   Violent people look scary—dirty, unshaven, or crazy. On the street, I avoid people who are obviously homeless or mentally ill. You can tell them by the look in their eyes.

Fact   Perpetrators are often normal looking and cannot be picked out of a crowd visually.

The Class and Status Myth

Would you characterize the person in your visualization as "scary"? If so, what made him or her scary? Did the image remind you of anyone in particular? Was your personal image of "homeless" a part of your visualization?

Attractive people, successful people, clean and popular people all sexually assault, beat, and attack other human beings. Rapists are often normal men from all social groups and classes, including corporation presidents, senators, and church leaders. Most are heterosexual, married, and young. A few perpetrators are sociopaths, psychopaths, or people with other serious mental illnesses. But, in general, people with a mental illness and people without a safe place to live are far more likely to be *victimized* than the rest of us. What looks scary to any one person is a subjective measurement, of course, but it's not a good idea to trust automatically someone you think looks safe.

In often duplicated studies of typical mainstream American college students, many of the male students agreed that there are some conditions in which it is acceptable for a man to force a woman to have sex (i.e., rape her), as well as some conditions under which they, themselves, would force a woman to have sex (primarily if they were certain they would not be caught). In fact, 1 in 12 men admit committing acts that meet the legal definition of sexual assault or attempted sexual assault (Warshaw, 1994). In another study, over 50 percent of high school boys and 42 percent of high school girls stated that there are times when it is "acceptable for a male to hold a female down and physically force her to engage in intercourse" (Warshaw, 1994). These kids aren't delusional, homeless psychopaths hiding in the park. They're products of a society that encourages healthy, well-adjusted people to blame the victims of sexual assault, not the perpetrators.

Awareness Drill 1.   *Visualize a Rapist*

Read the description of the imagined perpetrator that you wrote in your Practice Journal. Note the specific details that you included. How does your image of a rapist compare to the myths and facts we've discussed so far?

Success Check

- Visualize a rapist before you read the myths and facts.
- Write about your visualization in your Practice Journal.
- Compare your visualization to each myth and fact.

AWARENESS TECHNIQUES

In addition to unlearning some of the most common myths about the perpetrators of violence, you can develop many practical awareness techniques. Note that using awareness does not require you to live in constant fear, checking furtively over your shoulder and clutching your purse or passport close to your chest. As you read the techniques that follow, imagine enacting them with a feeling of cool, confident strength and assurance (figure 1.1).

- Notice your surroundings, including people on foot, in cars, in groups, and alone.
- Don't walk while talking on your cell phone. For that matter, don't drive while talking on your cell phone.
- Walk with your head up, your back straight, and your eyes on what is around you.
- Say no when you want to, without smiling, apologizing, or giving an excuse.

- Respond immediately to small signals your body gives you about being thirsty, hungry, or sleepy. When our inner voice is acknowledged, it gets louder and more reliable.
- Have a safety plan in place when you go out on a date. Tell someone you trust where you're going, when, and with whom. Know exactly how you will end the date early if you choose. Don't feel you have to protect your date from disappointment or hurt feelings.
- In public keep your drink with you, and don't accept already opened drinks.
- Choose not to drink or use mind-altering drugs when you're with acquaintances or in public.
- Look and act confident, even if you have to fake it.

Figure 1.1   Cool, Confident Strength

INCORRECT—DISTRACTED AND FEARFUL

1. Hands occupied
2. Distracted by phone conversation
3. Eyes on the ground
4. Fearful look, shoulders hunched

CORRECT—CONFIDENT AND ASSURED

1. Hands free
2. Head up, shoulders back
3. Confident gaze, not smiling or cringing

a
     b

Misstep

Mistaking a feeling of distraction and comfort for actual safety.

Correction

Although your cell phone may create the illusion that you're not alone, it cannot protect you if someone knocks you over when you didn't notice him approaching. Learn to be aware of and be able to tolerate feelings of discomfort or danger so that you can use that information to get safe, not just *feel* safe.

We all have blind spots—types of dangers and perpetrators that we've been trained not to notice. The ways in which you unlearn your training may differ from the way I've overcome mine. For example, if you grew up with a loud, violent, alcoholic father you may be able to spot his type a mile away and steer clear. But you may be unable to recognize the signals that quiet, repressed alcoholics give when they're about to become violent. Alternately, having a loud, violent alcoholic in the house could seem so normal to you that you don't even notice when your wife begins to drink and yell more and more over the course of a year.

ADVANCED AWARENESS TECHNIQUES

Most of us are capable, with just a small amount of prompting, to walk from our offices to our cars with our heads high, our shoulders back, and a look of alertness and awareness. But there are many awareness techniques at a more advanced level that take time, practice, and patience to develop. These techniques require that you become more aware, not just of your external environment, but also of your internal environment.

For example, maybe you've noticed that whenever you first begin dating someone, you tend to lose perspective on whether she or he is a good match or a trustworthy person. Using your awareness of this pattern, you may choose to ask friends for feedback on that new person before you take the commitment further. Or you may realize that, once you start drinking, you have a difficult time stopping. Awareness of this risk to your personal safety may mean that you choose to drink less often or only with trusted friends. Perhaps you have been aware for quite some time that a particular friend's father makes you uncomfortable. Your first reaction might be to ignore how you're feeling or to doubt your perceptions. Using advanced awareness techniques could include speaking to others about how he treats you and how it makes you feel, asking for help to develop a plan for confronting or avoiding him, and then getting support to follow through on your plan.

Advanced awareness techniques include the following:

- Develop friendships with people who can give you reality checks.

- Say yes to sexual activity only when you are certain that you want to. If you're not yet certain, say no.

- Learn to assess how impaired you are becoming if you use drugs or alcohol. Ask yourself if you are satisfied with how much and how often you drink or use drugs. Ask friends for help staying safe when you are planning to use them in public.

- Notice how drunk or impaired the people around you seem to be.

- Research the signs that indicate a person is controlling and likely to become abusive. Compare your friends, family members, and people you date to the signs you've researched.

- Learn to identify anger cues, which can be very different from person to person and culture to culture.

- Avoid people who hurt animals or children or destroy property.

- Develop a practice that helps keep you grounded in the present, not lost in the past or future. Activities that focus your attention on the current moment include meditation, playing music, tai chi, yoga, and gardening.

- Practice asking for help. Notice who in your life is available to help you and who is not.

- Do regular internal "spot checks" throughout the day in which you ask yourself "How am I feeling right now? What do I need right now?"

Misstep

Blaming yourself when something or someone else feels "wrong" by assuming you must be overreacting, confused, or mistaken.

Correction

Trust your instincts. We each have a natural and inborn sense of safety: listen to yours and learn to pay attention to it whenever someone feels "off."

Awareness Drill 2. *Incorporating Awareness Into Your Daily Life*

Making these techniques your own takes time, and practicing may feel uncomfortable at first. Don't stop! The gift that awareness brings to our lives is immeasurable. Choose two techniques from the basic or advanced lists and make a commitment to incorporate them into your life for the next 2 weeks. Try to pick at least one technique that you think will challenge you. For example, if it's very easy for you to say no but very rare for you to ever ask for help, pick the latter. Practice each one at least three times a week. Write about your experiences in your Practice Journal.

To Decrease Difficulty

- Ask a friend to practice with you.
- Tell someone about the exercise. Ask him or her to check in with you about how it's going.

- Choose one technique that you think will be easy and one that you think will be harder.
- Don't judge yourself harshly. You will benefit even from writing about your difficulties with the drill.

Score Your Success

Choose two techniques = 10 points

Practice a total of 6 or more times = 20 points

Practice a total of 3 to 5 times = 10 points

Practice 1 or 2 times = 5 points

Misstep

Getting isolated, buying into the myth that you should be able to handle, fix, control, change, or otherwise manage everything in your life with a minimum of help.

Correction

Practice asking for help, even with very small things. Reach out to others who can relate to your particular blind spots. It's normal for all of us to need help.

<hr>

Myth   Assailants lurk outside in public places such as parking lots, parks, fields, and dark alleys. You're safest if you stay at home, and you should be OK if you stay in after dark.

Fact   The majority of assaults occur at home or near the victim's own home. At least a third of sexual assaults occur in daylight hours. And the younger the victim is, the more that likelihood increases.

<hr>

According to the U.S. Bureau of Justice Statistics, in 2000, nearly two-thirds of all violent crimes took place in a residence (Durose et al., 2005). Only a fifth of all violence was committed in a public place. Furthermore, slightly more than half of all nonfamily violence took place in a residence. More than 41 percent of violence against a stranger and 29 percent of violence against a friend or acquaintance took place in a public setting. A relatively high percentage (25.5 percent) of violence against strangers took place on a highway or a road. Parking lots, eating or drinking establishments, and retail stores were each the site for about 10 percent of incidents of stranger violence.

In 2004, 51 percent of incidents of violent crime occurred during the day (6 a.m. to 6 p.m.);

less than two-thirds of sexual assaults occurred at night (6 p.m. to 6 a.m.) (U.S. Department of Justice, no year).

Only 10 percent of stranger attacks happen in parking lots? More than half of violent attacks by strangers occur in someone's home? This counters the emotional perception of danger that most of my students experience. Parking lots rank number one in the mythology of places to avoid. Obviously, I am not suggesting that you sleep in a parking lot and avoid your own residence. But, if we know that an assault can happen anywhere and usually happens at home, we can use that awareness to make our own decisions about where to go and when.

Awareness Drill 3.   *Awareness of Your Inner Voice*

Pay close attention to your surroundings for 1 week. Notice anytime you are uncomfortable, anxious, or afraid. Take a few seconds to write down when, where, and of whom you were afraid. If you get through a few days and never notice being afraid, talk to some other people in your life and ask them when, where, and of whom they tend to be afraid.

To Decrease Difficulty

Ask a friend to practice with you and share his or her results.

To Increase Difficulty

- Go to locations that are unknown to you, places with unfamiliar people.
- Add in one to two nights of media study. Who, where, and when is "scary" on TV? In movies?

Did you notice yourself feeling more afraid at night or during the day? Indoors or outdoors? In your home or outside of your home? At work? In familiar or unfamiliar surroundings? Now compare your results to some of the most common myths and facts about dangerous times, locations, and activities. Were you most often afraid in a residence? In public? Of strangers? Of acquaintances? During the day? After the sun went down?

Score Your Success

Note your fears in your Practice Journal for a full week = 20 points

Compare your results to the myths and facts about location of assaults = 20 points

HEALTHY BOUNDARIES

To be aware of inappropriate and potentially dangerous behavior, you must have healthy physical and emotional boundaries. Your physical boundaries delineate the area surrounding your body that you feel is your own space. When someone crosses into it, you feel violated or uncomfortable. The space can be sized differently based on your personality, family size, culture, and mood. It can be a different size for different people. If a friend comes up behind you at home and rubs your shoulders, it could be a lovely gesture. If your boss does the same at work, it could be an unwanted invasion of your personal space.

Before you can expect yourself to defend your boundaries, you must be able to notice when they've been violated. For example, you might notice that for some reason you're feeling uneasy and wishing you didn't have to work on the shoulder rubber's project. You can react immediately and directly by affirming the boundary, "Please do not touch me" or "You're too close."

Boundaries are also emotional. We each have our own level of comfort with sharing and hearing personal information, emotions, and intimate details. You may have one friend or family member who is completely happy to discuss the details of his digestive tract with you, whereas another would be shocked and appalled to hear it. An acquaintance might cross emotional boundaries by asking overly personal questions, by expecting you to do something for her without asking first, or by bursting into sobs at a professional meeting and expecting you to take care of him. Before you can defend your emotional boundaries, you must first recognize how you feel when they've been crossed.

Awareness Drill 4. *Healthy and Unhealthy Boundaries*

To begin to assess the current state of your physical and psychological boundaries, read each of the following statements and mark each trait with N (I Never do this), S (I Sometimes do this), F (I Frequently do this), or A (I Always do this). Examine the traits in light of your own relationships. Consider your behavior around family members, partners, coworkers, ex-partners, children, and friends. There are no right or wrong answers. Allow yourself to answer honestly; this information is only for you. Most of us (even self-defense instructors) display some healthy and some unhealthy boundaries from time to time.

Signs of Unhealthy Boundaries

_____ Trusting no one at all or everyone you meet

_____ Saying yes when you really want to say no

_____ Talking at an intimate level with people you've just met or when you don't really want to

_____ Talking at an intimate level because someone else does and you feel obligated to respond

_____ Falling in love immediately before you know someone

_____ Falling in love with anyone who reaches out to you

_____ Acting on your first sexual impulse

_____ Being sexual for your partner, not for yourself

_____ Going against your values to please others in your life or being afraid to displease anyone

_____ Not noticing when others seem to lack appropriate boundaries

_____ Not noticing when someone crosses your boundaries

_____ Accepting food, gifts, touch, or sex that you don't want

_____ Touching someone without asking first

_____ Taking as much as you can take for the sake of getting

_____ Giving as much as you can give for the sake of giving or allowing someone to take as much as they can from you

_____ Letting others make your decisions for you

_____ Expecting others to anticipate your needs

_____ Wanting others to fulfill your needs automatically

_____ Falling apart so that someone will take care of you

Signs of Healthy Boundaries

_____ Developing trust in other people gradually, over time, as you get to know them

_____ Being your own primary caregiver and protector

_____ Revealing a little of yourself at a time

_____ Moving step by step into social, emotional, and physical intimacy with others

_____ Making your own decision about whether a potential relationship will be good for you and not basing your decision on the other person's wish to be with you

_____ Keeping focused on yourself—your life, plans, and goals

_____ Weighing the consequences before acting on sexual impulses

_____ Being sexual when you want to

_____ Maintaining personal values despite what others say, do, or believe

_____ Talking to yourself gently, with respect, love, and appreciation

_____ Noticing when someone else displays inappropriate boundaries or invades yours

_____ Saying no to food, gifts, touch, or sex you don't want

_____ Asking a person before touching him or her

_____ Respecting others, not taking advantage of someone's generosity, time, or money

_____ Respecting yourself, not giving too much in the hope that you will make someone like you

_____ Not allowing someone else to take advantage of your generosity, time, or money

_____ Trusting your decisions

_____ Defining your truth as you see it

_____ Knowing who you are and what you want

_____ Recognizing that friends and partners are not mind readers and clearly communicating your wants and needs

To Increase Difficulty

Make a few copies of the traits, and then consider each one separately for three important people in your life. Look for patterns specific to one person or group of people. For example, do you always expect your partner to meet your needs but never expect this of your employees?

Score Your Success

Complete all questions = 20 points

Compare patterns in various relationships = 10 points

Misstep

Feeling intense discomfort when saying no to anyone for any reason.

Correction

Start small, be firm, don't give a reason or apologize.

Let's study a specific example of the setting and defending of healthy boundaries. Self-defense will require that you first set boundaries and then use your awareness skills to notice the other person's response. You will also be called on frequently to defend the boundary that you've set—verbally, emotionally, or physically. If you set a clear boundary and the other person ignores, mocks, or crosses it, you now have some very important information about your relationship. Let's look closely at how this plays out in a few scenarios.

Caroline and John have been out on five dates. They spent a great deal of time together over the last few weeks and enjoyed a classic whirlwind romance. Both are hoping the relationship will continue and deepen. Now it's fall and college classes have resumed. One Wednesday evening, John gives up on his homework, calls Caroline, and asks to come spend the night at her apartment. Caroline is studying for an important exam next week. What happens next?

1. Caroline wants to see him, but tells John that she really can't until the weekend (sets a boundary). He's disappointed and asks if she's sure (tests her boundary). She says she is (defends her boundary). They make plans for Saturday morning and, after talking for half an hour, both go back to studying. (Both John and Caroline hear and respect the boundary she set.)

2. Caroline wants to see him, but tells John he shouldn't ask because she'll feel bad and give in when she should really study (indirectly asks that John set a boundary for her). John tells her she's too serious and should have more fun. Caroline secretly thinks he's probably right and feels bad about herself. They talk on the phone for an hour and John asks four more times to come over (repeatedly pushes against Caroline's indirect boundary setting). He tells her that he'll

help her study and that she's smart like he is and doesn't have to study as long as she thinks she does. She says no the first three times but relents the fourth time, after he reminds her that he left work early last weekend to fix her car. (John and Caroline disrespect her boundary.)

3. Caroline wants to see him, but tells John she needs to study instead (sets a boundary). He tells her that she gets too worried about exams and that he used to do that too. They talk for 15 minutes and then she gets back to studying (respects her own boundary). He shows up 20 minutes later with a dozen red roses (ignores and crosses her boundary). He stands outside the window to her room, telling her that's she's beautiful and he can't stop thinking about her and playing love songs loudly on his car stereo. At first, Caroline tells him to go home, but then she sees that he's brought flowers, plus some photos he framed for her. He says he had to borrow gas money to get to her apartment, and so she lets him in. (She gives up on her boundary.)

4. Caroline wants to see him, but tells John she thinks she should study first (sets an indirect boundary). John begins to ask her questions about her day and reveals that he's already memorized her class schedule. He asks her to talk about the men in her group project for one class and tells her she's "always been a total flirt." Caroline was raised very conservatively and worries that maybe she has been flirtatious with the guys in her program. John gets angry and accuses her of cheating on him and demands to know if the guy is in her apartment right now (attacks her boundary). Caroline feels bad for upsetting him, assures him she's faithful, and tells him he can come over so she can prove that she's alone. (She gives up on her boundary under verbal and emotional attack.)

Misstep

Mistaking disrespectful boundary-crossing behavior for "love," "passion," or "normal" jealousy.

Correction

Set a clear boundary and pay attention to how it is received. It's essential to discover early in a relationship if your partner is able to accept not getting what she or he wants and able to respect your decisions. Even if it's difficult to say no, it's important to assess whether your new friend can *hear* no.

IDENTIFYING THE PERPETRATOR'S APPROACH

To identify the early warning signs of potential violence, listen carefully to your inner voice—including the emotional, verbal, and physical cues you receive when someone is exhibiting bad boundaries. This might mean a bad "gut feeling," a feeling of self-doubt (What's wrong with me? Why don't I trust her?), an unconscious desire to move away from someone physically, or a familiar feeling that something just isn't right.

Most assaults begin long before an assailant makes a physical move. Perpetrators test potential victims until they find someone they believe will be easy to control. In his excellent book *The Gift of Fear*, Gavin De Becker refers to this stage of the assault as the "interview" and delineates the most common elements of the perpetrator's approach (De Becker, 1997). During the interview, the perpetrator employs several techniques including the following:

- Siding with the potential victim (implying that he and the intended victim have something in common, whether accurate or not)

- Giving too many details (about him- or herself or the context)

- Loan sharking (insisting on giving help, a drink, a favor)

- Being charming (compliments, persuasion, flirtation)

- Typecasting the victim (challenging him or her to reveal details, trying to push the victim's buttons)

- Refusing to take no for an answer (usually starting with a relatively small issue)

Can you find examples of each of these techniques in John and Caroline's story? When and how does John use the perpetrator's "interview" techniques to get what he wants from Caroline? If you were in Caroline's shoes, which technique might be the hardest for you to say no to? Which would be the easiest for you to spot and resist? In the example of typecasting, what could someone you care about accuse you of that would trigger you into "proving him wrong"? (Hint: For Caroline, it was being labeled smart, too worried, or too flirtatious.)

SUCCESS SUMMARY

Developing your awareness is a lifelong process. You must unlearn myths about perpetrators and danger in general, and you must look closely at your own upbringing and habitual reactions in order to understand where you are most at risk. This requires that you examine your base assumptions and begin to study yourself. What are your personal challenges? Your beliefs? Your fears? How aware are you of your inner voice that indicates danger?

In Increasing Awareness of Your Surroundings, you have begun to use simple and advanced awareness techniques and to employ them in your daily life, noting those that are most difficult for you. You have assessed the state of your current physical and emotional boundaries as they relate to your relationships. You have also studied two personal stories of the use of awareness and compared them to your own skills and reactions.

Before Taking the Next Step

Before moving on to step 2, Defining Your Space, take time to reflect on what you have learned to this point. Answer the following questions honestly.

1. Have you pictured a rapist and compared your visualization to the myths noted in step 1, Increasing Awareness of Your Surroundings?
2. Have you incorporated two awareness techniques into your life for at least 2 weeks?
3. Have you studied your inner voice for 1 or more weeks, noting when you felt afraid or uncertain, and written about it in your Practice Journal?
4. Have you completed the checklists for healthy and unhealthy boundaries?
5. Have you analyzed John and Caroline's situation in light of the questions in Identifying the Perpetrator's Approach?

If you answered yes to all five questions, you are ready to move on to step 2, Defining Your Space.

Taking the Step Further. *Homework Assignments*

Memorize the myths in this step and write about them in your Practice Journal. Share some of your thoughts and feelings about the myths and facts with at least one other person. Does your conditioned intuition line up with the myths or the facts? How about other people you talk to?

Practice your chosen awareness techniques regularly for a full 2 weeks. It's generally more helpful to practice for 5 minutes every day than 35 minutes once a week. Continue to implement and develop those techniques that are difficult for you. If you find that you are unable to practice, get more support.

Defining Your Space

Can you shout really loudly? When was the last time you did? Could you do it if you were also very scared? What if you were woken up from a deep sleep? Can you tell someone, "Never touch me again" or "Get away from me"? What if you weren't sure whether that person meant any harm?

I commonly hear this response: "Sure, I could defend myself verbally if I had to. I don't really enjoy it, and I'm not planning on practicing—how embarrassing!—but, if I had to, I could. I do hate it when people think I'm rude or loud though." So the question remains—how do you *know* that you could defend yourself verbally? Could you truly claim to be able to drive if you had just imagined driving a few times but never actually gotten into a car? In this chapter, you will practice using your voice in a variety of ways, and, yes, it's essential that you practice.

Myth   Self-defense means hitting someone back if you are attacked.

Fact   Self-defense begins long before a single blow has been launched. Smart self-defense sometimes requires that you go on the offensive before anyone has hurt you, before you're certain of their intentions, and before your brain thinks you're ready.

This myth—that self-defense only means hitting someone who has already hit you—greatly hampers your ability to defend yourself. Assaults rarely begin on the physical level. Your success at physical defense depends on your ability to practice verbal techniques first. According to the FBI, you have a four times greater chance of breaking off an attempted assault if you practice a self-defense technique (Zawitz et al., 1993). The good news is that the study included shouting as a self-defense technique.

There are many reasons to practice your verbal skills seriously. After awareness, your voice is your second line of defense. Your voice can startle a perpetrator and send a loud and clear message that you are willing and prepared to defend yourself. A great many assailants would be deterred from their plans by such a verbal demonstration. If you've ever watched a martial arts class, you'll note that many practitioners let out a loud shout or grunt with each technique. This vocalization is an integral part of the moves.

The students' techniques are physically stronger when they yell and significantly weaker when they're silent. The sound is not just to seem mysterious or intimidating!

Finally and, perhaps, most importantly, when you're talking or shouting, you must breathe. And chances are that, in a real-life attempted assault, the first thing that will happen is that you will hold your breath. Preparing your body to talk, yell, or shout ensures that you will breathe to get the energy you need to break out of the natural freeze response and activate your defense.

SHOUTING

A strong shout comes not only from the vocal chords in your throat, but from a deeply relaxed belly that allows for maximum inhalation. Place your hands on the area below your belly button, take a deep breath in, and feel your hands rise (figure 2.1). Exhale. Do it again. Are you just reading along and imagining a deep breath? Please set the book down and take three deep breaths, pushing out your hands with each inhalation and feeling your hands sink in on each exhalation.

Now do another deep inhalation and, on the exhale, say no in your regular speaking voice.

Do it again louder. And louder. And louder! It may seem obvious that a loud shout requires a deep breath, but it does take practice. When you're feeling fear or uncertainty about setting a boundary, you will very likely experience some part of the fight-flight-freeze response. This may involve increased heart rate, shallow respirations, or complete freezing of the diaphragm and temporary holding of the breath. Preparing to shout allows you to mobilize these physiological responses for your defense.

Figure 2.1   Shouting

1. Stand up straight
2. Put your hands on your belly
3. Take a deep breath
4. Shout *NO!*

Misstep

Tensing up and shouting from the throat, limiting your force and volume.

Correction

Begin with a deep breath and make sure your hands on your belly move.

Practice the *no* shout several times now at your own speed. Practice at least 20 shouts until you're getting a consistent, loud, solid sound.

A great number of people, often women and teens, are unwilling or unable to be loud. It may be that in your family you experienced years of being punished for raising your voice, or perhaps your community judges loud people as rude, selfish, crazy, or uncouth. Practice shouting 5 minutes a day in the car or some time when you can be alone. Know that it's OK to feel awkward, silly, or strange. For inspiration, study a toddler having a tantrum or rowdy fans watching sports.

Another common error in shouting is getting too caught up in what to say. You don't have to carry the burden of a rational conversation. The word *no* is a complete sentence. In an actual assault, shouting will force you to breathe deeply. It will also startle your attacker and attract any available help, in that order. There's no need to shout "*I think it might have been an accident and I don't want to offend you, but you bumped into me just now and groped my breast, and I'm not happy about that, but I'm sorry if you didn't mean to!*" A simple *No!* will meet all three objectives very effectively.

What Should You Yell in a Real-Life Attack?

That's up to you; there's no perfect answer. I'm a big fan of just yelling *no*. It's clear, concise, and to the point. I have heard the suggestion never to yell *help* or *rape*, but instead to yell *911* or *fire*. The sad possibility behind this suggestion is that helpers would be more likely to intervene if they think they too are in danger. Given that many people are loathe to intervene in cases of domestic violence, some people suggest that you yell *I don't know this man*—whether you do or not.

Misstep

Giving too much explanation, trying to give a rational explanation, or engaging in conversation.

Correction

Simply shout *no* or stick to short phrases such as *Stop it! Go away! or Don't touch me!* Try the broken-record technique of repeating the same strong statement over and over again.

Misstep

Being unwilling or unable to be loud or to make a scene.

Correction

Practice in the car, with a group of friends, or with kids. Start with making a scene in other, small ways in your daily life.

Defining Space Drill 1. *Shouting*

If you can gather together a few friends or kids (who love this exercise), this drill will help you address some of the more difficult elements of shouting. First you will shout together as a group. Start with one person counting off for the group "1, 2, 3, *NO!*" Try this several times until you're getting a consistently loud shout from everyone in the group. Next, have the counter point to just one person when it's time to shout. Take turns being the lone shouter.

How does it feel? Easy? Hard? Fine in a group but embarrassing when you have to shout on your own? Familiar? Freeing? Did you laugh or smile after? Watch your friends. What elements make for a strong, forceful *no*? Are you able to commit your full voice each time? Why or why not?

Quick Thinking

One great example of verbal self-defense is the true story of a college student who met a man at a fraternity party who offered to drive her home. Although she felt uncomfortable, she agreed because her friends had already left the party without her. On the way, he parked in a secluded area and began to kiss her. Although she said no repeatedly, he refused to stop. She quickly realized that she was unsafe and brilliantly lied to him, suggesting that they go to a motel together. As they pulled up to the motel, she offered to go inside herself to get them a room. He stayed in the car while she called the sheriff's office. The man was arrested for sexual assault! (Danylewich, 2001)

Defining Space Drill 2. *Studying Success*

Answer the following questions in your Practice Journal. If you like, discuss the Quick Thinking success story and your answers with a friend or study partner.

1. When did the student begin her self-defense?

2. How many kinds of self-defense did she use? List each one. Include the use of awareness and verbal, emotional, and psychological techniques, not just physical ones.

3. What might you have done differently in the same situation? Why?

4. What surprised you about this survivor's experience?

5. What satisfied or empowered you most about this survivor's experience?

PROTECTIVE STANCE

One way to enhance the power of your voice is to take a protective stance (figure 2.2). Protective stance is a good position to assume anytime that you would like to set a boundary; you may be feeling threatened or assessing a potential danger. You can assume protective stance in an elevator or a grocery store line if you feel that someone is standing too close to you. You may use the stance as a part of saying no to a pushy date, to an angry drunk in a bar, or to someone coming toward you in the conference room at work.

Stand with your feet approximately shoulder-width apart and your knees very slightly bent. It's important not to lock your knees such that your legs are rigidly straight. Place your dominant foot (probably the same as your dominant hand) slightly behind your other foot and slightly angled out. Your hands should be flat palmed, facing your potential attacker, and your elbows should be in close to your body and relaxed. Study figure 2.2 carefully; this is the core position from which most of your future techniques will arise.

Now get into a protective stance several times. Compare your stance in the mirror to the photos in figure 2.2. Experiment with your hand and foot positions and practice both variations of the stance.

Figure 2.2   Protective Stance

a

b

FEMALE

1. Feet shoulder-width apart
2. Dominant foot slightly back and angled
3. Hands up, flat, facing out
4. Knees slightly bent

MALE

1. Feet shoulder-width apart
2. Dominant foot slightly back and angled
3. Hands up, flat, facing out, slightly lower and further apart
4. Knees slightly bent

Now stand normally and practice getting into protective stance 20 times, shouting *no* with your full voice each time you raise your hands.

Notice the difference between the two figures? Although no single rule covers all circumstances, in general, women are best protected by the hand position in figure 2.2a and men by the hand position in figure 2.2b. You'll note the woman's hands are closer together and closer to her face. The man's hands are located slightly further apart and lower down.

Perpetrators assaulting men often assume that their intended victim will fight back. These assailants expect you to stand and throw punches; in fact, they may be hoping to provoke you into a physical fight. The protective stance for men sends a message that the intended victim is willing to defend himself but cannot be goaded into a fight against his will and that he is therefore not a good target for violence.

Perpetrators who assault women assume that their intended victim will not fight back and have generally visualized an assault in which a "helpless and weak" woman is instantly overpowered and injured. The protective stance for women sends a message that she is willing and prepared to defend herself physically and is therefore not a good target for violence.

Misstep

Crouching, bending knees too low, bending at the waist.

Correction

Keep your center of gravity over your hips. Keep your knees loose, and your legs mostly straight.

When to Assume Protective Stance

If someone is coming toward you and you feel uncomfortable, how close is too close? Note that, in a defensive situation, a single arm's length away may be unsafe if it enables your attacker to hit you. You will be best protected if you are already in the protective stance before an attacker gets within one arm's length of you. The stance is also an excellent position if you get knocked down from behind. Your weight is balanced, you're grounded with a low center of gravity, and your raised arms can protect your face and head if you fall forward.

Defining Space Drill 3. *Stopping Lines*

If you're studying this book with a group or can gather up four or five others, form two lines facing each other on either side of the room. Each line should have the same number of students, enabling you to identify a partner—the person directly across from you.

1. Make eye contact with your partner. On the count of 3, members in line 1 walk forward. When line 2 members are ready, they get into protective stance and say *stop.* The stopping distance will be different for each pairing. Take a moment to note the differences.

2. Repeat the exercise, but this time the walking line will shout *hey, you!* and begin to stride forward with a sense of purpose toward those in line 2. Again, line 2 members choose independently when to stop their partners.

3. Finally, all together on the count of 3, line 1 members yell *hey!* and begin to run toward those in line 2. Again, line 2 members choose independently when to get into protective stance and say *stop!*

Mix up the lines internally so that each student has a new partner, and then repeat the three parts of the drill so that each person gets a chance to be a walker and a defender.

What was it like to be a member of the line of walkers? How did the exercise change when you tried parts 1, 2, and 3? Did it make a difference for you who your partner was? How did you feel when you were shouting *stop!*? How did it feel when someone shouted *stop!* at you? Did anyone laugh? When?

Misstep

Getting into protective stance too late.

Correction

You do not have to wait. Protective stance is a great position for whenever you feel unsure, uncomfortable, or would like a very nice person to stand a little further away from you.

Protective stance is not the position to assume when someone takes a swing at you. In an emergency situation, the mind lags behind the body. Many survivors of violence report that, even after a physical assault began, a voice in their head was still struggling to get past the thoughts "This can't really be happening. Did he just hit me?" The solution? You must be prepared internally to trust your instincts even if you fear that you will make a scene or be perceived as crazy, controlling, hypersensitive, too feminine, or too masculine.

In most of us, the desire to rationalize the world and the behavior of others is very strong. When another human behaves irrationally by attempting to harm you, you have to push aside that desire in order to practice effective self-defense. Consider the following: What if someone sincerely just wants to know the time, and you whip around to face him, putting your hands in protective stance? Would it be the worst thing in the world? What if a room full of people laughed at you? Most of us can acknowledge mentally that our personal safety far outweighs any potential embarrassment to ourselves or others, but you need to practice releasing any lingering fear.

Tracking From Protective Stance

In addition to holding a static protective stance, practice moving in the stance or tracking the aggressor. Keep your upraised hands between yourself and your attacker, turning to face him or her when he or she moves. Without lifting your right foot from the ground, practice using your left foot to pivot in a circle (figure 2.3) while your arms and hands remain in position. It's fine to move both feet while tracking as long as you're certain you aren't moving either toward or away from the aggressor.

a   *b*

Figure 2.3   Two people, one circling the other who is positioned in protective stance.

Defining Space Drill 4.   *Tracking*

Choose a partner and pick one person to play the defender and one to play the aggressor. The aggressor's goal is to get behind the defender. The defender's goal is to keep his raised hands ready in protective stance and follow the partner's movements so that he is always facing the attacker. Place a $20 bill underneath the defender's stationary foot to help him hold his ground. Each pairing should have at least a 6-foot radius in which to work. The aggressor should remain an arm's length or further away from the defender. Take turns as defender and aggressor.

Did the aggressor ever manage to get behind the defender? How? Or why not? Did anyone want to move toward or away from the aggressor? Did anyone step off the $20 bill? How did you feel when you played the aggressor? How did it feel to play the defender?

To Decrease Difficulty

- Have the aggressor move more slowly.
- Put a $100 bill underneath the defender's foot.

To Increase Difficulty

- The aggressor gradually builds up speed and switches direction rapidly.
- Practice this drill several times with different partners.

Success Check

- Both partners get a chance to be defender and aggressor.

Score your success

Defender stays in protective stance = 5 points

Defender stays on the bill = 5 points

Defender never has his back to the aggressor = 10 points

VERBAL SELF-DEFENSE

In addition to getting into protective stance and shouting, there are many other choices for defining your space. Verbal self-defense can be defined as using your words to prevent, de-escalate, or end an attempted assault.

You do not have to wait until the point of physical violence to use verbal self-defense. Perpetrators don't wait; they know that verbally attacking someone is an effective way to get what they want. The majority of sexual assaults include verbal coercion, abuse, and threats, but only some sexual assaults include physical violence as well. Perpetrators rely on the power of words to threaten, paralyze, coerce, or otherwise frighten their intended victims into physical compliance.

Myth   It's better just to ignore verbal assaults. If you pay attention to them, you'll just encourage the abuser or worsen the situation.

Fact   Ignoring a verbal assault is very rarely a good idea. You are much better protected if, instead, you make an assessment of your safety and choose how to react.

Verbal self-defense could mean simply saying no to someone. It could be repeatedly refusing a request or telling someone who has violated a boundary what you want, or it could entail a more complicated scenario in which you are called on to refuse to engage verbally with someone manipulative, to set limits, and to end the conversation. Consider the following examples:

- **Cheryl at the bus stop.** A large young white man at a bus stop has been chatting with Cheryl and moving closer and closer. He sits down very close to her on the bench. At first, Cheryl feels uncomfortable and tries to figure out if he's flirting with her or planning to steal her purse. Then, without smiling, she puts up one hand, flat palm out, and says "You're too close. Please move away." He looks surprised and moves to the other end of the bench. When he's joined five minutes later by a friend, he mutters, "She's crazy. Don't go near her."

- **Josh on the airplane.** Josh normally enjoys chatting with people on his long business flights. But this time, the man in the next seat is drinking heavily and making sexual comments about the flight attendant. After a few minutes of this Josh says, "I'm not comfortable with that kind of talk. What's that book you're reading?"

The drunk man makes a mocking face and asks Josh if he's gay. Josh says, "That's enough now. Have a nice flight" and turns and looks out the window.

- **Tanya and her sister Mechelle.** Tanya's little sister Mechelle has always known how to manipulate her. Tanya frequently winds up driving her around all weekend long, even when she has promised herself that she's not going to give in this time. Mechelle shows up at Tanya's apartment Saturday afternoon and asks to be taken to the mall. When Tanya says no, Mechelle gets angry and starts to cry. She storms off and threatens not to invite Tanya to her niece's birthday party. After Mechelle leaves, Tanya calls a friend to talk. She thinks maybe she should call Mechelle and apologize, but her friend encourages her to stick to the boundary she set. Tanya decides she's willing to drive Mechelle once a week, but no more.

- **Soledad at the club.** Soledad has gone out dancing with a group of friends from work that she doesn't know very well. Early in the evening, a man brings a drink to her table and asks her to dance. When Soledad says no to both, he tries to talk her into it for a long time. But she doesn't back down. Later on, he comes up behind her on the dance floor and starts dancing suggestively near her. She feels embarrassed and thinks, "I should just leave." But instead she turns toward him, looks him in the eye, and says, "Please go away." He laughs and grabs her wrist. She gets into protective stance and shouts as loudly as she can, "Let go of me right now!" Her workmates look at her in shock. The man drops her hand, calls her a name, and walks away.

The first thing you need to understand about effective verbal self-defense is that the intention of the person you're defending yourself from is not important. What if the man at the bus stop was only flirting? It doesn't matter. If Cheryl feels uncomfortable, she has a right to tell him to sit further away. What if the man on the plane was just drunk and trying to be funny? Again, it doesn't matter. Josh feels uncomfortable and doesn't have to pretend he's not.

Do you remember the myth at the beginning of the step? Many people believe that self-defense means hitting someone when you are physically attacked. Cheryl might be afraid that, if she asks the man at the bus stop to move away from her, he'll get mad and attack her. But the vast majority of perpetrators plan their attacks. You cannot cause a well-meaning person to attack you by setting a verbal boundary, but, if someone is planning to attack you, you can stop him by being verbally assertive.

Note that none of the verbal defenders in these examples gave an explanation for their behavior. Cheryl is not required to say, "I'm sorry, I'm sure you're a very nice guy, but I've had a long day and I don't really feel like chatting right now." Josh does not owe his seatmate an explanation of his feelings about language that degrades women or the fact that he might be feeling triggered because his father is a heavy drinker. Nor does he have to lie and pretend that he has work to do or that he's sleeping.

What if you want to say no, but you've said yes many times in the past? This is Tanya's predicament with her sister. When we're setting new boundaries, especially with someone who knows us well, we often feel intense discomfort. It may be far easier for Soledad to yell at a stranger on a dance floor than it is for Tanya to refuse to drive her sister to the mall. Keep in mind that feelings of guilt or even fear do not mean you're doing anything wrong. It's common for friends and family members to test our newly set boundaries. Mechelle will probably come back over to Tanya's house several more times demanding a ride, and Tanya's job will be to remain firm and clear and to repeat herself.

Finally, verbal self-defense often requires that you be willing to make a scene. The first thing that happens when Soledad shouts, "Let go of me!" on the dance floor is that all of her coworkers turn to stare at *her*. For some people, that would be no big deal. Others would wilt with embarrassment and shame. But Soledad's safety, her right to set boundaries, and her self-worth are more important than anyone's embarrassment, including her own!

Defining Space Drill 5. *Using Verbal Self-Defense Techniques*

The following is a list of verbal self-defense techniques. Go through the list for each of the four verbal defenders in the situations just described and jot down a few ideas for how each one could use each technique.

After you have considered all eight techniques for each defender, think about a situation from your own past. This may have been a time when you felt uncomfortable but didn't know what to say or a situation in which you wanted to speak up for yourself but didn't know how. Or perhaps there is a person you expect to see in the future with whom you'd like to set a verbal boundary. Now fill in the blanks for each technique for your own situation.

1. Say no. When might each defender say no? To what?

Cheryl _____

Josh _____

Tanya _____

Soledad_____

Me _____

2. Say what you want. Use simple sentences such as "Move away from me" or "Let go of me."

Cheryl _____

Josh _____

Tanya _____

Soledad_____

Me _____

3. Be a broken record; repeat yourself. What might each verbal defender repeat in his or her situation?

Cheryl _____

Josh _____

Tanya _____

Soledad_____

Me _____

4. Say what just happened. Without judging or explaining, describe out loud what the boundary crosser has just done.

Cheryl _____

Josh _____

Tanya _____

Soledad_____

Me _____

5. Lie.

Cheryl _____

Josh _____

Tanya _____

Soledad_____

Me _____

6. Leave. Leave the room, leave the relationship, remove yourself from the situation. How or when could the defenders have left?

Cheryl _____

Josh _____

Tanya _____

Soledad_____

Me _____

7. Increase verbal intensity. If you're not heard the first time, you may need to either get louder or drop the pitch of your voice.

Cheryl _____

Josh _____

Tanya _____

Soledad_____

Me _____

8. Make a scene, attract attention, ask for help from others.

Cheryl _____

Josh _____

Tanya _____

Soledad_____

Me _____

To Decrease Difficulty

Ask a friend to read the scenarios and contribute his or her ideas.

Success Check

• Complete each blank.

Score Your Success

Fill in the blanks for Cheryl, Josh, Tanya, and Soledad = 25 points

Fill in the blanks for a personal situation = 25 points

When you look at the answers for your own situation, what do you notice? Can you go back and take any of these actions now? What support would you need to be able to defend yourself verbally in the future? Is there someone you could practice with first?

"Say what just happened" is one of my favorite verbal techniques. By simply describing the perpetrator's actions out loud, you make his or her actions public in a sense. You place the burden where it belongs—on the person who has been inappropriate. A great example of this technique has been talked about for years in the self-defense community. I don't know its origin, but it's incredibly creative! On a crowded train, a perpetrator began to physically assault another passenger by groping her. The woman grabbed his wrist and held it up in the air, shouting "Does anyone know whose hand this is? I found it on my ass!"

 Misstep

Responding passively by smiling, looking away, or merely giving a "look."

Correction

Looking angrily at someone is generally not read by perpetrators as an assertive response. Be firm, say what you want, say *no*.

In order to master verbal self-defense, you must unlearn the misinformation most of us have been taught about the meanings of the words passive, aggressive, and assertive. Study these characteristics of each style:

• **Passive.** Ignoring your own rights and wishes, not noticing when you are angry, refusing to say what you really want, communicating how you feel only indirectly (by rolling your eyes, complaining to others, gossiping behind someone's back), going along with something so as not to hurt another person's feelings. Other physical qualities that may convey passivity include looking down, turning away from the other person, being unable to take up space, and slouching.

- **Aggressive.** Controlling others, ignoring their rights and wishes, refusing to listen to others, demanding to get your own way, being willing to hurt others to get what you want, intimidating others with anger, manipulation, or direct force, and blaming others for your anger. Physical qualities that may convey aggression include speaking in a loud voice, showing teeth, stepping in toward other people, frequently being angry, clenching fists, stony silence.

- **Assertive.** Respecting your own rights and wishes and taking into account the rights and wishes of others, respectfully stating your own opinions, making your own choices, listening to others but not allowing their opinions to control you, communicating directly (saying what you want honestly, being willing to say yes or no). Physical qualities that may convey assertiveness include assuming a protective stance, holding your ground, and maintaining a neutral face (not smiling or frowning).

If you grew up witnessing violence, you may have an underdeveloped reaction to aggres-sion. It may seem acceptable and even normal to you when people act verbally, emotionally, or physically aggressive toward you or others. Some survivors of violence feel quite numb and lack an appropriate fear response in these situations. These students may sometimes respond instinctively with either aggression or passivity. You can unlearn these reactions in order to protect yourself.

Another misconception is the belief that being assertive is the same as being aggressive. This is especially common for those who were taught that appeasing someone is the only way to avoid danger. These students may freeze up when they are exposed to any new aggressor. It may actually feel quite dangerous and over the top for you to turn toward another person, put your hands up, and say, "Don't touch me." But this is an asser-tive response, not an aggressive one.

Many of our communities also train boys and men to believe that their only option in the face of violence is to respond with violence. The man who chooses to be assertive rather than aggressive is sometimes labeled passive, weak, feminine, or homosexual. Unlearning this early training is essential to men's ability to practice self-defense. If you believe the lie that assertive-ness in men equals passivity, you are enslaved to the desire of any perpetrator at any time who wishes to force you into a fight.

Defining Space Drill 6. *Saying No*

The following drill is a very simple one. Some would say simple, but not easy. Sometime this week, say no to something you'd normally go along with. This requires that you use your aware-ness skills (to notice that you don't want to go along with something) and your verbal skills (to say no). After you do so, write about how it felt in your Practice Journal. Was it easy to do? Difficult? Impossible? Did you see an opportunity to say no and then give in anyway? If you have any trouble completing the drill, read through some students' responses for inspiration.

"The assignment to say no was a lot harder than I thought it would be. This girl asked me for some of my fries and I remembered, so I said no, but she looked so hurt! I gave up and said 'I'm just kidding, here! Here!' I can't believe how hard this was. I had a lot of other chances too. My mom wanted me to watch my cousins. I gave my brother $50. I had no idea how many things I go along with in a week. Bummer." *You're not alone. When I assign this drill to my students, invariably half of them find they can't do it—even when it's a graded assignment! I encourage you to keep trying. This is great practice for all of life, not just self-defense against violence. Pay attention to how you feel before, during, and after saying no. What do you notice? Don't give up; it's worth it.*

- "This homework was perfect timing for me. I finally said no to my boss about working late on Fridays. It felt really hard though. I was actually shaking afterward. I don't know if I thought I was going to get fired or what. The other moms I work with say no all the time. He looked surprised for a minute, and then he just said. 'Have a nice weekend.'" *Congratulations! You did it! It's perfectly normal to find that it feels bad when you first start setting boundaries. Many people find that their own emotional discomfort is a lot worse than the other person's reaction. Just because it felt uncomfortable, unfamiliar, or scary doesn't mean you did anything wrong.*

- "I said no to letting my girlfriend smoke in my apartment. It felt great. I've wanted to do that for a really long time. I don't think she believed me at first, like she was shocked or something. And then she lit up again the next morning and I had to tell her again! I'm really glad I did it. It felt weird but good too, like it was my apartment again." *I'm so happy to hear that. Nice work! When we set new boundaries with people who know us, it's quite common for them to test us, to push against the boundary to see if we really mean it. It's great that you stood firm the next morning too. You have a right to say no.*

To Increase Difficulty

Choose a more difficult opportunity, perhaps one in which you expect the other person will feel hurt or angry if you say no.

Score Your Success

You said no = 100 points

You noticed an opportunity but were unable to say no = 25 points

Imperfect Self-Defense Is Still Self-Defense

I have a personal story of successful verbal self-defense. A few years ago, I gave a presentation to a community group of which I am a member. Afterward, a well-respected member walked up to me. I had always mistrusted him, although I wasn't sure why. He put one hand on my shoulder and with the other began to rub my belly while he thanked me for my talk. I felt disgusted and confused. My first reaction was to do nothing. I held my breath, stood still, and felt deeply uncomfortable. Just then someone walked around the corner, and the man let go of me and walked away.

I drove home hating and blaming myself. I remember thinking, "I'm a self-defense instructor, why did I let him get away with that?!" After an hour or so, I realized I needed to get help with my self-criticism. (Have you ever heard "My head is a dangerous neighborhood, I shouldn't go in there alone"?) I called some friends and described to them what had happened. They agreed that his behavior was inappropriate, and none of them blamed me or claimed that I had somehow "allowed" or "caused" his actions. With their help, I realized that I could still set a boundary with him, and I practiced what I wanted to say.

One week later, I walked right up to him in protective stance and said, "After my talk here, you put your arm around me and rubbed my stomach" (say what happened). "I didn't like that, and I never want you to touch me again" (say what you want). I was prepared for him to deny his actions, or get angry, or call me a liar. But, in fact, his response was to look terrified and say, "I'm sorry, I don't know why I did that," and then he got away from me as quickly as possible!

I count my experience as a success story even though I wasn't perfect. Self-defense very rarely is. Most of us feel some discomfort, denial, fear, shame, or confusion when our boundaries are crossed. I had a right to confront the belly rubber, even though a week had passed, even though I was worried that people would think I was making a big deal out of nothing. We are all worth defending. Even when we feel we've made a mistake, even if we wished we'd spoken up sooner, even if we're scared we can't do it perfectly. And that man never touched me again!

Defining Space Drill 7. *Studying Success*

Answer the following questions in your Practice Journal. If you like, discuss the Imperfect Self-Defense success story and your answers with a friend or study partner.

1. When did I begin my self-defense? (Hint: It was *before* he touched me)

2. How many kinds of self-defense did I use? List each one. Include the use of awareness and verbal, emotional, and psychological techniques, not just physical ones.

3. What might you have done differently in the same situation? Why?

4. What surprised you about this experience?

5. What satisfied or empowered you most about this experience?

SUCCESS SUMMARY

In step 2, Defining Your Space, you began to practice a variety of self-defense skills, including yelling, taking a protective stance, and tracking. Using your developing awareness, you have chosen a style of protective stance best suited to you. You've studied some of the most common psychological barriers to verbal self-defense and have begun to train against them in your daily life. You've incorporated the boundary lessons from step 1, Increasing Awareness of Your Surroundings, by practicing physically with others. You've applied eight common verbal techniques to several situations calling for self-defense against boundary crossers, and you've examined your own history to consider how these techniques might benefit you in the future.

Before Taking the Next Step

Before moving on to step 3, Striking With Hands and Arms, take time to reflect on what you have learned to this point. Answer the following questions honestly.

1. Have you shouted *no* loudly at least 40 times?
2. Have you studied the protective stance and chosen a hand position best suited to you?
3. Have you practiced tracking with a partner?
4. Have you filled in the verbal self-defense blanks for Cheryl, Josh, Tanya, Soledad, and your own scenario?
5. Have you said no to something you would normally just go along with? Have you tried to say no? Did you write about your experience in your Practice Journal?

If you answered yes to all five questions, you are ready to move on to step 3, Striking With Hands and Arms.

Taking the Step Further.   *Homework Assignments*

Memorize the myths in this step and write about them in your Practice Journal. Share some of your thoughts and feelings about the myths and facts with at least one other person. Has someone ever violated your boundaries and you responded by doubting yourself? Have you ever tried to ignore verbal abuse? How can you tell if someone is about to become violent?

Physical practice—Spend 5 to 20 minutes a day practicing the moves from step 2, Defining Your Space, particularly shouting and taking a protective stance, until you begin step 3, Striking With Hands and Arms. If you're uncomfortable with being loud, practice in your car or in the shower. It's generally more helpful to practice for 5 minutes every day than 35 minutes once a week.

Striking With Hands and Arms

Even a clear and firm verbal boundary is sometimes crossed. If the skills you learned and practiced in steps 1 and 2 do not deter an assailant, you have many other options available to you. In step 3, you will learn a variety of strikes using your hands and arms. These techniques are designed for people with low or average arm strength, and they work even if you have the use of only one of your arms. You do not have to be able to split boards with your bare hands or bench-press 200 pounds to break off an attack using hand and arm strikes. And if you don't use your arms at all, don't worry. You may skip ahead to step 4, Kicking With Feet and Legs.

Myth   Don't fight back; you'll just make him mad and then you'll be hurt worse.

Fact   The majority of assailants look for a victim, not for a fair fight, and therefore they can be deterred by even the simplest and least physical display of meaningful resistance.

According to a Brandeis University study, the most passive victims of sexual assault actually sustain more injuries and more severe physical injuries than those who fight back (Ullman and Knight, 1993). Many women and men have avoided assault by fighting back. According to the FBI, many assaults are broken off when the intended victim physically resists in any determined way (Zawitz et al., 1993). When a person defends herself effectively, the attacker tends to become more concerned with his own safety than with trying to assault her. Many, many more people have been hurt being raped than by escaping rape. Anyone assaulting another human being is already disturbed. You can't "make him mad" by attempting to defend yourself.

A word first about what we *won't* be learning in step 3, Striking With Hands and Arms—punches. I invite you to forget for the time being every punch you've ever seen thrown on television or in the movies. Punching can be complicated to learn, plus you run the risk of injuring your own wrists and knuckles. In self-defense situations, it can also be a liability. A punch may be exactly what the assailant is expecting, particularly those assailants who target men. Your attacker may be well versed in blocking those types of strikes. It's also easy to broadcast your intentions accidentally when you pull your arm back to punch, thus taking away the advantage of surprise.

We also won't be learning martial art-style strikes. Martial art forms take years to master. The perfect placement and angle of your hands, forearms, legs, and feet can be essential to the successful execution of a strike. Some styles require a great deal of balance and grace. And practicing martial art strikes usually requires an experienced sparring partner who knows exactly what you're going to do and can respond appropriately.

Instead, you will be learning strikes that are simple, accessible to most bodies, and do not require years of practice to perfect. If you've ever witnessed an actual, nonprofessional fight, you may have noticed that assaults and defenses look messy, confusing, and inelegant. People stumble and fall, they miss, and they try a strike several times before they even make contact. They get surprised, they get blocked, and then they try something new. This is how real self-defense looks—scrappy, imperfect, unchoreographed, and effective.

EYE STRIKE

The first strike uses your hands to strike an attacker in the eye or the eye region. Some of my students have heard rumors about driving the attacker's eyeballs out of the sockets. Never fear; we will not be learning any such technique. There will be no gouging, no plucking, and no blinding. The primary goal of the eye strike is to put the attacker into defensive mode and to create some space between you so that you can plan your next move. You're unlikely to hit your target perfectly, and, even if you did, there is sufficient space in the socket to protect the eye.

Your fingers are very slightly curved so that your thumb is tucked inside and the tips of your fingers are touching each other (figure 3.1). Include all of your fingers, and do not pull them back toward your palm.

The Eye Strike (figure 3.2) is a very quick jabbing motion. Practice it now against the palm of your hand. Use both the correct and incorrect hand positions. Do you notice the difference in power? Can you feel how much stronger the technique is with all of the fingers supporting

each other? Gently aim an Eye Strike at the bony sinus areas surrounding your own eyes. Push just a little harder and then a little harder yet. Did you notice something? You do not need much force at all with this strike to create discomfort and recoil.

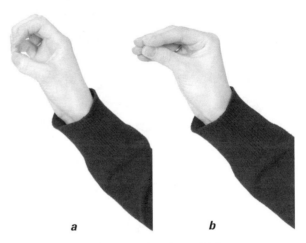

a　　　　*b*

Figure 3.1 Eye Strike hand position: *(a)* incorrect position with fingers excessively curved and pulled back toward palm; *(b)* correct position with fingers straight or curved slightly, thumb tucked, and fingertips together.

Figure 3.2   Eye Strike

APPROACH

1. Begin in protective stance

EXECUTION

1. Form hands into Eye Strike position
2. Strike toward eye region
3. Shout *NO!*

FOLLOW-THROUGH

1. Bring hands back quickly to protective stance
2. Repeat if necessary

a

b

Starting in protective stance, practice the Eye Strike several times at your own speed. Practice 20 repetitions, shouting *no* with each one.

Misstep

Pulling away from the attacker during the attempted Eye Strike.

Correction

Hold your protective stance and lean into the strike slightly. At the end of the strike, your arms will still be slightly bent, not fully extended.

Misstep

You want to punch with clenched fists instead.

Correction

Reread the first page of step 3, Striking With Hands and Arms. And practice, practice, practice!

Hand and Arm Strikes Drill 1. *Eye Strike Surprise*

This drill requires a partner. I'd like you to experience an Eye Strike from the point of view of an attacker. Take up positions on either side of a glass door or window; stand as close to the glass as possible. When you are ready to strike, try to surprise your partner by aiming an Eye Strike at the glass in front of his or her face. Do not, of course, hit your own fingers on the glass. Your partner then tries to surprise you with an Eye Strike as well. Experiment with your timing and placement to achieve a moment of surprise and be sure to include a strong *no* shout with each strike. To give yourself and your partner the full benefit of the surprise factor, allow yourself to enter into the drill fully instead of just acting it out or going slowly.

Score Your Success

Talk someone into doing this drill with you = 10 points

Manage to surprise your partner when striking = 20 points

Shout *no* with your strike = 10 points

Hand and Arm Strikes Drill 2. *Eye Strike Execution*

Another option for practicing the Eye Strike with a partner is to have someone hold a piece of tough fabric (denim works well) at or above eye level in front of you. The fabric should be held firmly and taut enough to provide both some resistance and some give. Your partner should be sure not to hold the fabric directly in front of his or her own face. Practice the Eye Strike 5 to 10 consecutive times, using your voice and jabbing at the fabric each time.

To Increase Difficulty

- Practice it one-handed.
- Practice it with your nondominant hand.

Success Check

- Keep your fingers together, thumb on the inside.
- Use a quick, jabbing motion.
- Return to protective stance after each strike.
- Use your voice with each strike.

Score Your Success

Complete the drill = 20 points

Return fully to protective stance after each strike = 10 points

Shout *no* with your strike = 10 points

ELBOW STRIKES

There are at least two ways to use your elbow in self-defense. These are surprisingly powerful strikes. Because your elbow is small and pointy (probably), you can channel all of the power of your arm, shoulder, back, and hips through a relatively small surface area. Elbow strikes can effectively disarm or even temporarily disable an attacker.

Low Elbow

The first strike you'll practice is one to use against someone behind you. From protective stance, reach forward with your dominant hand in a fist and thrust your arm directly back, striking the attacker in the gut, ribs, or just under the breast bone with the point of your elbow (figure 3.3). Bring your elbow straight back, right along your own side. Do not move your elbow out to the side in a rounded motion; your target is directly behind you. Remember to reach forward to give yourself maximum range of motion for your strike. You must thrust it back forcefully, similar to the force that is required to start a lawn mower. Your strike will be more powerful if you yank your elbow back 3 feet than if you only have 1 foot in which to strike.

Figure 3.3   Low Elbow Strike

APPROACH

1. Take the protective stance
2. Bring striking arm forward
3. Make a fist
4. Lean slightly forward

EXECUTION

1. Thrust elbow straight back
2. Transfer weight to back leg
3. Move entire torso, not just arm
4. Shout *NO!*

a

b

Starting in protective stance, practice the Low Elbow Strike several times at your own speed. Practice it with both arms. Use a mirror, a friend, or an instructor to check your alignment. Practice for 20 repetitions, shouting *no* with each blow.

Misstep

Moving only the arm, not fully integrating the force of your entire body.

Correction

Be sure that your striking arm is on the same side as your back leg. Your back foot should be angled slightly out. (Review Protective Stance, figure 2.2, page 18.)

Hand and Arm Strikes Drill 3. *Low Elbow Strike*

Now practice the Low Elbow Strike and actually make contact with a target. It's important to set up your drill carefully in order to protect both the target and your own body. You'll need a striking pad or extremely firm couch cushion and, if you like, friends or classmates to help you (optional: a couch or a car). Choose a target for your low elbow. If practicing with friends, they should hold the pad or cushion behind you and slightly to the side of your striking arm (figure 3.4). The pad or cushion must be large enough to allow for range of motion (2 by 3 feet is good) and firm enough to protect the holder (pillows won't work).

Alternatively, you may do this drill while seated on a well-cushioned couch or in a car (not while driving, please). First ensure that your couch or car seat is adequately cushioned, by striking slowly. Use 25 percent of your full power, then 50 percent, and then 75 percent. The Low Elbow Strike is the same movement whether you are seated or standing.

Finally, be prepared to shout as loudly as possible. Do you have family or roommates in the next room? Are you worried about frightening someone in the apartment upstairs? This drill (and the others to follow in subsequent steps) must include the *no* shouts, so do what you need to do to let people know what to expect.

For the drill itself, you will execute two separate and distinct moves. For the first, you will shout *no* while you get into protective stance. In the second move, you will reach forward and then strike with a low elbow as you shout *no* a second time. Go slowly, but use full force. If applicable, check in with your instructor or friend holding the pad to make sure he or she is ready for you to begin. Check your foot and arm position before you strike. When you are ready to begin, use full force to strike the pad as hard as you can. Complete 10 repetitions of the Low Elbow Strike using your dominant arm and 10 repetitions using your nondominant arm. Use your voice each time.

To Decrease Difficulty

- Do fewer repetitions. Give yourself plenty of time.
- Use only the dominant arm.
- If you're uncomfortable shouting or practicing with others, start with the car seat drill.

To Increase Difficulty

- Increase repetitions to 40.
- Use mostly your nondominant arm.
- Hold your breath and complete five repetitions silently.
- Increase the speed and force of your strikes.

Figure 3.4   Low Elbow Strike.

Success Check

- Begin from protective stance.
- Bring striking arm forward and lean forward slightly.
- Make contact with full force.
- Use voice on each contact.
- Return to protective stance after each strike.

High Elbow Strike

You may also use an elbow strike to reach a target behind and above you. The High Elbow Strike targets the face of an assailant who has grabbed you from behind. As in the Low Elbow Strike, you strike first with your dominant side. Check your alignment to be sure that your dominant leg is back and that your foot is angled slightly out from your body. From the protective stance, look over your shoulder for your target (imagine someone standing behind you) and then strike backward with your elbow (figure 3.5). It's important to include your entire body while you strike so turn in to face the attacker. At the end of the move, you will have turned 180 degrees and be facing directly behind you. This ensures that you don't twist and strain your back, and it also allows you to bring the strength of your entire body into the strike.

Figure 3.5 | **High Elbow Strike**

APPROACH

1. Take the protective stance
2. Look for your target

EXECUTION

1. Strike with your elbow
2. Shout *NO!*
3. Turn in toward attacker

a

b

FOLLOW-THROUGH

1. Face attacker
2. Resume the protective stance

c

Try the High Elbow Strike to the air at your own speed several times. Check your alignment in a mirror and turn your feet all the way around. It's OK to feel awkward; in fact, it's quite normal when you're practicing any new physical skill. The High Elbow Strike can feel quite strange at first.

Misstep

Not turning in; moving only your arm and ending the strike still facing forward.

Correction

Move your feet. This doesn't have to be elegant. You may take several tiny steps, spin on the balls of your feet, or lunge. Just be sure to bring your feet, hips, and back along with you when you turn in.

High Elbow, Prone Position

You can also use the High Elbow Strike while you are lying down. Just like the standing High Elbow Strike, it's important to move your entire body with the prone position strike. Instead of turning your feet around to face the attacker, roll your entire body in toward the attacker.

Begin by lying on your side on a bed or floor. Make sure that you have plenty of open space behind you for striking and rolling. Come up onto your bottom elbow and look behind you for your target, in this case the face of an attacker who is lying down behind you (figure 3.6). Reach forward with your top arm, then coordinate striking back with your elbow, shouting *no*, and rolling in with the strike. At the end of your strike, you will be facing the opposite direction. Remember, rolling in ensures that you don't strain your back and allows you to bring the strength of your entire body into your High Elbow Strike.

Figure 3.6 | **High Elbow Strike, Prone Position**

APPROACH

1. Lie on side

PREPARE

1. Reach forward with your top, striking arm
2. Make a fist
3. Look for your target

EXECUTION

1. Strike with your elbow
2. Shout *NO!*
3. Roll in with your strike

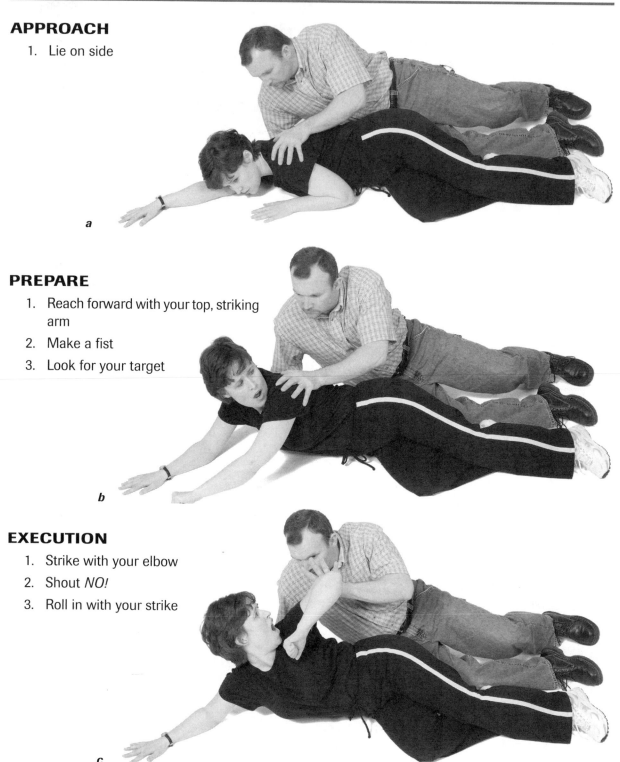

a

b

c

FOLLOW-THROUGH

1. Face the attacker you've just struck

2. Return your top hand to protective stance position (flat, palm out)

Practice the High Elbow Strike from the ground several times at your own speed and force. Check your alignment in a mirror and be sure to roll all the way over with each strike.

Misstep

Not rolling in; throwing the elbow back while trying to move the rest of your body forward.

Correction

Roll! Practice the drill in slow motion until you're consistently facing the opposite direction at the end of the strike. Although it may feel scary to be on the ground and facing an attacker, it's far safer than keeping your back toward someone trying to hurt you.

Hand and Arm Strikes Drill 4. *High Elbow*

Repeat the drill for the low elbow, this time with the target padding held high (figure 3.7). You will complete two separate and distinct moves. In the first, you will shout *no* while you get into protective stance. In the second move, you will strike with a high elbow as you shout *no* and turn in toward the target. Go slowly, but use full force. If available, you may choose to use a smaller, handheld striking pad.

Check with your friend holding the pad to make sure he or she is ready for you to begin. Establish which arm you're going to strike with. Check your foot and arm position. When you are ready to begin, hit the pad as hard as you can.

If you don't have someone to hold a target for you, you may drill the High Elbow Strike in the prone position by lying down and striking the back of a well-padded couch. Just be sure to roll all the way in so that you're facing the back of the couch when you've completed the blow.

Beginning in protective stance, complete 10 repetitions of the High Elbow Strike with voice using your dominant arm and 10 repetitions using your nondominant arm. Complete the same 20 repetitions of the drill lying down. If you do not have a suitable couch, you can practice the High Elbow Strike in the standing position only.

To Decrease Difficulty

- Do fewer repetitions. Give yourself plenty of time.
- Use only your dominant arm.
- Use the larger cushion or pad.

To Increase Difficulty

- Increase repetitions to 40.
- Use only your nondominant arm.
- Use a smaller striking pad or mark a small area of the couch with masking tape to sharpen your targeting accuracy.
- Increase the speed and force of your strikes.

Figure 3.7 High elbow drill, standing.

Success Check

- Begin from protective stance.
- Look over your shoulder for the target.
- Make contact with full force.
- Shout *no* with each contact.
- Face the target fully at the end of the strike.
- Return to protective stance after each strike.

Complete all 40 repetitions = 30 points

Shout *no* with all repetitions = 10 points

Shout *no* with half the repetitions = 5 points

Face your target at the end of each strike = 30 points

Targeting

In all of the strikes covered in this step, your target is not the rib, the nose, or the face. Your target is actually *behind* the rib, *behind* the nose, or *behind* the face. You want to strike so forcefully that you plan to hit through or beyond the target. In the case of the High Elbow Strike, for example, picture your target as about 1 foot behind the attacker's head. This prevents you from "pulling your punches" and thus lessening their impact. It takes true physical and psychological commitment to plan to elbow *through* someone's face. This blunt description frequently elicits some of the following questions from my students:

But what if I miss and the attacker gets mad?
But what if I gouge the attacker's eyes out?
But what if I can't hit hard enough?
But what if he grabs my hands?
But this won't work, and it looks dumb!
But why can't I just run away?
But what if I get prosecuted for defending myself?
But what if I don't do it right?
But what if I *do* do it right?

Often these questions arise along with an underlying feeling that it's not right to hurt someone else. It's understandable if you notice an uneasiness when you imagine having to do one of these techniques or even feel queasy just thinking about it. I hope that none of us ever has to harm someone in this way. But sometimes the most loving, compassionate, and nonviolent action you can take is to stop someone from hurting you. And sometimes the best way to achieve that is to strike hard with an elbow to the face.

HAMMER FIST

The Hammer Fist Strike (figure 3.8) is another move you can use if assaulted from behind. In this move, you strike a male assailant's groin with your fist. You'll be striking with the flat, outside surface of your fist (the pinky side). Note that your target is not the front of the body, but up and under—between his legs. From protective stance, make a fist with your dominant hand and swing it down and back and then up to make contact with the attacker's testicles. Keep your arm straight as you swing your fist back. For some of us, this move requires that we first shift our own hips out of the way. Looking for your target beforehand can be helpful in making contact.

Figure 3.8 — Hammer Fist Strike

APPROACH

1. Begin in protective stance
2. Look for target
3. Shift your hips to the side, opposite your dominant hand

EXECUTION

1. Swing your dominant arm back and make contact with the groin
2. Shout *NO!*

a

b

Misstep

You hit the attacker in the stomach or miss entirely.

Correction

You must be quite close to the target to be effective. Be sure to target up and under, not at the front of the body.

Misstep

You lack force on contact.

Correction

Discuss your feelings about this strike with someone. It's common to feel some discomfort or even disgust about striking an attacker in the groin, but you cannot destroy a man's ability to procreate with this blow. You do not deserve to be attacked, and you have a right to defend yourself powerfully and with force.

Practice the Hammer Fist Strike several times. Begin in protective stance and incorporate your voice with each strike. Consider that, depending on your own height and the height of your attacker, you will probably need to bend both of your knees, perhaps considerably, given the probable location of the attacker's groin.

Hand and Arm Strikes Drill 5. *Hammer Fist*

As with the elbow strikes, practice the Hammer Fist Strike with an actual target to hit. The pad should be held horizontally so that you can practice hammering up and underneath it. Be sure to use your voice with each strike. Complete at least 20 repetitions, varying which arm you use.

To Increase Difficulty

- Increase repetitions to 40.
- Mark a small area of the pad with masking tape to sharpen your targeting skills.
- Increase the speed and force of your strikes.

Success Check

- Begin from protective stance.
- Bend your knees slightly while swinging your striking arm back.
- Make contact with full force.
- Use your voice on each contact.

Score Your Success

Complete all 20 repetitions = 30 points

Shout *no* with all repetitions = 10 points

Shout *no* with half of your repetitions = 5 points

HEEL PALM

For the final technique in this step, you use the heel of your outstretched palm to strike an attacker in the throat, chin, or nose region (figure 3.9). When combined with the momentum of an attacker moving toward you, this technique can effectively end an assault. Study the correct form to protect your own wrists.

Starting in protective stance, strike out and up with the heel (base) of your open palm. Target the attacker's nose. Imagine your palm sweeping up the buttons of his shirt before connecting with his face. Keep your fingers pulled back and step in toward your target as you strike.

Figure 3.9   Heel Palm Strike

APPROACH

1. Begin in protective stance
2. Use dominant arm (the one slightly back)

EXECUTION

1. Step in
2. Strike out and up, targeting the bottom of the nose
3. Shout *NO!*

a   b

Starting in protective stance, practice the Heel Palm Strike several times at your own speed. Practice with both hands. Use a mirror or ask a friend to check your alignment. Complete 20 repetitions, shouting *no* and stepping forward with each executed strike.

Misstep

Attempting to strike from a static position and overextending the arm.

Correction

Be sure to step in while striking.

Angle and distance are important to a Heel Palm Strike. It helps to be closer than an arm's length away from the attacker. Remember, you're striking through the nose, not just trying to reach the tip of it. You want to aim for a diagonal line up the attacker's shirt buttons, about a 45-degree angle. Do not strike straight up toward the sky or straight out horizontally (figure 3.10).

Figure 3.10 Heel palm distance and angle: *(a)* incorrect, defender strikes out horizontally; *(b)* correct, defender strikes out in diagonal line.

 Misstep

Striking straight forward or up.

Correction

Strike at an angle of about 45 degrees.

TURNING IN

One of the most common errors in the practice of all of the techniques in this step—and in almost all self-defense moves—is the urge to pull away from the assailant instead of turning in and moving closer. It's a natural reaction. If you have a clear escape route, are a fast runner, and are not being chased, running from an assailant can be a great choice. But most of the techniques in *Self-Defense: Steps to Survival* require that you move closer to the attacker. These techniques work at close range and depend on both the momentum of your attacker and your own willingness to strike back with force and intention. If half of your focus and attention is on getting away, you dilute the power of your strike.

Elevator Escape

In *Her Wits About Her*, self-defense instructor Tamar Hosansky recounts the time a man lunged at her in a New York City elevator. In order to defend herself, she used a combination of techniques, including the physical and psychological need to *turn in*.

Because she was trapped in an elevator with no immediate escape route, she instinctively knew she could not afford to turn away physically or mentally. The man in the elevator, a messenger she knew who worked in her building, lunged at her in an attempt to grab and kiss her. She hit him in the chest, and he backed away and said, "I'm sorry, I'm sorry, don't hit me." At this point she took "a fighter stance" and began to yell at him to get off the elevator.

Throughout the attack, Hosansky thought to herself repeatedly that she had to keep her eyes on him, remain alert, and be willing to seriously and effectively hurt him, given the small enclosed space. She hit buttons on the elevator to get it to stop at the next floor. He fled. With the help of her partner, Hosansky called security who locked down the building. Hosansky identified her attacker and spoke to the police about her options for prosecution. Though she experienced some emotional reactions after the attack, Hosansky writes that in the actual moments of the assault "[I] responded without fear and with the certainty that I was going to handle the situation no matter what it took—that I wasn't going to let him rape me."

Adapted from *Her Wits About Her*, edited by D. Caignon and G. Groves, 1987. New York: Perennial Library. Pages 212–213.

Hand and Arm Strikes Drill 6. *Studying Success*

Answer the following questions in your Practice Journal about the Elevator Escape success story. If you like, discuss the success story and your answers with a friend or study partner.

1. When did Tamar Hosansky begin her self-defense?

2. How many kinds of self-defense did she use? List each one, including the use of awareness and verbal, emotional, and psychological techniques, not just physical ones.

3. What might you have done differently in the same situation? Why?

4. What surprised you about Hosansky's experience?

5. What satisfied or empowered you most about her experience?

SUCCESS SUMMARY

Getting safe sometimes requires that you move beyond awareness and verbal techniques to strike with your hands and arms. In step 3, Striking With Hands and Arms, you learned the Eye Strike, the Low Elbow and High Elbow Strikes, the Hammer Fist Strike, and the Heel Palm Strike. All of these techniques require you to turn in and focus your attention on the attacker, rather than turning away physically or psychologically. You've hit your targets with full force. And you've explored some of the possible psychological barriers that could cause you to hold back or strike ineffectively.

Before Taking the Next Step

Before moving on to step 4, Kicking With Feet and Legs, take time to reflect on what you have learned to this point. Answer the following questions honestly.

1. Have you practiced the Low Elbow Strike both to the air and while making contact with something?
2. Have you drilled the High Elbow Strike from both standing and prone positions?
3. Have you practiced the Hammer Fist Strike both with and without a target?
4. Have you practiced the Eye Strike to the air as well as on your own palm?
5. Have you practiced the Heel Palm Strike? Did you shout *no* throughout your drill?

If you answered yes to all five questions, you are ready to move on to step 4, Kicking With Feet and Legs.

Taking the Step Further. *Homework Assignments*

Memorize the myth in this step and write about it in your Practice Journal. Share some of your thoughts and feelings about the myth and fact with at least one other person. Do you think a lot of people believe this myth? Do you remember the first time you heard the false idea that fighting back would make an attack worse? How does this myth benefit perpetrators of violence?

Physical practice—Spend 5 to 20 minutes a day practicing the moves from step 3, Striking With Hands and Arms, until you begin step 4, Kicking With Feet and Legs. Remember to incorporate your voice with each technique, do each one with full force, and use padding or cushions for targets.

Watch for moves from step 3, Striking With Hands and Arms, (or the missed opportunity to use them) in movies or television depictions of violence. Take notes. Write down the scenario and the techniques the victim could have used, including protective stance, shouting, and Low Elbow, High Elbow, Hammer Fist, Eye, or Heel Palm Strikes.

Kicking With Feet and Legs

Most of us who use our legs in daily life have a tremendous amount of power available in these muscles. You might be surprised by the force of your own stomps and kicks. For example, it only takes about 40 pounds (18 kg) of pressure to break a kneecap. Most of us can quite easily muster a kick of that force! Women in particular often concentrate their most significant muscle power in the hips, buttocks, and legs.

Myth   Women can't defend themselves because they are weaker than men. A small person will always lose in a fight with a bigger person.

Fact   There is not as much difference between male and female strength as we have been taught to believe. Women and children have effectively defended themselves against attackers of all sizes. Regardless of size and strength, all men and all large people have vulnerable areas, including the eyes, nose, throat, groin, and knees.

It's not the size of the woman in the fight, it's the size of the fight in the woman. Commitment and training are a lot more important than size. In step 4, Kicking With Feet and Legs, you'll have a chance to practice both standing and ground techniques using the feet and legs. One of the great benefits to using kicks in self-defense is the fact that attackers have seen all of the same movies and believe all of the same myths as defenders. The majority of us have internalized the false idea that "fighting" requires standing and throwing punches. For a defender to drop to the ground suddenly and deliver a potent kick to the attacker's groin is an extremely unexpected move to an assailant who harbors the false belief that his gender ensures his victory! This element of surprise, added to the remarkable force of a strong kick, can effectively bring to an end many attempted assaults.

STOMP

Stomping on the instep of an assailant (figure 4.1) is a sturdy technique that can end an attack almost before it begins. To stomp safely and avoid injury to your own body, bring your

47

foot down directly underneath you. Stomping far out in front or to your side may compromise your knees. You bring more force to your stomp if you bend both of your knees on impact. This brings the weight of your entire body into the force of your stomp, whether that's 80 pounds (36 kg) or 800 pounds (362 kg). Have you ever dropped anything that weighed even *half* your body weight onto your own foot? I hope not! Bending both knees also protects them from becoming hyperextended or jammed on impact.

Figure 4.1　　Stomp

APPROACH

1. Take a protective stance
2. Look for your target
3. Lift your foot, turning it out

EXECUTION

1. Stomp directly beneath you
2. Shout *NO!*
3. Bend both knees on impact

a　　　　　　　　　　　　　　　　　*b*

Misstep

Forgetting to look for your target and stomping the ground instead of the attacker.

Correction

Simply stomp again. In a realistic attack or defense scenario, your body is moving much faster than you think. You have enough time to repeat a stomp two, three, or four times before most startled attackers can react.

Turn your toes outward in most cases. One common use of the Stomp is to startle someone who has grabbed you from behind. Your stomp packs more power when your foot comes down *across* the foot of the attacker, rather than facing in the same direction as his or her foot (figure 4.2).

With respect to shoes, a shoe cushions your foot from the ground but it also cushions the ground from your foot, so the Stomp technique

a   b

Figure 4.2 Stomp target: *(a)* incorrect, defender's foot in same direction as attacker's; *(b)* correct, defender's foot comes down across attacker's.

is just as effective barefoot as shod. For the purpose of real-life self-defense, don't worry too much about high heels. Chances are that you would break a shoe heel (and you are more likely to twist your own ankle), but, in an adrenalized state, you'll be unlikely to register such an injury until you get to safety. For the purposes of drilling the Stomp, wear comfortably padded shoes. Exercise shoes work well.

Starting in protective stance, practice the Stomp several times at your own speed. If you don't have cushiony mats underneath, begin slowly. You might practice the Stomp outside on the grass or on thick carpeting first. Use a mirror or ask a friend to check your alignment. Complete 20 repetitions, alternating sides and shouting *no* with each one.

Feet and Leg Kicks Drill 1.   *Stomp*

After you feel completely comfortable and well balanced with your stomp, place a shoe on the ground next to and slightly behind you. It should be quite close to your own foot, just as it would be if someone grabbed you and gave you a bear hug from behind. Choose a shoe to play the assailant, one you're not particularly fond of. Begin by standing normally. Your first move is to shout *no* and get into protective stance. Your second is to maintain your stance while looking down for your target. Your third move is to lift and turn your foot and stomp that blasted shoe. Complete 20 repetitions, shouting *no* with each stomp.

To Increase Difficulty

Close your eyes and ask a friend to place the shoe behind you. On the count of 3, open your

eyes and assess which side the shoe is on before you stomp.

Success Check

- Make three separate moves.
- Hit your target 8 out of 10 times or more.
- Bend both of your knees with each stomp.
- Turn your foot out each time.
- Shout *no* each time.

Score Your Success

Complete 20 stomps = 1 point per repetition, up to 20 points

Shout *no* with each stomp = 1 point per *no*, up to 20 points

KNEE TO GROIN

Kneeing an attacker in the groin is the celebrity technique of self-defense. It's the one most of us have already heard of and the first idea that

comes to mind when I ask most groups for an example of self-defense. It's a good technique, a powerful one, and potentially a knockout blow.

Unfortunately, there are also many common misconceptions about it, so be prepared to unlearn some of what you believe.

First, the defender's knee never enters into the equation. The technique could be more accurately named the leg-to-groin or the upper-thigh technique. There are also many misconceptions about the target. The defender's upper thigh should strike the attacker between his legs, in an area both up and under (figure 4.3). On a male attacker, this targets the testicles, not the lower abdomen or the front of his body. This technique also works against female attackers (as any woman who's ever fallen off the seat of a boy's bike can tell you).

a b

Figure 4.3 Knee to Groin target: *(a)* incorrect target, defender knees abdomen; *(b)* correct target, defender brings upper thigh up and under.

Misstep

Incorrect targeting, aiming for the penis or abdomen rather than the testicles.

Correction

Remember that your true target is beyond the area where you make contact, in this case *above* the testicles.

To use this technique, you must be extremely close to the attacker (figure 4.4). This distance feels counterintuitive to most people, but you cannot thigh anyone in the groin from an arm's length away. During the execution of the technique, follow through by taking a large step even closer.

Figure 4.4 | Knee to Groin

APPROACH

1. Take a protective stance, with your knees slightly bent
2. Stand less than an arm's length away

EXECUTION

1. Take a large step in
2. Strike the groin with top of your thigh
3. Shout *NO!*

a

b

FOLLOW-THROUGH

1. Use the protective stance
2. End the movement where the attacker was standing

c

Starting in protective stance, practice the Knee to Groin several times at your own speed. Make sure you have the space to take three to four large strides forward. Keep your hands in protective stance throughout the move; they will protect your face if the attacker falls forward. It may also help to bend your knees very slightly and tighten your stomach muscles to maintain your own balance. Your foot should land about 3 feet in front of you and stay there at the end of the strike. Do not bring your foot back to its starting position.

Practice with both legs. The striking thigh is the one that is slightly back when you are in protective stance (probably the same side as your dominant hand). Use a mirror or ask a friend to check your alignment. Practice 20 repetitions using alternate legs, striding back and forth across your living room as needed, shouting *no* with each strike.

Misstep

Pulling away during the strike, avoiding contact with the attacker, pushing him out of range of your strike.

Correction

Move *in*! At the end of the strike, you should be standing in the exact location where the attacker was standing at the beginning of the technique.

Misstep

Losing your balance, your leg swings out wildly or you stumble on contact.

Correction

Tighten your abdomen and crunch very slightly forward. In protective stance, bend your knees and bounce up and down slightly to locate your own center of gravity. Make sure you are not holding your breath during practice. Shouting helps.

Feet and Leg Kicks Drill 2. *Knee to Groin*

It is helpful to make actual contact when you practice the Knee to Groin. See figure 4.5 for the correct way to hold the strike pad. Take a few moments to ensure that you are correctly positioned. The padding should be directly in front of you, held about groin height for an average attacker. The holder should be off to the side, because you're about to stride right through the pad and end up several feet in front of where you are now. Depending on your height, you may need to bend your knees slightly to target the pad properly.

Get into protective stance. When you're ready, strike the pad with the upper thigh of your dominant leg. Maintain your stance while your helper repositions the pad and repeat, this time with the other leg. Depending on the size of the room, repeat this move 5 to 10 times, shouting *no* with each strike. When you run out of space, turn around and come back across the room. If you don't have access to a strike pad, slap your upper thigh with your hands to simulate each moment of impact. Be sure to return your hands to protective stance after each strike.

Figure 4.5 Knee to Groin drill.

You can practice the setup for the Knee to Groin with a friend in order to give yourself a sense of how close you need to be, but, obviously, you do not want to hurt your friend with an actual blow. Practicing the Knee to Groin in slow motion without any force will not work. You'd be tempted to shove your friend instead of the popping or punching movement that you actually need. Getting a physical sense of powerlessness is not helpful to you at this important time in your training. Don't practice with friends.

To Decrease Difficulty

- Do fewer repetitions and give yourself adequate time.
- Use only your dominant leg.
- Ask your helper to give you a 1-2-3 count to prepare you to strike.

To Increase Difficulty

- Add movement. Walk toward the strike pad on your own or have the helper bring the pad toward you as you assess when to strike.
- Use a smaller pad for a target.

Success Check

- Begin in protective stance.
- Strike with the upper thigh, up and under.
- Step through your target.
- Keep your hands in protective stance throughout the strike.
- Use your voice with each strike.

Score Your Success

Complete 20 strikes = 1 point per repetition, up to 20 points

Move forward with each strike = 5 points per strike

Shout *no* with each strike = 1 point per *no*, up to 20 points

Knee to Groin Reactions

I rarely encounter a student who feels neutral about the Knee to Groin. This technique seems to occupy its own special place in the human psyche. Love it or hate it, you've probably heard whispers about it on the playground and seen it used for a laugh in 100 bad movies.

My students usually aren't shy about expressing their feelings about this technique. "I hate this more than anything else we learned today," one student told me. "It was just drilled into me growing up that you never, ever hit a boy there. My mother used to tell us that if we hit our brothers there they couldn't have children. It feels really nasty, like good girls don't do that." My response to her is that it's not true that you can make a man infertile by kneeing him in the groin. And you have a right to defend yourself by any means necessary. This is not roughhousing between children, this is your life. Remember rule 4 of the essential rules of self-defense? There are no rules.

Another student expressed a different view. "I love this," she said. "I've never felt so powerful in my whole life. It makes me feel really good to know that even this huge rapist is so completely vulnerable and now I know how to hurt him back. I want to use this all the time." Great! How wonderful to feel fully committed to your own life and safety!

"I was skeptical at first," one male student told me. "As a man, I never thought I'd do this to another guy. I keep thinking 'don't fight dirty' or 'fight fair.' But I figure if someone's coming after me or my family, I'm willing to do whatever it takes." Some students feel the same way when they imagine using the Knee to Groin in defense against a woman, as though it's somehow not fair to fight that way. But I absolutely agree that the effective practice of self-defense is not a sport with rules to follow.

(continued)

(continued)

"Totally gross," one blunt student said. "I don't even want to hear the word *groin*. I mean, what if he likes it? Or gets excited? I don't want to get anywhere near it. I'd rather just run away." Running can be an excellent technique if you have the chance to do it, and it will be even more effective if you've first delivered a blow that stops the assailant from chasing you. If you believe you have an opportunity to leave a situation, start with backing up several feet in protective stance. If you are followed, stop and hold your ground. Believe me, no one enjoys a knee to the groin. And it's OK to feel grossed out or uncomfortable while you're learning self-defense, especially when contemplating moving toward an area of the attacker's body you'd prefer to move away from. You don't have to let that feeling stop you from practicing.

FRONT SNAP KICK

The Front Snap Kick also targets the attacker's groin, in a slightly different fashion. This technique is a particularly good one for children and small people who might not be able to reach an attacker's groin with their upper thigh. It's similar in form and function to the Hammer Fist in step 3, Striking With Hands and Arms. Depending on the length of your legs, you may be able to use the Front Snap Kick from a greater distance than the Knee to Groin. It also requires slightly more balance, so, if you felt unbalanced by the Knee to Groin or if you struggle with balance issues in general, you may want to stick with the previous technique.

Target the groin with the top of your foot (figure 4.6). The "snap" refers to the quick motion of the kick as well as the flex of your ankle on contact. Leave your ankle and foot loose and allow them to snap upward on contact. Keep the height of your target in mind. There's no need to fling your foot up to head level. Keep your balance by leaving your hands in protective stance position, your knees unlocked, and your weight over your own hips. Just as in the Knee to Groin, slightly tightening or crunching your stomach muscles will help you stay upright.

Starting in protective stance, practice the Front Snap Kick several times at your own speed. Use both legs and use a mirror or ask a friend to check your alignment. Practice 20 repetitions, shouting *no* with each kick.

Misstep

Lunging forward, losing your balance, or grabbing the attacker with your hands.

Correction

Practice. Keep your hands in protective stance. Test to see if it's easier to balance on one foot or the other.

Figure 4.6   Front Snap Kick

APPROACH

1. Begin in protective stance

a

EXECUTION

1. Kick groin
2. Snap your foot on impact
3. Shout *NO!*

b

Feet and Leg Kicks Drill 3. *Front Snap Kick*

You can drill the Front Snap Kick to the air or to a target. You'll need a soft target about groin height. You may be able to use the bottom of a hanging body bag in a gym or a friend holding a kick pad horizontally, as in the Knee to Groin drill.

To Decrease Difficulty

- Do fewer repetitions and give yourself adequate time.
- Practice first with one hand resting on a table to improve your balance.
- Use the Knee to Groin or the Hammer Fist instead.

To Increase Difficulty

- Use a smaller cushion or strike pad to refine your targeting abilities.
- Practice with a thrown soccer ball to practice hitting a moving target.

- Add movement by walking toward the strike pad or have your helper walk the pad to you.

Success Check

- Begin in protective stance.
- Hit the target with the top of your kicking foot.
- Keep your hands in protective stance throughout the kick.
- Use your voice with each kick.

Score Your Success

Complete 20 kicks = 1 point per repetition, up to 20 points

Keep your hands up in protective stance = 10 points

Shout *no* with each kick = 1 point per *no*, up to 20 points

SIDE THRUST KICK

The Side Thrust Kick is the meat and potatoes, or the beans and rice, of your self-defense toolbox. This is a powerful technique you can return to over and over again. You can use it to target many vulnerable areas, including knees, groin, and head. It's such an important tool that you'll be returning to this kick in step 10, Delivering Knockout Blows, to refine and develop it. For now, learn the basics.

Unlike in the Eye Strike or the Low Elbow Strike, the defender's alignment for the Side Thrust Kick is extremely important. Taking the time to learn it correctly now will pay off in the future. Begin by lying flat on your left side on the ground. Rest your left forearm and elbow on the ground in front of your face. Bring both hands to rest flat on the ground in front of you.

Leave your legs together and bend both of them at the knee, bringing your feet as close to your bottom as you can. Point your top (right)

knee and toe directly at the ceiling. Your left leg remains on the ground. Plant the toe of your left foot on the ground, anchoring yourself in place. This is the Side Thrust Kick position (figure 4.7).

Figure 4.7 Side Thrust Kick position.

Got it? The feeling is a little odd, isn't it? If you're not working with someone experienced with the Side Thrust Kick, read through these instructions one or two more times before you go on to the drill.

Once you've got your alignment correct, kick out slowly, turning your top hip and shoulder over toward the ground in front of you (figure 4.8). Your striking surface is the heel of your right foot. When your leg is fully extended, your toe will point to the ground and you will be looking back over your right shoulder toward the target.

Figure 4.8 | **Side Thrust Kick**

APPROACH

1. Take the Side Thrust Kick position
2. Keep your knee and toe pointed up
3. Keep both hands on the ground in front of you

EXECUTION

1. Kick out
2. Roll your hip over toward the ground
3. Keep both hands flat in front of you
4. Shout *NO!*

a

b

FOLLOW-THROUGH

1. Extend your body in a straight line
2. Face away from the target, but look back over your shoulder
3. Return to the Side Thrust Kick position

c

Starting in the Side Thrust Kick position, practice the Side Thrust Kick several times at your own speed. Practice on both sides. Use a mirror or ask a friend to check your alignment. Practice 20 repetitions, shouting *no* with each kick. Return fully to the Side Thrust Kick position at the end of each kick. Pull your leg all the way in, keeping your top knee and toe pointed toward the ceiling and your bottom leg tucked in close.

Misstep

Kicking from your back instead of your side (figure 4.9).

Correction

Do not begin until both of your hands are on the ground in front of you. Keep your entire body tightly coiled, not extended out flat onto the ground.

Figure 4.9 Side Thrust Kick: incorrect, man kicking from his back.

Misstep

Not rotating your hip (figure 4.10).

Correction

When you are kicking, your top hip must roll over toward the ground. The defender faces away from the attacker at the end of the kick.

Figure 4.10 Side Thrust Kick rotation: incorrect, kicker's extended leg not rotated.

Feet and Leg Kicks Drill 4. *Side Thrust Kick Position*

For the Side Thrust Kick drills, you need a friend or partner willing to lean on you. Begin by checking your alignment against the figures. Plant your hands in front of you and your bottom toe on the ground. Kick out once but, instead of pulling your leg back into position, leave your leg extended. The standing partner should hold your extended foot and lean into your leg, gradually adding his or her entire body weight. If you are properly aligned, you leg will remain straight and extended. If, by leaning on your leg, your knee bends, thus bringing the stander in toward your face, you have not rotated your hip. Practice the move now. After you have checked your alignment, switch places and check your partner's alignment.

Success Check

- Both hands are on the same side.
- Top hip is rotated toward the ground.
- Leg remains extended despite partner's weight.

Score Your Success

Complete the drill = 20 points

Experiment until you discern correct alignment = 20 points

Feet and Leg Kicks Drill 5. *Side Thrust Kick Impact*

Use a strong exercise pad or cushion as a target. The pad holder kneels in front of the defender, holding the pad as shown in figure 4.11. When you, the defender, have checked your alignment, do three Side Thrust Kicks in a row, shouting *no* with each one. Allow time for the pad holder to reset the padding after each kick. Repeat on the other side using the other leg. Complete 20 kicks, taking breaks between them to check your alignment against figures 4.7 through 4.10. Don't rush. Take your time and set up in correct alignment prior to each kick.

To Decrease Difficulty

- Do fewer repetitions and give yourself adequate time.
- Use just your dominant leg.

To Increase Difficulty

Have the pad holder quickly back up 3 to 5 feet between kicks. This requires the defender to scoot in toward the target before kicking.

Success Check

- Both hands remain flat on the ground on the same side of your body.

- The top hip is rotated toward the ground.
- Return fully to the Side Thrust Kick position after each kick.

Figure 4.11 Side Thrust Kick drill.

(continued)

Feet and Leg Kicks Drill 5. *(continued)*

Score Your Success

Complete 20 kicks = 20 points

Maintain your position for each kick = 1 point per kick

Shout *no* with each kick = 1 point per shout

Dora's Story

One great self-defense success story comes from Dora Gonzalez, which she shares in *Her Wits About Her*. At a party, she noticed a group of three men attacking another man, and her male cousin went to the man's defense. She kept an eye on the group of attackers, knowing them to be dangerous and hoping to protect her cousin as well. Eventually, they started coming toward her, and one of them picked up a beer bottle on his way. Dora had studied some karate, and she said "I knew I had to be really fast, to catch them off guard. They weren't expecting retaliation, not from me, anyway." She shocked the assailants by kicking the first one in the groin and giving another a bloody nose with a heel palm-type strike, thus breaking off their attack. Later, she ran across one of the group in public and he stayed far away from her. She says it was "one of the most empowering experiences I've had."

Adapted from *Her Wits About Her*, edited by D. Caignon and G. Groves, 1987. New York: Perennial Library. Pages 153-156.

Feet and Leg Kicks Drill 6. *Studying Success*

Answer the following questions in your Practice Journal. If you like, discuss Dora's success story and your answers with a friend or study partner.

1. When did Dora Gonzalez begin her self-defense?

2. How many kinds of self-defense did she use? List each one. Include the use of awareness and verbal, emotional, and psychological techniques, not just the physical forms of self-defense.

3. What might you have done differently in the same situation? Why?

4. What surprised you about this survivor's experience?

5. What satisfied or empowered you most about this survivor's experience?

SUCCESS SUMMARY

Successful strikes using your feet and legs require careful positioning and maximum force. These techniques provide the core of your self-defense skills. You've now learned and practiced the Stomp, Knee to Groin, Side Thrust Kick, and perhaps the Front Snap Kick as well. Each strike builds on either the protective stance or Side Thrust Kick position and can be used against a variety of targets, including the knees, groin, and head.

Before Taking the Next Step

Before moving on to step 5, Breaking Holds, take time to reflect on what you have learned to this point. Answer the following questions honestly.

1. Have you practiced stomping? Did you start in protective stance?
2. Have you practiced the Knee to Groin technique?
3. Have you read the student comments about this technique?
4. Are you certain that you've physically mastered the correct positioning of the Side Thrust Kick? If not, have you asked someone to help by reading the instructions and checking your alignment?
5. Have you drilled the Side Thrust Kick full-force against padding?

If you answered yes to all five questions, you are ready to move on to step 5, Breaking Holds.

Taking the Step Further. Homework Assignments

Memorize the myth in this step and write about it in your Practice Journal. Share some of your thoughts and feelings about the myth with at least one other person. When was the first time you remember being exposed to the idea that women can't defend themselves because they are weaker than men? In what other areas of life besides self-defense do you hear that men are more capable than women? Can you think of three movies, television shows, or fairy tales that support this myth? Can you think of three that support the fact?

Search for five examples that disprove this myth online, in the news, in stories, in your own life, or in the lives of people you know. Seek out stories in which, against all odds, little people triumph over the powerful. Or share a story with a friend about a time that you achieved something you didn't think was possible. Inspire yourself!

Physical practice—Spend 5 to 20 minutes a day practicing the moves from step 4, Kicking With Feet and Legs, until you begin step 5, Breaking Holds. Incorporate your voice with each technique. Hit hard. Don't pull your punches or just act out the technique. Actually do it.

Breaking Holds

In step 5, Breaking Holds, you will learn a variety of ways to free yourself if someone is grabbing you. This step focuses on standing attacks. Holds on the ground (or pins) are covered in step 6, Getting to the Ground Safely, and step 7, Fighting From the Ground.

There are a variety of verbal, psychological, and physical techniques for breaking someone's hold on you. Breaking holds is both easier and more complicated than simply hitting a pressure point or using a karate chop to a wrist. One of the best ways to break an attempted hold is to avoid getting grabbed in the first place.

Myth   It's important to be certain of the attacker's intention. It's best to wait until you're absolutely certain that someone means to harm you. It would be terrible to make a mistake.

Fact   It's best to respond firmly and immediately when an assailant tests your boundaries. Attacks begin before the attacker grabs, and victims usually doubt their perceptions long after an attack has begun. It's far better to react than to wait.

Remember the perpetrator's approach from step 1, Increasing Awareness of Your Surroundings? Many perpetrators test your physical boundaries after testing you verbally. She or he may put an arm around you, rub your back, squeeze your shoulder, or try to hug you. If you want to be hugged, that's great! But if you'd rather not be hugged by this person and you don't respond firmly when he or she has done it anyway, you just sent a message that you will not stick up for yourself. This could be welcome news to a perpetrator looking for a victim.

Start with some defenses against boundary invasions from people that you like. These great nonviolent techniques send a clear message that you are in charge of whether you are touched or not. You could use them against an acquaintance who is testing the waters or even a beloved friend just because you don't feel like being touched right then. Many of us have the opportunity to practice these techniques at parties, support group meetings, family reunions, or church.

THE BRUSH OFF

This technique stops someone who is trying to put a hand on your shoulder or is trying to place an arm around you. When the toucher reaches out, simply raise your own arm on that same side, with a flat palm, and gently push the arm away (figure 5.1). It's a brushing off movement. If you've watched martial arts classes (or have ever seen *The Karate Kid*), it's a familiar move.

Figure 5.1 | Brush Off

APPROACH

1. Stand near a friend
2. Your friend reaches out to place an arm around your shoulders

EXECUTION

1. Bring your hand up, inside the friend's arm, with flat palm, as in a protective stance
2. Move out in a circular motion

a

b

THE HUGGER

This technique enables you to say no to being hugged and is basically a two-handed version of the Brush Off. When approached by a hugger, bring both of your arms up into protective stance and then sweep them up and out to your sides (figure 5.2). If you like, you can clasp the hugger's hands warmly at the end of the move and then return them.

Figure 5.2 | **Hugger**

APPROACH

1. Using awareness, decide if you want to hug or not

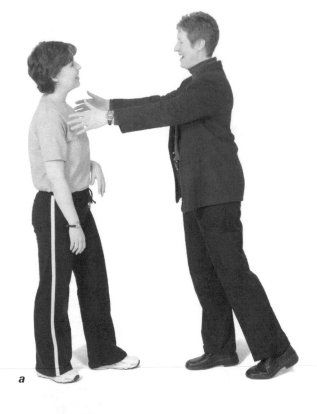

EXECUTION

1. Bring hands with flat palms up between hugger's arms
2. Move arms up and out to the side
3. Brush the hugger's arms away from you

a

b

FOLLOW-THROUGH

1. Take hugger's hands
2. Give them back to her

c

Misstep

Waiting until the toucher or hugger is too close.

Correction

Move early. Depending on the speed and distance of the toucher or hugger, you need to move at least as soon as she or he is an arm's length away and closing in.

Stand with your arms at your sides and practice the single-arm Brush Off and the double-armed Hugger to the air. Use a mirror or ask a friend to check your positioning.

I have successfully used both of these techniques on many occasions. Once I used the Brush Off with a drunken stranger on the street who was trying to lean on me in a friendly if unwelcome manner. I probably get a chance to stop someone from hugging me at least once a week. I'm a member of several communities where hugging is the norm, but I'm just not a big hugger. Usually, my friends look surprised

and, once in a while, someone seems offended. Even then, it's worth it. I get to decide who touches me.

Some students of self-defense, particularly women, find it almost unbearable to imagine indicating (even in this gentle, silent way) that they would prefer not to be touched. If you can relate, it's essential that you practice these techniques in the real world. You need to develop the internal willingness to make yourself and, perhaps, others uncomfortable. You will be unable to kick someone in the head if you are unable to brush his arm gently off your shoulder.

THE "FRIENDLY" WRIST GRAB

You can use this nonviolent technique if someone has grabbed you by the wrist. I no longer have "friends" who grab me by the wrist, but I've found that this technique is frequently useful to my college-aged students. They describe drunken friends at parties who try to get them on the dance floor or to come to another room. Rather than get into a tug of war with someone who may have more upper-body strength or mass than you do, simply clasp your own hand and then yell *no* while dropping your body

weight and yanking your own arm down and away (figure 5.3). Much like the Stomp, this move requires that you use the weight and movement of your entire body, not just the strength of your free arm. And voice is important. If you're hesitant, or smiling uncomfortably, or wishing your friend would change his or her mind, this technique won't work. Although nonviolent, it's considerably more forceful than the Brush Off or the Hugger.

Figure 5.3 **Wrist Grab**

APPROACH

1. Grabbed by the wrist

a

CLASP

1. Clasp your own hand

b

YANK

1. Shout *NO!*
2. Drop body weight
3. Yank arm down

c

Start with one arm extended. Practice the friendly Wrist Grab several times at your own speed. Use both arms and use a mirror or ask a friend to check your alignment. Practice 20 repetitions, shouting *no* with each clasp, drop, and yank motion.

Misstep

Not using enough force, being too embarrassed to shout, or getting into a tug of war.

Correction

Develop your willingness to make a scene.

Breaking Holds Drill 1. *Friendly Boundary Invaders*

All three of these techniques are great to practice with a friend. Ask someone you trust to hug you normally or to put his or her arm around your shoulder. Take turns being the toucher or hugger and the person setting a physical boundary. When you get to the friendly Wrist Grab, the grabber seizes the defender's wrist, not the hand. Although I'm asking you to practice with a friend, the Wrist Grab defense requires force and shouting.

Success Check

- Each partner gets a chance to be the toucher or hugger and the boundary setter for all three techniques.

Score Your Success

Use the Brush Off on the toucher on both sides = 20 points

Successfully avoid being hugged = 20 points

Get your arm free on the Wrist Grab = 20 points

Escaping Touchers, Huggers, and Grabbers

You have a right to decide who touches you and when. It's your body, not theirs. One student shared that she really liked these techniques and was planning to use the Hugger on one particular man at church, whom everyone else seemed to like. "I don't mind hugging some people, but I can see myself doing this move when I wouldn't scream 'Don't touch me!' at him, you know?" she shared. It doesn't matter if other people like the hugger or not; you get to choose when you're touched. Not only that, it's essential to trust your instincts. Your feeling of not wanting to touch him is valuable information. When you trust and respond to your instincts, they get louder. You need access to that internal information.

Another student shared that she was unsure when to use the various wrist grabbing techniques. "I'd much rather grab my own hand and yell than do that Eye Strike or knee somebody! Shouldn't I start with the lowest one and see if it works?" she said. That decision is entirely up to you. I recommend that you only use the friendly Wrist Grab (yelling and grabbing your own hand) very rarely, in the case of a close friend you trust but who, for some reason, is not responding to verbal boundary setting. If a stranger or someone who has hurt you before grabs you by the wrist, an assault has already begun. You may be best protected at that point by responding forcefully with a strike of your own.

TURN-INS

The next group of techniques for breaking holds are considerably less friendly than the first is, but they all share one element in common: They require that you turn in and move toward the attacker. Although this may be counterintuitive (in an actual assault, it's likely that at least part of you will want to close your eyes or run away instead), you are best protected if you turn in and face your assailant, just as you practiced with the strikes in step 3, Striking With Hands and Arms. The following descriptions describe turning in when someone attempts to grab your shoulder, wrist, or hair.

Shoulder or Wrist Grab

Imagine a perpetrator grabbing you by the shoulder or by the wrist from behind. Your first move in both instances is to turn in and face the grabber with one palm (Wrist Grab) or two palms (Shoulder Grab) in protective stance position (figure 5.4). While you are turning in, shout *no*.

a

b

Figure 5.4   Shoulder or wrist grab reactions: *(a)* incorrect, pulling away; *(b)* correct, moving in.

Then look at the grabber. Is it your grandmother trying to stop you from accidentally walking into traffic? Is it your best friend who forgot you're studying self-defense and just did something really stupid? That's OK; it's great that you responded forcefully!

If it's *not* your grandmother or your best friend, what can you do next? (Hint: Think back to step 3, Striking With Hands and Arms.) What parts of your body are free? What targets on the perpetrator are facing you? From this position, you might choose an Eye Strike with one or both hands or a Heel Palm Strike (figure 5.5). Or you could strike with a Stomp or a Knee to Groin. Keep in mind that, depending on the attacker's grip on you, you will probably be quite close, less than an arm's length away. Don't pull away; you do not have to get into a tug of war using upper-body strength. Being close is your best chance of effectively striking the attacker and getting him to loosen his grip on you. Focus first on striking; you can run later if you choose.

Figure 5.5   Shoulder or Wrist Grab

APPROACH

1. Attacker has grabbed your wrist
2. Turn in and assume protective stance

a

(continued)

Figure 5.5   *(continued)*

EXECUTION

1. Shout *NO!*
2. Perform Eye Strike

FOLLOW-THROUGH

1. If necessary, perform Knee to Groin

b

c

Breaking Holds Drill 2.   *Shoulder and Wrist Grab*

Practice this combination of moves to the air. Begin by standing normally. Imagine someone has grabbed your shoulder from behind. Turn around to face that person with both hands up in protective stance while you shout *no*. Now do a quick Eye Strike to the air, followed by a Knee to Groin. Remember to step through; do not pull your leg back after the Knee to the Groin. Repeat this series five times. Do another five repetitions as if you'd been grabbed by the wrist. For these, after turning in and shouting *no*, practice a one-handed Eye Strike.

Success Check

- Use full force to the air.

- Shout *no* with each strike, including the turn-in.
- Keep your hands flat in protective stance.
- Step through on the Knee to Groin strike.

Score Your Success

Practice 20 repetitions of the entire series = 20 points

Separate each move—turning in, Eye Strike, Knee to Groin = 10 points

Shout *no* three times for each series = 20 points

Step through on the Knee to Groin = 10 points

Hair Grab

Another variation of the turn-in can be used if someone grabs you by the hair. Your first technique is to regain control of your head by clasping both of your hands to the perpetrator's and clamping down against your head (figure 5.6). This prevents him from yanking your head around or from pulling your hair out. Maintain this clamp with both of your hands and then turn in. What can you do next? What do you have free?

Figure 5.6	**Hair Grab**

APPROACH

1. Clamp the perpetrator's hands to your head

EXECUTION

1. Turn in
2. Shout *NO!*
3. Knee to Groin

FOLLOW-THROUGH

1. Step through the Knee to Groin strike
2. Maintain the protective stance

a   b   c

Breaking Holds Drill 3. *Hair Grab*

Practice this combination of moves to the air. Begin by standing normally. Imagine someone grabbing you by the hair from behind. First clamp your own hands to the back of your head while you turn in and shout *no*. Now do a Knee to Groin strike. Remember to step through. Repeat this series five times.

Success Check

- Use your full force to the air.
- Use your full voice on each strike, including the turn-in.
- Step through on the Knee to Groin strike.

Score Your Success

Practice 20 repetitions of the entire series = 20 points

Separate each move—hand clamp, turning in, knee = 10 points

Shout *no* three times for each series = 20 points

Step through on the Knee to Groin strike = 10 points

ARM BAR CHOKE HOLD

You can also break the hold of someone trying to choke you from behind with his forearm. Obviously, any choking hold is serious and requires that you move quickly to ensure your own safety. The first move is to free your airway. Turn your head to the side so that your chin is pointing into the crook of the assailant's elbow (figure 5.7). This will move your throat into a small empty space, thus freeing your airway from the pressure of the forearm.

After you've made sure that you can breathe, bring both of your hands up and clamp onto the attacker's forearm (figure 5.8). You do *not* have to pull or yank or force his or her arm away from you. You may or may not have the arm strength to do so. Simply clamp the arm to your chest for your next move. Next, bend over from the waist, taking the attacker with you. The force of your entire torso collapsing will force the attacker off balance. Still holding on to his forearm, you are in perfect range for a Stomp.

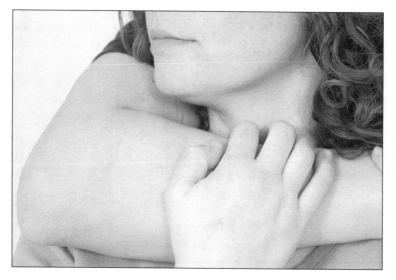

Figure 5.7 Secure your airway.

Figure 5.8 | **Arm Bar Choke Hold**

AIRWAY

1. Turn your head toward the crook of the attacker's elbow
2. Clamp the attacker's forearm to your chest

a

EXECUTION

1. Bend from the waist
2. Shout *NO!*

b

FOLLOW-THROUGH

1. Stomp

c

This move is not easy to practice with a friend. Your friend would be unwilling to actually choke you, and you would be unwilling to use the force necessary on the waist bend to throw your friend off balance. In fact, given the element of surprise and depending on your own weight, you could accidentally throw someone over your back with this move. But more likely, you wouldn't be able to get free, thus giving your body a physical memory of failure.

It's possible that a perpetrator could use this grab to catch you unaware and drag you off your feet. In that case, start with the first two moves (securing your airway and clamping your hands to his forearm) and then wait. You do not have to break the hold or drag his arm away. You will get an opportunity when the attacker stops, stumbles, or needs to catch his breath. Then, complete your move and get free.

Breaking Holds Drill 4. *Arm Bar Choke Hold*

Start in a standing position. Practice these moves several times at your own speed. Make sure you're doing four separate moves: 1) Head Turn; 2) Forearm Clamp; 3) Bend From Waist; 4) Stomp. Use a mirror or ask a friend or instructor to check your alignment. Practice 10 repetitions, shouting *no* with each waist bend and with each stomp. Practice bending to both sides.

Success Check

- Use four separate moves.

- Use your full force with the waist bend and stomp.
- Use your full voice during each bend and stomp.

Score Your Success

Practice 10 repetitions of the entire series = 20 points

Separate each move—Head Turn, Arm Clamp, Bend, Stomp = 20 points

Shout *no* with each move, starting with the Arm Clamp = 20 points

Breaking Holds Drill 5. *Bring Protective Stance Into the Real World*

Find or create an opportunity to practice protective stance at least three times in the next 1 to 2 weeks. Use it to set a physical boundary with someone at work, school, in your family, or in public. Note in your Practice Journal how it makes you feel and what, exactly, is the response of the other person. Imagine what could you do next if the person angrily grabbed you; write about it.

Score Your Success

Practice 1 or 2 times = 20 points

Practice 3 times = 40 points

Write about your reaction = 20 points

Two Gutsy Women

Two smart and powerful women told the editors of *Her Wits About Her* about their successful escape from a convicted felon. Their experience reveals how much time a defender has to think, plan, and react during an attempted assault, even in the presence of a weapon.

Chris Weir had taken only a couple of one-day self-defense workshops and a few months of judo classes when she and her partner, Sally, were grabbed at knifepoint by a man in their neighborhood. When he pushed something into her abdomen and said, "I have a knife," several things happened at once. Sally moved several feet away, and Weir started wishing this weren't happening. She wondered about reversing time and changing their walking route; she wondered if Sally should stay or run for help; she wondered what this guy wanted.

Weir told him they didn't have any money. His reaction was to say "I don't care" and gesture her toward a secluded area at the side of the road. This behavior told her he was planning a sexual assault. Weir considered submitting, fearing she'd be hurt, but then she remembered a community speaker who taught that resistance usually works. Weir decided to resist.

After making her decision, Weir said, "No, I won't do anything you want me to do. I'm not going anywhere with you. This is my neighborhood and you can't get away with this. I'm going to yell and people are going to come out. You'd better get out of here right now. Go away! Leave us alone!" Sally repeatedly circled behind the man, ignoring his demands that she get in front of him and stand near Weir. Although the assailant had a good grip on her and kept the knife close to her abdomen, Weir moved toward the knife to get under a street lamp. When she moved toward the knife, the man backed away and let go of her arm. He grabbed her other arm. At one point, Weir saw the weapon, a 6-inch hunting knife. She jerked herself out of his grasp, prompting him to jump back several feet.

At the moment both women were clear of the range of the knife, they began to yell in earnest. They called for their neighbors by name and shouted that there was a man with a knife outside. As porch lights came on, the attacker took off running. After chasing him briefly, Sally returned. He was later caught, tried, sentenced to 14 years. He already had served time in prison on multiple rape charges.

Not until he had run away that afternoon did Weir feel overcome by emotion, "…terrified of what could have happened, and amazed we had saved ourselves. We had done it well, we had fought back, we had chased him out of the neighborhood. We said no, and it worked."

Adapted from *Her Wits About Her*, edited by D. Caignon and G. Groves, 1987. New York: Perennial Library. Pages 214 and 215.

Breaking Holds Drill 6. *Studying Success*

Answer the following questions in your Practice Journal about the Two Gutsy Women success story. If you like, discuss the success story and your answers with a friend or study partner.

1. When did Chris Weir and Sally begin their self-defense?

2. How many kinds of self-defense did they use? List each one, including the use of awareness and verbal, emotional, and psychological techniques, not just physical ones.

3. What might you have done differently in the same situation? Why?

4. What surprised you about their experience?

5. What satisfied or empowered you most about their experience?

Breaking Holds Drill 7. *Match the Photo to the Technique*

Study the series of photos. Each shows a different defender and attacker position. Decide for yourself which techniques you could use in each situation and then check your answers against the answer key (page 78). Choose techniques from all five previous steps. The defenders will have more than one choice available in each photo. (Hint: There will be at least five self-defense options for each photo.)

1. Defender's wrist grabbed from behind.

2. Sitting on a bench, arm around defender.

3. Arm bar choke from behind.

4. Wrist grab, adult pulling a child.

5. Mugger grabs wrist and purse.

Score Your Success

4 or 5 correct answers for one photo = 10 points each

2 or 3 correct answers for one photo = 5 points each

SUCCESS SUMMARY

Successfully breaking holds may require that you raise your awareness, prevent someone from getting close enough to grab you, deflect a grab, or break free from a surprise attack. In step 5, Breaking Holds, you have studied and practiced each of these skills. You brought your techniques into the real world by practicing full force and by making connections between the drills and the rest of your life.

Before Taking the Next Step

Before moving on to step 6, Getting to the Ground Safely, take time to reflect on what you have learned to this point. Answer the following questions honestly.

1. Have you practiced the nonviolent boundary techniques (the Brush Off, the Hugger, and the "friendly" Wrist Grab) with a partner?

2. Can you identify three types of perpetrator approach to which you would respond by turning in?

3. Have you drilled all three turn-in techniques on your own?

4. Have you practiced the defense against a choke from behind?

5. Have you brought the protective stance into the real world by using it at least three times and writing about the results in your Practice Journal?

If you answered yes to all five questions, you are ready to move on to step 6, Getting to the Ground Safely.

Taking the Step Further. *Homework Assignments*

Memorize the myth in this step and write about it in your Practice Journal. Share some of your thoughts and feelings about the myth and fact with at least one other person. Can you imagine hitting someone in self-defense who hasn't hit you first? Why or why not? How important is intention? What is the worst thing that could happen if you misjudged someone's intention?

Physical practice—Spend 5 to 20 minutes a day practicing the moves from step 5, Breaking Holds, until you begin step 6, Getting to the Ground

Safely. Remember to incorporate your voice with each technique!

Watch for five examples on television or in movies of opportunities for victims to use one of these techniques for breaking holds. You might begin by asking yourself what the victim has free (voice, hand, foot, knee, etc.) and what targets are accessible on the assailant (eyes, groin, throat, knee, etc.). Get help if necessary to come up with options for the defender. There will always be an opening.

Answer Key

Answers for Breaking Holds Drill 7. Match the Figure to the Technique (pages 76 and 77)

1. Defender's wrist grabbed from behind—Turn in, protective stance, assess, one or more of the following: Eye Strike, Heel Palm, Knee to Groin, Front Snap Kick, Stomp

2. Sitting on a bench, arm around defender—Brush Off, set verbal boundary, Eye Strike, Heel Palm, Hammer Fist to Groin

3. Arm bar choke from behind—Turn head, clamp, bend, use Stomp, Low Elbow Strike, High Elbow Strike, and Knee to Groin

4. Wrist grab, adult pulling a child—Hand clasp, yank away, Eye Strike, Front Snap Kick, Stomp

5. Mugger grabs wrist and purse—First drop purse, protective stance, see if attacker runs; could then use Eye Strike, Heel Palm, Stomp, Knee to Groin, Front Snap Kick

Getting to the Ground Safely

In a typical American horror movie, when the pretty, young, white girl twists her ankle and falls down, you know that the jig is up; she's about to be raped or eaten by aliens. In typical heroic dramas, our man falling to the ground is inevitably a plot device to indicate shame and failure. He's lost the battle—unless and until he dramatically rises again. These visual images get into our subconscious and prevent us from learning to defend ourselves.

I can remember the exact moment in my own childhood that I came to believe it was impossible to prevent sexual assault. I was about 12 years old and I was watching a TV movie alone, probably while babysitting. A woman was knocked down in a parking structure by a bad guy, and she cried and screamed and struggled ineffectively while he raped her. I remember thinking to myself, *Oh, I always thought that I'd fight back if someone tried to grab me, but look, there's nothing she can do!*

Myth   Once you get knocked to the ground in a fight, you will lose.

Fact   The ground is actually one of the safest places you can be in an attack. Your legs are probably stronger than the perpetrator's arms. In many self-defense scenarios, the best choice you can make is to get down on the ground and kick.

In step 6, Getting to the Ground Safely, you will learn all of the basics for ground fighting, beginning with the timing of when to choose to get down on the ground, a variety of ways to do so safely, basic mobility once you're down there, and techniques to employ if someone grabs your kicking leg.

THE DROP

There are at least two ways to drop to the ground safely. Choose the one that works best for your body. The basic concept behind both is getting as low to the ground as possible and then moving into Side Thrust Kick position. You might want to review your Side Thrust Kick position in figures 4.7 through 4.10 (pages 56 to 58) as a refresher.

Drop A

The first style of drop (drop A) is to place one knee on the ground behind you and then fall over. This may not be the best choice if you have previous knee injuries or if it's painful for you to kneel for short periods. Starting in protective stance, come down onto your non-dominant knee (probably the left one) so that you're kneeling, almost in a marriage proposal position, except with your hands up in protective stance (figure 6.1). Then sink back toward your left knee, sitting your butt down on the ground. Your right leg comes up and ready to kick. Remember to bring both hands down to one side in front of you.

Figure 6.1   Drop A

APPROACH
1. Take a protective stance

KNEEL
1. Kneel on one knee

SIDE THRUST KICK POSITION
1. Fall back into Side Thrust Kick position
2. Shout *NO!*

FOLLOW-THROUGH
1. Remain ready to kick

a *b* *c* *d*

Drop B

Drop B is slightly less structured and may work well for students with knee pain. Crouch as close to the ground as possible by bending both knees and then fall over (figure 6.2). It's important to land in Side Thrust Kick position. Are your hands both on one side? Is your kicking leg (toe and knee) pointed up? Is your bottom leg tucked in close to your bottom?

Figure 6.2	Drop B

APPROACH

1. Take a protective stance

EXECUTION

1. Crouch down
2. Fall to the side into Side Thrust Kick position
3. Shout *NO!*

FOLLOW-THROUGH

1. Remain ready to kick

a

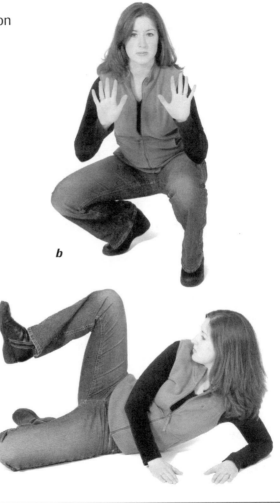

b

c

Starting in protective stance, practice the drop several times. I recommend starting on padding, thick carpet, or grass. Begin slowly at first, particularly when you drop back onto your arms.

Practice both styles, using a mirror or asking a friend to check your alignment. Practice 20 repetitions, shouting *no* each time you drop.

Misstep

Dropping down onto your hands or wrists.

Correction

Keep your hands flat on the ground and rest on your entire forearm.

Misstep

Trying to combine the drop and kick all in one flying motion.

Correction

Allow the drop to be its own separate move, by shouting *no* and getting into Side Thrust Kick position only. Chances are the drop may be preventive and you won't even have to kick!

Ground Drill 1. *Drop*

This drill draws from and adds to the third drill in step 2, Defining Your Space, in which you walked toward a partner who got into protective stance and said *stop* (page 19). Make sure that you have a well-padded space on which to drop. You should also have a minimum of 4 to 5 feet (1.2 to 1.5 m) of open space behind you. Partners each take a turn being the walker and the dropper. The walker begins about 10 to 20 feet (3 to 6 m) from the dropper. Make eye contact with each other. On the count of 3, the walker walks forward and, at his or her own speed, the dropper drops. Include the *no* shout. Give each partner a chance to drop 10 times.

To Increase Difficulty

- Gradually repeat the drill with the walker moving faster, jogging, running, and yelling.

- Practice both styles of drop.
- Drop onto both sides (left and right).

Success Check

- Both partners have a chance to be the walker and the dropper.
- Practice both styles of drop if they are right for your body.
- End on your side in the Side Thrust Kick position each time.

Score Your Success

Practice 10 drops = 20 points

End in Side Thrust Kick position each drop = 20 points

Shout *no* with each drop = 20 points

When to Drop

You should drop anytime you suspect that an attacker may be getting ready to punch you. Learn to hone and develop that suspicion. It will probably take some practice to be willing to drop. Yes, trained fighters can learn to block punches. Yes, it's possible that, if you move quickly enough, you can avoid a punch by stepping in toward the attacker. However, those techniques can be complicated to master, and you want to do everything in your power to avoid being hit in the head.

Warning signs that an assailant may be getting ready to punch can be culturally specific. Some

signs include a wind-up (pulling his clenched fist back in preparation for a blow), an intense display of anger—including finger pointing, yelling, or moving closer than two arm's lengths away—or other evidence of generally menacing behavior. Another clue? If someone is shouting that he's going to hit you, take him at his word and drop. That assailant is informing you of his or her intention. There is no reason to wait until the wind-up to get safely to the ground.

Other reasons to drop include being choked from the front. You may or may not have the arm power to break someone's hold, but chances are that they cannot hold your entire weight in the air. If someone is trying to hold you by the throat, dropping gets you safely to the ground, breaks or loosens his or her grip on your neck, and pulls the attacker into excellent striking range.

You should also drop if someone is charging at you. If you are standing in protective stance and someone is running directly at you, you have very little time before that attacker closes the gap and reaches you. To avoid being knocked to the ground at this speed, drop before he reaches you.

Memorize these three reasons to drop. Can you think of others? You may choose to use the drop any time that you like. You're well protected on the ground and you have some of your strongest techniques available to you there (figure 6.3), so the drop can be a good response to a wide variety of threats.

The discussion of dropping brings up an interesting question: What if, in the process of developing your awareness skills, you misjudge someone's intention and drop and shout *no* at a charming neighbor who is merely out jogging late at night? The official self-defense expert answer is "So what?" Your safety is more important than anyone's embarrassment, including your own. I would much rather err on the side of caution than on the side of protecting the feelings of a person who is planning to assault me. I choose to honor my intuition, rather than ignore it and hope for the best. Anyway, it could teach your neighbor not to run directly at people late at night, advice that could protect him in the future as well.

If you don't drop, but you get knocked to the ground unexpectedly, don't worry. When you're

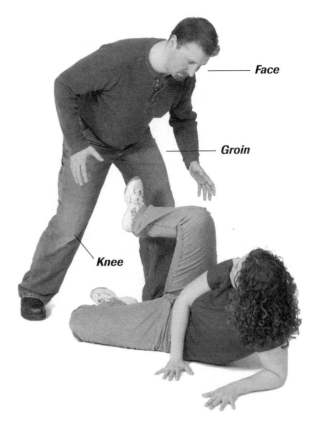

Figure 6.3 Side Thrust Kick targets available after dropping: face, groin, and knee.

falling, you have more time than you might think. The actual moment of falling is not the time to struggle or tense up. Once you get to the ground, you can scramble quickly into Side Thrust Kick position. In a real-life assault, this is one of those unchoreographed experiences for which you cannot plan. Don't worry too much about it. Adrenaline and a will to defend yourself go a long way if you are knocked to the ground.

GROUND MOBILITY: SCOOT AND SWITCH

Use these techniques to move closer to your target or to track an assailant who is circling you. Practice being mobile, moving quickly, and keeping your body coiled in the Side Thrust Kick position, always ready to kick defensively.

There are two basic ways to move safely on the ground. Scooting is extremely easy to learn. The basic concept is to stay in Side Thrust Kick position

(hands on your side, with the toe and knee of your top leg pointing up) and then scoot forward. Use your arms to push yourself, and anchor yourself by pushing your bottom toe into the ground. It's not unlike the way young toddlers scramble on the ground when they don't want to walk. The main difference is that you stay in Side Thrust Kick position rather than crawling on all fours.

The Switch (figure 6.4) is a way to get quickly from one side to the other in Side Thrust Kick position. This may be one of the least elegant moves you'll learn in this book, so prepare to roll around foolishly a bit as you get the hang of it. The Switch has two important elements. First, make sure that you are fully in Side Thrust Kick position. If your legs are extended and you want to switch sides, first pull them in close. Second, make sure both of your hands hit the floor on your new side when you switch.

The actual Switch itself just requires that you flip over. If you are in Side Thrust Kick position with your right leg ready to kick, push off your left side, onto your back, and then over onto your right side. Because your legs are coiled in tightly, they are already in kick position when you flip over. Practice the Switch slowly at first and gradually build up speed. Keep both of your legs tucked in at all times and remember that your top knee and toe should point to the ceiling. The forearm of your bottom arm should rest on the floor.

Figure 6.4   **Switch**

APPROACH

1. Side Thrust Kick position

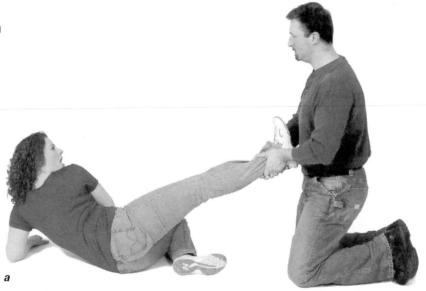

a

EXECUTION

1. Pull leg in close
2. Push into ground with arms and bottom leg
3. Shout *NO!*

b

FOLLOW-THROUGH

1. Flip over
2. Remain prepared to kick with top leg

c

Starting in Side Thrust Kick position, practice the Switch several times at your own speed. Practice both directions (starting with your right leg up and then with your left leg up). Use a mirror or ask a friend to check your alignment. Practice 20 repetitions, shouting *no* with each Switch.

Misstep

Landing on your back, not your side.

Correction

Smack both your hands on the mat or carpet when you shout *no* loudly. Plant yourself firmly on your new side before attempting to kick.

Ground Drill 2. *Switch and Scoot*

Find a drill partner and start on the ground in Side Thrust Kick position. The standing partner does not have to be familiar with the Side Thrust Kick position; even a child older than 6 years or so might enjoy this drill. The standing partner's job is to walk in a circle around the defender, always staying about an arm's length away. The defender's job is to keep his or her feet between the stander and the defender's own head by using the Scoot or the Switch, depending on the needs of the moment.

If the stander walks toward the front of the defender's body, it's easiest for the defender to use the Scoot in a circle, keeping his or her top leg up, always ready to kick. If the stander walks toward the back of the defender's body, it's easiest for the defender to use the Switch onto the other side. Practice this to get a physical sense of how it works. As the stander gradually builds up speed, he or she should randomly begin to change directions and actively attempt to get to the defender's head.

To Decrease Difficulty

- Do fewer repetitions and give yourself adequate time.
- Ask the stander to move more slowly or to move only in one direction.
- Take frequent breaks if your legs get tired.

To Increase Difficulty

- As you begin to feel more confident, have the stander gradually increase speed.
- Have the stander build up to a run as he or she tries to get to the defender's head.

(continued)

Ground Drill 2.   *(continued)*

Success Check

- Both partners have a chance to be the walker and the defender.
- Remain in Side Thrust Kick position except in the middle of the Switch.
- Keep your legs between your head and the walker at all times.
- Practice both the Switch and the Scoot, depending on the walker's direction.

Score Your Success

Practice both the Scoot and the Switch = 20 points

Remain in Side Thrust Kick position except in the middle of the Switch = 20 points

Keep your legs between your head and the walker at all times = 20 points

LEG GRAB

What if you manage a perfect Side Thrust Kick, but the attacker is lucky enough to grab your outstretched leg? You can regain control of your defense by adding one more move to the Switch. All you have to do is bend the leg that's been grabbed, thus pulling your knee in toward your nose (figure 6.5). This works even if the attacker is stronger than you are (in which case, bending your knee will slide you in toward the attacker). *After* bending the grabbed leg, use the Switch and shout *no*. This places you in perfect alignment to deliver a Side Thrust Kick to the attacker's head with your other leg.

Figure 6.5	Single-Leg Grab

APPROACH

1. Side Thrust Kick position
2. Kicking leg grabbed

a

EXECUTION

1. Bend knee of grabbed leg
2. Pull in and shout *NO!*
3. Use the Switch and shout *NO!*

b

FOLLOW-THROUGH

1. Kick with the other leg

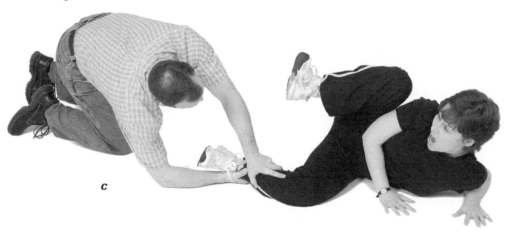

c

Misstep

Trying to combine both the Single-Leg Grab and the Switch at the same moment.

Correction

Shout *no* with each separate move and slow yourself down.

Ground Drill 3. *Leg Grab*

Start in Side Thrust Kick position, with your top or kicking leg extended, and practice the Single-Leg Grab Switch several times at your own speed. Practice with both legs, using a mirror or asking a friend to check your alignment. Practice 20 repetitions. Shout *no* twice for each Single-Leg Grab, once when pulling in and again when switching.

(continued)

Ground Drill 3. (continued)

Success Check

- Remain in Side Thrust Kick position except in the middle of the Switch.
- Shout *no* twice, first when pulling in your leg and then again for the Switch.
- End in Side Thrust Kick position with both hands on one side.

Score Your Success

Each switch is two separate moves = 20 points

Use your voice twice for each switch = 20 points

End in Side Thrust Kick position with both hands on one side = 20 points

---

In addition to the Switch for dealing with a Single-Leg Grab, there are several other techniques to maximize the mobility of your kicking legs while defending yourself on the ground: the Cycle Kick, the Bunny Kick, and the Toppler.

CYCLE KICK

If, by some chance, an assailant were able to grab both of your feet or legs, you still have options. One is to sit up and do an Eye Strike or a Heel Palm Strike. An assailant's head has to be close to you for him to grab both of your legs in Side Thrust Kick position, so both strikes could work well. You can also deal with a double-leg grab by kicking vigorously in a bicycling motion (figure 6.6). Rapidly cycle your feet, scraping closely along the length of your own shin. At the end of each scraping motion, make contact with the attacker's forearms, thus loosening his grasp. When you free even one of your legs, you're ready to aim a Side Thrust Kick to the assailant's face or groin.

Figure 6.6	Cycle Kick and Scrape

APPROACH

1. Side Thrust Kick position
2. Attacker has grabbed both of your legs

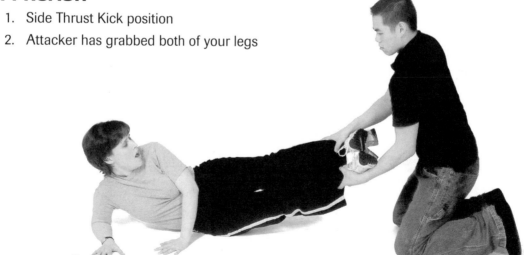

a

EXECUTION

1. Cycle both legs rapidly
2. Scrape along your own shin
3. Shout *NO!*

b

FOLLOW-THROUGH

1. Kick with your free leg

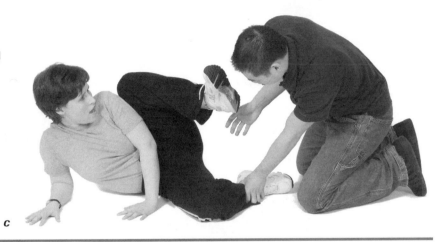

c

Start in Side Thrust Kick position with both of your legs extended, and practice the Cycle Kick and scrape several times at your own speed. This will probably feel somewhat awkward. It's actually easier to do when someone is holding your legs (for the same reason that sit-ups are easier with someone sitting on your feet). Practice several times on each side. Complete the scenario by ending in Side Thrust Kick position.

Misstep

Not using enough force.

Correction

Use your voice, loudly, to inspire your legs to cycle and scrape.

BUNNY KICK

Another technique to free yourself when an attacker has grabbed both of your legs is a swift kick to the chest or groin with both feet together (figure 6.7). Don't let the goofy name fool you, the Bunny Kick can pack a powerful punch. This move works best when you use 100 percent voice and power. Start with your legs bent, almost as if both of your legs were preparing for a Side Thrust Kick.

Figure 6.7   Bunny Kick

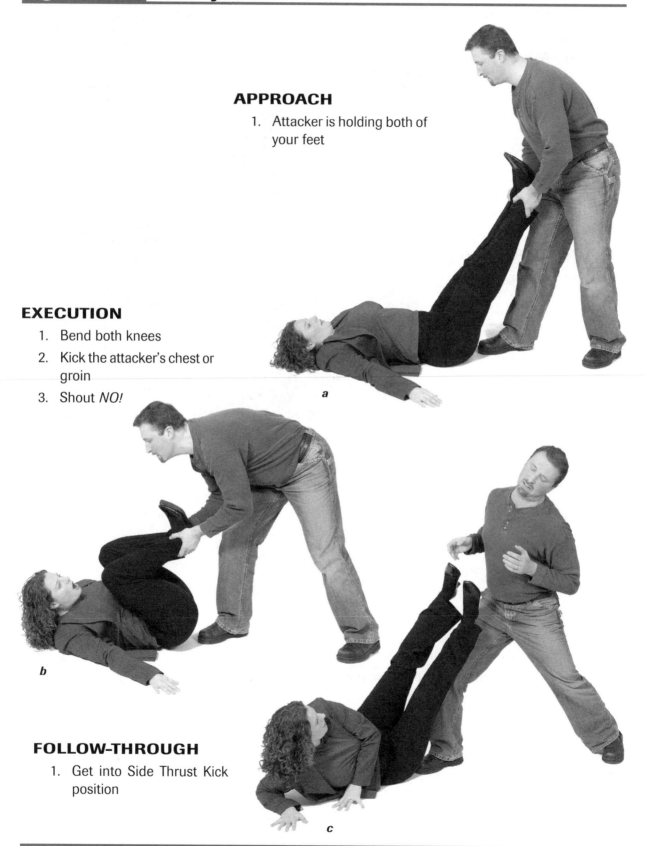

APPROACH

1. Attacker is holding both of your feet

EXECUTION

1. Bend both knees
2. Kick the attacker's chest or groin
3. Shout *NO!*

a

b

FOLLOW-THROUGH

1. Get into Side Thrust Kick position

c

Starting on your side, in Side Thrust Kick position, pull both of your knees to your chest and practice the Bunny Kick several times at your own speed. Use a mirror or ask a friend to check your alignment. Practice 10 kicks, shouting *no* with each one. This movement will probably feel somewhat awkward when performed to the air. If you have access to a large, heavy body bag, it can be very satisfying to use the bag as a target for this kick.

Misstep

Beginning with your legs extended; extended legs don't allow enough range of motion to provide the impact you need.

Correction

Bend both of your knees first.

THE TOPPLER

The Toppler is a great example of using an attacker's momentum to your own advantage and requires minimum effort for the payoff you get. Should the opportunity ever arise that an assailant is dragging you by both feet, all you have to do is bend your knees. This will bring the top of your body close enough to the attacker's feet that you can grab on to his or her ankles (figure 6.8). You stop the attacker's feet unexpectedly, and the rest of his or her body will continue its backward motion, thus ensuring that the attacker topples to the ground. When the attacker lands on his or her back, you can easily use the Scoot to move into the Side Thrust Kick position.

Figure 6.8   Toppler

APPROACH
1. Being dragged
2. Shout *NO!*

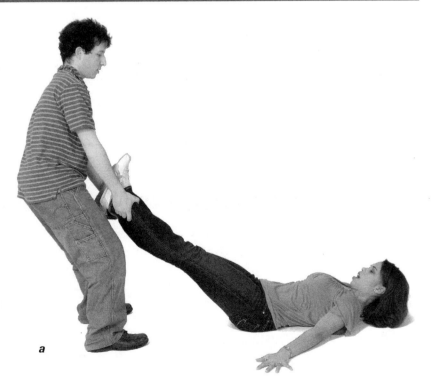

a

(continued)

Figure 6.8   *(continued)*

EXECUTION

1. Grab the attacker's ankles
2. Shout *NO!*
3. Allow gravity to do its work

b

FOLLOW-THROUGH

1. Scoot out into Side Thrust Kick position, ready to kick the attacker's groin or knees

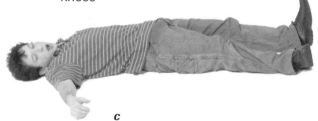

c

GROUND FIGHTING BASICS

Many of my students dislike the whole concept of choosing to defend themselves from the ground. Most think they would be better off standing and throwing punches or, better yet, running away. But unless you're a professional fighter, there's every chance that an assailant will be a better puncher than you are. Even if you feel confident about your punching skills, remember that many attackers are fully prepared to block your punches and throw their own. The stand-ing hand and arm strikes you've learned in step 3, Striking With Hands and Arms, are generally fast and unpredictable, but, if someone is trying to punch you in the face or head, you're much safer on the ground, where you can use your kicks to keep the attacker away from your head and end the assault quickly.

Running is a good self-defense technique in some situations, particularly if you are a very fast runner and your attacker has very low motivation to hurt you. If an assailant wants your purse or wallet, I generally recommend dropping it, backing away several yards in the protective stance, and then turning and running. But running from an attacker who is close and is determined to hurt you requires that you turn your back on danger. How will you know if you are being chased? How do you know how fast the attacker can run? How will you avoid being hit from behind? It's safer to remain facing the assailant, drop to the ground, and strike hard with your legs and feet.

Here are some comments from my students about dropping to the ground:

- "I'm not crazy about the drop. It still feels weak to me. It seems like if I'm standing I should just punch somebody. But when we did the walking drill I was amazed by how it looks to the perpetrator. When my partner dropped, he just totally disappeared from view, and there was this foot looking back at me!" *It's an amazing point of view, isn't it! Just that small amount of resistance and confusion could deter many attackers, and it gets you to breathe, shout, and assume a protected position, all at a time when you could be experiencing an adrenaline-based freeze response.*

- "The Side Thrust Kick is really hard for me. I've never done sports or taken a class like this. I feel clumsy, like I'm doing everything wrong. But, after I figured out the alignment, I could feel how much stronger my kicks were. I was surprised at how good it felt to kick that pad. It would really hurt if I kicked someone that hard!" *Absolutely, I'm glad you got to feel the difference that correct positioning makes. Keep practicing. The more Side Thrust Kicks you try full force, the better you'll get at setting up and really delivering some power.*

- "I actually used this on a German Shepherd in my neighborhood; it was so cool. It was running right at me and barking, and I was wondering if they had one of those invisible fences, but the next thing I knew I was dropping and yelling *no*. My body just responded! It stopped about 15 feet away from me and growled, but I felt good." *Congratulations! Most dogs are probably better at respecting clear physical and verbal boundaries than most people!!*

Mark's Story

Mark had taken an IMPACT padded attacker class years earlier at his girlfriend's insistence, but he hadn't practiced or needed to use the skills since. He'd never felt extremely confident physically, but he had managed to talk himself out of several scary situations in college and figured he could always rely on that skill if he were threatened again. One night, while leaving a concert, he was getting jostled by a large crowd, all trying to get through the doorway at once. One guy he bumped took offense and shoved him hard up against the wall with a nasty comment. He apologized and walked quickly away. About half a block down the street, he realized the shover and his friend were following, shouting and cursing him. He crossed the street. They followed. He heard their footsteps speed up into a jog behind him and quickly scanned the street; he didn't see anyone else around. He turned toward them, already in protective stance. He'd planned to try to talk them out of their anger, but, as he turned, he saw one swinging something (it turned out to be a hammer); they were both very close. He dropped to the ground and delivered a Side Thrust Kick to the leg of the attacker closest to him. He later said, "I didn't even think, it happened really fast, but I also had that feeling where time slows down, like I had all the time in the world to do what I needed to. I didn't even feel scared until an hour later at the police station!" As soon as he kicked the first attacker, the second attacker, the one with the hammer, took off running. The first yelled at him and took several ineffective swipes at him where he remained on the ground in Side Thrust Kick position before jogging off with a pronounced limp.

Ground Drill 4. *Studying Success*

Answer the following questions in your Practice Journal. If you like, discuss the Success Story and your answers with a friend or study partner.

1. When did Mark begin his self-defense?

2. How many kinds of self-defense did he use? List each one, including the use of awareness and verbal, emotional, and psychological techniques, not just physical ones.

3. What might you have done differently in the same situation? Why?

4. What surprised you about Mark's experience?

5. What satisfied or empowered you most about this survivor's experience?

SUCCESS SUMMARY

Step 6, Getting to the Ground Safely, discussed all of the basic skills you need to get to the ground safely and stay mobile once you're there. Each mobility technique—the Switch and the Scoot, the Single-Leg Grab, the Cycle Kick, the Bunny Kick, and the Toppler—works to return you as quickly as possible to your power move, the Side Thrust Kick.

Before Taking the Next Step

Before moving on to step 7, Fighting From the Ground, take time to reflect on what you have learned to this point. Answer the following questions honestly.

1. Have you studied both techniques for dropping and chosen the one that suits you best?

2. Have you memorized at least three reasons to drop to the ground? Do you know which targets are available to you if you are on the ground and the assailant is still standing?

3. Have you practiced both the Switch and the Scoot?

4. Do you know two techniques to use if an assailant grabs your kicking leg or legs?

5. Have you practiced both of them?

If you answered yes to all five questions, you are ready to move on to step 7, Fighting From the Ground.

Taking the Step Further. *Homework Assignments*

Memorize the myth in this step and write about it in your Practice Journal. Share some of your thoughts and feelings about the myth and fact with at least one other person. Can you find any images online, on television, or in movies of physically powerful people defending themselves on the ground? Has your image of ground fighting changed after completing this step? How?

Physical practice—Spend 5 to 20 minutes a day practicing the moves from step 6, Getting to the Ground Safely, until you begin step 7, Fighting From the Ground. Remember to incorporate your voice with each technique, including the drop. For extra credit, do the drop in public, including voice, in an area where you will be seen by others. Write in your Practice Journal about the response you get from others. (Choose a carpeted or grassy area to avoid getting scraped on concrete or asphalt.)

Fighting From the Ground

Step 7 includes more techniques available to you during ground fighting, including some for assaults that begin with the defender in a seated position or lying down. The majority of sexual assaults begin from or progress to a prone position. These assailants attempt to surround an intended victim and get him or her to the ground as quickly as possible. In addition to the physical techniques you will use in ground fighting, step 7 addresses the necessary mental skills. These include awareness, psychological and emotional preparedness, and your own natural will to defend yourself. Step 7 helps you connect to and activate that willpower.

Myth   People who are sexually assaulted must have wanted it to happen: if she was on a date with him, dressed provocatively, and was willing to go to his apartment . . . if he was gay, hanging out in that park, flirting at the bar . . . they must have brought it on themselves. Some people are just asking for it.

Fact   No one causes, invites, enjoys, asks for, or deserves being sexually assaulted. It is *always* the rapist's fault. It is *never* the victim's fault. Never.

Sexual assault is sexual contact without the consent of the victim. Consent is an unequivocal agreement between two people to have sex. True consent never exists in the face of physical force, verbal coercion, or intimidation. For someone to give consent, she or he must be free to revoke consent at any point, for any reason or for no reason at all. The answer *yes* is completely meaningless if someone is too scared, too drunk, too weak, or too young to feel free to say *no*. Submission does not equal consent.

Children are incapable of consenting to sex with adults. They do not have the social power or skills to understand fully what they are consenting to. Age of consent laws, which permit adults to "have sex" with children legally in some states, do not change this fact. There are no exceptions. "Even if a 16-year-old girl walks into her living room naked and throws herself on her father, he is still not justified in touching her sexually. A responsible father would say, 'There seems to be a problem here.' He would tell her to put her clothes on; he'd discuss it with her, get professional help if necessary. Regardless of age or circumstance, there is never an excuse for sexual abuse" (Bass and Davis, 1994).

OVERCOMING THE FREEZE RESPONSE

The first thing to know about defense that begins on the ground is that you will freeze. It's normal, it's natural, and it's not a problem. Whether you freeze for half a second, a minute, 5 minutes, or longer, you can come out of your frozen state and defend yourself. This natural response is not a sign that you have done anything wrong, nor is it a sign of weakness. It's merely a sign that you are human and that your body has a physiological response to fear.

Almost everyone has already experienced this at some point. Perhaps you are terrified of heights and got surprised on a hike or at the top of a tall building by your inability to back away from the edge. Maybe you've struggled with a terror of public speaking and had to battle the sweaty palms and stuttering that arise just before a presentation at work. Maybe you were assaulted previously and, when you tried to scream, you found you had no voice. Please don't criticize yourself or your body for its humanity. You didn't do anything wrong. You are not still frozen. If you're reading this book, you didn't stay stuck on the mountain, on the stage, or in the experience of being assaulted. You and your body found a way to move forward and to learn more. You can do this.

The basic psychology of how to rebound from a freeze response includes the following four elements:

1. **Focus on the present.** You can do this by opening your eyes, breathing, wiggling your toes, or noting the color or shape of something right in front of you. Fear has a way of sweeping you into the past or the future. Your self-defense happens in the present.

2. **Watch for an opening.** Know that there will always be an opening. Assailants are troubled, distracted, and frightened humans. They will close their eyes, let go of your arm, get confused, loosen their grip, or turn their backs. You don't have to despair. There will always be an opening for you to defend yourself. Watch for it.

3. **Pay attention to your body.** Pay more attention to your body than to your brain. Your brain is frequently operating in the past ("Why did I accept a ride from him?") or the future ("Oh no, where is he taking me now?"). The body is always in the present. Breathe. What parts of your body do you have free? Where are your hands and feet? You don't have to stop your brain, but you don't have to get stuck there either.

4. **Go from 0 to 100 percent in a moment.** When you have an opening, use the element of surprise, act decisively, and employ 100 percent of your physical power and your loudest *no* shout all at once. Being at 0 percent might look like compliance or weakness, but it makes going to 100 percent even more powerful. Avoid wasting your energy or broadcasting your intention to fight by struggling or tensing when you are at 0 percent.

Being at Zero

"This is the scariest thing we've learned so far. I hate being at zero. It was really, really awful to practice lying there and waiting. Just my worst nightmare. But it helped a lot to watch the other women in the class. There were some really tiny women. I loved watching how fierce and determined they were; it helped me to realize that, if they could do it, I could do it too. I could cheer for them, watch for their openings, and it looked so strong when they just went for it! I can hardly remember my fight, but I remember some of theirs!"

It isn't unusual to feel uncomfortable at zero. Staying at zero, breathing, and waiting for an opening takes commitment and practice. If you want realistic practice with the freeze response and going from 0 to 100 percent, I suggest taking an IMPACT class. Look for a class in your area that allows for a lot of physical practice and offers an emotionally safe environment that encourages students to have and to express feelings.

Ground Fighting Drill 1. *Overcome the Freeze Response*

Memorize the four elements of coming out of the freeze response. List in your Practice Journal times in your life when you have used them. Think beyond physical self-defense. For example, anyone who has given birth to a child is already an expert in going from 0 to 100 percent. When you are resting in the brief moments between contractions, you are at zero. When the contraction hits and you begin to push, you move instantaneously to 100 percent.

Other real-life examples include meditation (focus on the present moment), biofeedback (body awareness), military basic training (0 to 100 percent), getting through a difficult exam (focus on the present), overcoming a serious illness or accident (body awareness), merging into a traffic circle during rush hour in Boston (waiting for your opening), practicing yoga or being an athlete (body awareness), or sticking it out at a horrible job while you submit your resume elsewhere (waiting for your opening).

Work on this drill until you come up with at least two personal successes in overcoming the freeze response. Consider sharing your successes with someone else and having a celebration!

Score Your Success

Find one personal example = 20 points

Find two personal examples = 40 points

Share your success with someone else = 20 points

EYE STRIKE FROM THE GROUND

The Eye Strike that you learned in step 3, Striking With Hands and Arms, is a great technique to use in ground fighting, because you are frequently in perfect striking range to target someone's eyes. A defender lying on his or her back will often have at least one hand free to do an Eye Strike. The Eye Strike from this position creates enough of a recoil on the part of the attacker to enable you to use the Scoot to move into the Side Thrust Kick position (figure 7.1).

| Figure 7.1 | Eye Strike From the Ground |

APPROACH

1. Lying on ground
2. Defender is not struggling or tensing

a

(continued)

Figure 7.1 *(continued)*

EXECUTION

1. Opening—attacker releases one of defender's hands
2. Eye Strike
3. Shout *NO!*

b

FOLLOW-THROUGH

1. Scoot out
2. Get into Side Thrust Kick position
3. Kick to the attacker's head or groin

c

Starting off lying on your back on the ground, practice the Eye Strike from the ground several times at your own speed. Begin by lying on your back at zero (loose, relaxed, without struggling). Then perform the Eye Strike to the air, and sit up into the Side Thrust Kick position. Practice using both arms and coming up onto both sides. Use a mirror or ask a friend to check your alignment. Practice 20 repetitions, shouting *no* with each Eye Strike and *no* again when you get into the Side Thrust Kick position. Start slowly to get the feel of it, and then allow yourself to practice at full force, at full speed, and with full voice.

Misstep

Sitting up straight, with an arm on both sides and staying on your back.

Correction

On your side! Review Side Thrust Kick position and figures 4.7 through 4.10 (pages 56-58).

Misstep

Feeling exposed in Side Thrust Kick position, angling your knee and toe to the side instead of to the ceiling.

Correction

Keep your knee and toe pointing up. Your kicks will be stronger, your head will be better protected, and you will end the assault sooner.

Ground Fighting Drill 2. *Eye Strike From the Ground*

To get a sense of doing an Eye Strike from the ground, practice with a large pillow or a light medicine ball. A large beanbag chair is ideal for this drill. Start off lying on the ground, and place the pillow or bag on your abdomen. Take a few moments to practice being at zero, breathe, and wait for your opening. Count to 3, and with a strong *no* shout, do an Eye Strike to the air (or to that pesky beanbag if it's large and firm enough). After the Eye Strike, scoot out from underneath the bag and get immediately into Side Thrust Kick position. Finish the drill by kicking either to the air or at the prop you've been using. Remember to shout with both the Eye Strike and the Side Thrust Kick. Repeat 10 times, practicing on each side.

To Decrease Difficulty

- Do fewer repetitions and give yourself adequate time.
- Use your dominant leg only.
- Practice without the bag.
- Roll over onto your side before you sit up to minimize any strain on your abdomen.

To Increase Difficulty

- Use your nondominant hand.
- Do the Eye Strike with both hands at once.
- Use a heavier bag.
- While you are at zero and waiting for your opening, hold your breath.

Success Check

- Explode from 0 to 100 percent, with full voice, into the Eye Strike.
- Use your voice during the Side Thrust Kick.
- End in the Side Thrust Kick position, with both hands on one side.

Score Your Success

Begin at 0 percent and breathe = 10 points

Use your voice twice, once with the Eye Strike and once with the Side Thrust Kick = 20 points

End in the Side Thrust Kick position, with both hands on one side = 20 points

BUTT STRIKE

This technique ends in the Side Thrust Kick position, just as in the previous move. One difference is that you start off lying on your front instead of your back. In this defense, the attacker is behind you and attempting to get you up on your hands and knees. Instead, you come up onto your knees and forearms, shift your hips backward quickly to knock the attacker off balance, and then lunge forward into the Side Thrust Kick position (figure 7.2). Getting up onto your forearms instead of your hands makes you more stable and grounded and less likely to be knocked off balance than if you were balanced on your wrists alone (figure 7.3).

Figure 7.2 | **Butt Strike**

APPROACH

1. On your front
2. Assailant cues you to get on your hands and knees

a

EXECUTION

1. Come up onto your knees and forearms
2. Strike back with your hips and butt
3. Shout *NO!*

b

FOLLOW-THROUGH

1. Lunge forward, shouting *NO!*
2. Get into the Side Thrust Kick position
3. Do a Side Thrust Kick to the attacker's head or groin

c

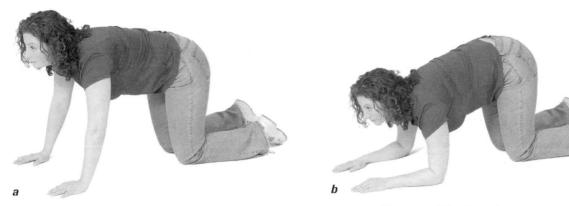

Figure 7.3 Butt Strike arm position: *(a)* incorrect, defender up on hands; *(b)* correct, defender on forearms.

Starting by lying facedown, practice the Butt Strike several times. You may wind up lunging 5 or 6 feet (1.5 to 1.8 m) forward from your starting position, so make sure you have enough room above your head for the Scoot. Use a mirror or ask a friend to check your alignment. Practice 20 repetitions, shouting *no* with each strike backward and each lunge forward. End in the Side Thrust Kick position each time.

Misstep

Thinking you have to lift or shove the attacker off with brute force.

Correction

The purpose of the Butt Strike is to create just the necessary amount of space and time for you to lunge forward and get into the Side Thrust Kick position. You do not have to overpower the assailant or be larger or stronger.

Ground Fighting Drill 3. *Butt Strike*

You can drill the Butt Strike in the same way as you did the Eye Strike from the ground, using a large pillow or beanbag chair. Start by lying on the ground and placing the pillow or bag over your bottom and legs. Take a few moments while lying on your front to practice being at zero. Breathe and wait for your opening. When you are ready, count to 3, and with a strong *no* shout, come up onto your elbows and forearms and lunge backward into the Butt Strike and then forward into the Side Thrust Kick position. Finish the drill by kicking to the air. Remember to shout with both the Butt Strike backward and the lunge forward. Repeat 10 times.

To Decrease Difficulty

- Do fewer repetitions and give yourself adequate time.
- Practice without the bag.

To Increase Difficulty

- Use a heavier bag.
- While you are at zero and waiting for your opening, hold your breath.

(continued)

Ground Fighting Drill 3. *(continued)*

Success Check

- Begin at 0 percent, lying on your front.
- Come up onto your knees and forearms.
- Explode from 0 to 100 percent, with full voice, into the Butt Strike.
- Strike backward and then lunge forward.
- End in the Side Thrust Kick position, with both hands on one side.

Score Your Success

Come up onto your knees and forearms = 20 points

Explode from 0 to 100 percent with full voice = 20 points

End in the Side Thrust Kick position, with both hands on one side = 20 points

WAIT AND KICK

This technique enables you to defend yourself from someone who is trying to remove your pants. Take a breath. The good news is that there's something you can do in this terrible situation, and it works even if you begin the assault frozen or unable to move. In fact, it works better if you're keeping still and waiting at zero at the beginning.

As with the other ground techniques, wait for an opening and then move quickly into the Side Thrust Kick position. Your opening comes when the attacker gets below your knees. Once your pants are below your knees, your legs are free enough to kick and get into position. Go to 100 percent, using your voice to shout *no* and your legs to kick (figure 7.4). Depending on your pants, you may need to do the Cycle Kick and scrape from step 6, Getting to the Ground Safely, to be able to get into the Side Thrust Kick position (see page 56). At that point, all you have to do is to sit up onto your side and kick. Likely targets for this technique are the attacker's groin or head.

Figure 7.4 | **Wait and Kick**

APPROACH

1. On your back
2. Wait at zero until your pants are below your knees

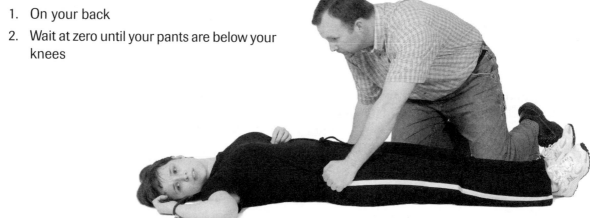

a

EXECUTION

1. Go to 100 percent and shout *NO!*
2. Free your legs by kicking

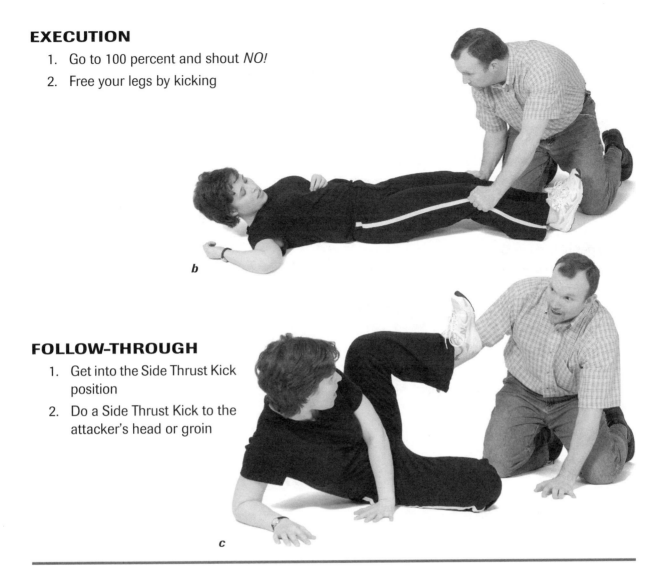

b

FOLLOW-THROUGH

1. Get into the Side Thrust Kick position
2. Do a Side Thrust Kick to the attacker's head or groin

c

Starting lying on your back, count to 3, then shout *no* and get into the Side Thrust Kick position. Roll slightly onto your side first if that helps you to sit up. Do this several times at your own speed. Then add in a Cycle Kick and scrape, after the *no* shout but before getting onto your side. Practice 20 repetitions. Begin at 0 percent and then go to 100 percent with a strong *no* shout.

One of my students had this to say about the Wait And Kick: "I guess I always thought, like you said, that I couldn't do anything from the ground. But, when we practiced the one where he pulls your pants down, it was amazing. When I was the one [in the role of attacker], her leg just came out of nowhere; her foot was right in my face! Even though I knew she was going to do it, she still scared me!" *Exactly. The benefit of having the element of surprise is huge. We've all been taught a bunch of lies about the invincibility of the attacker in sexual assault. You have a lot of choices, including a very powerful kick.*

Misstep

Worrying too much about the physics of fabric and your legs getting tangled.

Correction

Focus instead on going from 0 to 100 percent with your voice and your commitment.

Ground Fighting Drill 4.   *Wait and Kick*

If you have a friend to practice with, a great way to drill Wait And Kick is to act it out up to the point of getting into the Side Thrust Kick position. Start with one person kneeling at the side of the defender, who is on his or her back on the floor. The kneeler should place his or her hands at the defender's hips and mimic pulling down the defender's pants. Make sure the defender can actually feel you yanking your hands down along the sides of his or her legs. When the kneeler's hands get below the knees, the defender should shout *no* while sitting up into the Side Thrust Kick position. Make sure you both get a turn seeing what this looks like from the attacker's point of view.

To Increase Difficulty

Wear two pairs of pants and have your practice partner actually pull down the top pair. Hint: Wear pants that you don't mind ripping.

Success Check

- Take turns as attacker and defender.
- Wait at 0 percent until the attacker is below your knees.
- Go to 100 percent with a *no* shout.
- Sit up into the Side Thrust Kick position.

Score Your Success

Stay at zero until the attacker is below your knees = 20 points

Explode from 0 to 100 percent with your *no* shout = 20 points

Get into proper Side Thrust Kick position with each attempt = 10 points

Ground Fighting Drill 5.   *Self-Diagnostic*

Before going further, let's run a brief self-diagnostic. I've noticed that those students of self-defense who have the most trouble learning ground techniques are usually the ones with the strongest commitment to not having feelings. After all, we're not learning how to dribble a basketball or kick a field goal. It's impossible to read about and act out defenses against sexual assault without having feelings of some sort. Ignoring your feelings in this case takes a tremendous amount of energy. That energy is needed for the physical and intellectual task at hand.

Answer the following questions, either by discussing them with a friend or writing about them in your Practice Journal.

How are you?

Are you breathing? Are you holding your breath or breathing shallowly?

Are you reading quickly?

Are you skipping the drills?

Do you need to take a break?

Are you thinking about quitting *Self-Defense: Steps to Survival?*

Do you want to quit?

Is it possible that you're feeling angry, scared, or overwhelmed?

If you don't want to quit, what help could you get?

What do you need right now?

If you don't have any uncomfortable feelings and want to continue, that's fine. It's also acceptable to go slowly, ask for help, and only use the steps in a way that's right for you. If you are feeling overwhelmed, make sure that you are using your voice loudly and firmly each time you practice. Acting out the drills silently, or reading them and thinking about them without doing them physically, could contribute to a sense of fear, despair, or exhaustion. You don't have to give up on your decision to learn self-defense, and you don't have to muscle through it by ignoring your need for breaks and support either.

Overcoming the Past

Self-defense isn't simple. It's complicated, and learning and practicing these techniques can bring up a lot of unexpected and sometimes painful memories. After a lesson on ground fighting, one of my students expressed her discomfort. "Last week's class really felt bad. I thought about not coming back after that," she said. "I wasn't sure why until last night, when I had a dream about what happened to me in high school. I didn't do any of this! It didn't even occur to me to yell or hit him or try to lie. I was just totally frozen. I feel terrible. I mean why couldn't I have tried something at least? It seems so simple now, and I didn't do anything. I don't think I can ever forgive myself for that."

First of all, she didn't deserve what happened to her in high school, and it wasn't her fault for not fighting back. There are many reasons that people are unable to defend themselves, and it takes a lot of time and help to overcome them. Some of the reasons that victims can't fight include the following: the freeze response, thinking that they'll be hurt worse, loving the person who's hurting them, or being dependent on them financially or emotionally, not knowing how to fight, not wanting to believe it's really happening, thinking it's their fault and being unable to get angry at the assailant, not thinking they're worth defending, having been assaulted in the past and re-experiencing that assault, or feeling ashamed or incapacitated by drug or alcohol use. Learning how to defend yourself *now* does *not* mean that you should have been able to defend yourself in the past. I told my student that she had nothing to forgive herself for. She did the right thing then, and I was glad she was here now.

OTHER GROUND FIGHTING CHOICES

In addition to the Eye Strike, the Butt Strike, and the Wait And Kick techniques, you can negotiate, lie, pretend to acquiesce, or go to 0 percent to lull the assailant into a false sense of security before you fight or escape. Here are some examples of verbal techniques:

"OK sure, I just have to go to the bathroom first."

"Just let me go tell my friend not to wait for me."

"I'll do anything you want."

"These pants are tight. If you let go of my hands, I'll help you with that."

"I promise not to scream."

"Yes, I have money. It's in my purse on the table in the other room."

The goal of these verbal techniques is to get yourself into a position to fight back full force (or to run if safety and other people are very close). You may also choose to get into Side Thrust Kick position at any point—if you hear someone in your house at night, or if your date has been ignoring your verbal demands to stop. You don't have to wait to be pinned.

I'm not a fan of some of the verbal techniques with the goal of getting the rapist to change his mind. Some people suggest that you appeal to his sense of decency or his love for his mother or the fact that he'll be frightened if you have your period or HIV. I suspect that most men who are willing to force others into unwanted sex have lost their empathy and their fear of consequences. But I've also heard legends of these techniques working. Trust your instincts. One woman, who successfully avoided rape by telling a group of men that she had her period, had this to say about the technique: "They said they were going to rape me. I told them I was menstruating and it scared them off. I think nowadays it wouldn't be that big a deal, but, in the South in the forties, it was a big deal. People were more inhibited. You just didn't tell people you were menstruating" (Caignon and Groves, 1987).

Misstep

Holding your breath, closing your eyes, focusing on what the attacker is saying.

Correction

Breathe, open your eyes, and focus on your body. Threats and verbal abuse are used to frighten an intended victim and are less important than watching for your opening and going to 100 percent when it arrives.

Battle in the Cemetery

In *Her Wits About Her*, Rashida describes using many of the defenses covered in step 7 when she was trapped in a car by multiple assailants. While Rashida was walking home at night, a group of five young men pulled up next to her and forced her into the backseat of their car. She describes her emotional process in the car, moving from extremely frightened to extremely angry and focused. She says, "I stopped struggling . . . I began to get angry . . . I sat quietly . . . my anger helped me to relax, slipping into a state I call my 'battle awareness' . . . when they stopped the car in the middle of the dark cemetery, I was ready." One of the men held her prone in the backseat, while a second started to climb in on top of her with his pants down. From her battle-ready state (being at 0), she exploded (going to 100). All in the same movement, she bit the arm holding her, hit the same perpetrator in the gut with her elbow, and kicked the one coming toward her. The man she bit released her, and the second perpetrator, also injured, backed out of the car in astonishment. She leapt from the car and ran. The men were so shocked only one chased her briefly. She heard the others call him off. She hid in the cemetery until they drove off, and then sought help nearby at a friend's house. The police captured one of the perpetrators later that same night when a man with a "severe human bite that required stitches" turned up in the emergency room.

Adapted from *Her Wits About Her*, edited by D. Caignon and G. Groves, 1987. New York: Perennial Library. Pages 182–184.

Ground Fighting Drill 6.   *Studying Success*

Answer the following questions in your Practice Journal about the Battle in the Cemetery success story. If you like, discuss the success story and your answers with a friend or study partner.

1. When did Rashida begin her self-defense?

2. How many kinds of self-defense did she use? List each one, including the use of awareness and verbal, emotional, and psychological techniques, not just physical ones.

3. What might you have done differently in the same situation? Why?

4. What surprised you about Rashida's experience?

5. What satisfied or empowered you most about her experience?

SUCCESS SUMMARY

The core techniques of step 7, Fighting From the Ground, are emotional and psychological. You have already had some opportunity to practice these in your own life—staying focused on the present moment and aware of your body, maintaining hope when you need to wait for an opportunity, and going from 0 to 100 percent with all of your energy and commitment. Each of these skills will deepen and improve your physical self-defense techniques. Consider ways in which you could continue to practice these core techniques in your current life. During the self-diagnostic drill you returned to the present moment, enhanced your body awareness, and chose your own next right action.

Before Taking the Next Step

Before moving on to step 8, Avoiding Blows, take time to reflect on what you have learned to this point. Answer the following questions honestly.

1. Have you learned the four elements for overcoming the freeze response?
2. Have you identified at least two of these you have already used in your own life?
3. Have you drilled the Eye Strike from the ground position?
4. Have you drilled both the Butt Strike (facedown) and the Wait and Kick (faceup)?
5. Have you completed the self-diagnostic drill and shared your results with a friend or written about it in your Practice Journal?

If you answered yes to all five questions, you are ready to move on to step 8, Avoiding Blows.

Taking the Step Further. *Homework Assignments*

Memorize the myth at the beginning of this step and write about it in your Practice Journal. Share some of your thoughts and feelings about the myth and fact with at least one other person. Why do you think blaming the victim is so prevalent when people talk about sexual assault in particular? How does victim blaming help rapists? If we cannot cause someone to sexually assault us, why is this myth so common?

Physical practice—Spend 5 to 20 minutes a day practicing the moves from step 7, Fighting From the Ground, until you begin step 8, Avoiding Blows. Remember to incorporate your voice with each technique.

What are five possible obstacles that could stop you from studying *Self-Defense: Steps to Survival* at this point? Some students struggle with finding enough time, finding enough support, getting overwhelmed, trying to do too much, or needing help to understand the drills. What help could you get to overcome your obstacles?

Avoiding Blows

It's a smart strategy in self-defense to avoid being hit, particularly in the face or head. Your best defense in any particular assault may be varied—using awareness to help you act before a punch is thrown, using verbal techniques to talk yourself into a better protected position, or launching an offense before a blow ever hits you. For men, avoiding blows may require a 100 percent commitment, including being willing to back down, to listen to verbal abuse without responding, and to refuse to be goaded into a fight. For women, avoiding blows may require a willingness to take threats seriously, to mistrust someone you'd like to believe, or to throw the first punch. Let's review three of the essential techniques you've already studied in previous steps.

- **Awareness (step 1).** Can you think of some examples in which awareness could help you avoid blows? How about paying attention to verbal and nonverbal cues, being aware of others' level of intoxication, choosing not to make eye contact or otherwise engage with an unsafe driver trying to bait you with road rage. If someone angrily demands that you leave his or her house, neighborhood or office, you

can do so by backing away slowly in protective stance. If he or she follows or chases you, hold your ground. As you learned in previous steps, it is usually safer to face an attacker than to turn your back on danger.

- **Turn-ins (step 5).** The turn-in techniques (shoulder, hair, and wrist grabs) can all be effective defenses against blows as well. Because you are turning in when grabbed, instead of turning away or attempting to flee, you have two advantages. You move closer than an arm's length from the attacker, which is unexpected and makes it more difficult for him to target you. And you are now on the offensive. Rather than waiting to try to block incoming punches, you are responding swiftly by delivering an Eye Strike, Heel Palm, or Knee to Groin.

- **Drop (step 6).** Anytime you have a suspicion that someone might be getting ready to hit you, the drop is an excellent choice of technique. The most statistically significant indicator that someone is likely to hit you is whether he or she has hit you in the past. Using this technique effectively means being willing to drop *before* you are hit.

Myth   Self-defense doesn't work for battered women. It's too dangerous to teach them self-defense skills. Fighting back will just make the batterer angrier and put her in more danger. And anyway, she'll never leave him, so why bother?

Fact   Escaping a batterer is courageous and complicated, and it may well be the hardest thing a victim will ever do. It requires emotional, psychological, *and* physical self-defense. Women leave every day. A survivor of battering —no one else—is the best person to decide whether it is the right time to get self-defense training.

Batterers may increase their violence and tighten their control over their victims at any sign of independence or self-care. But who would insist that an illiterate battered woman "should never be taught how to read; it might just make him mad"? Some survivors are not ready to take self-defense training until they are safely away from their batterers; some survivors will not feel empowered to leave their batterer until they've gotten some self-defense training.

A battered partner is at the highest risk of being killed *after* she leaves the abuser. Knowing this instinctively, many choose not to leave because they do not have enough support to do so safely. Surviving an abusive partner requires more than learning a couple of physical moves, and step 8, Avoiding Blows, offers a range of verbal, emotional, social, and physical self-defense techniques for escaping from a violent partner.

HEAD BLOCK FROM THE GROUND

If someone is throwing a punch at your head while you are standing, your best bet is to drop to the ground and kick. But, if you are being held on the ground and someone tries to hit you, you can block and strike. Form two fists, thumbs on the outside, and place them at the back of your neck so that your arms and elbows form a cage protecting your head (figure 8.1). Ensure that your fingers are not interlaced; your hands should be two fists, separate from each other. Your hands need to be as free and mobile as possible for their next move. Place just one arm in this position; you can see that it's very difficult to hit your own head with the other arm.

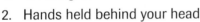

Figure 8.1   **Head Block**

APPROACH

1. On the ground
2. Hands held behind your head

a

EXECUTION

1. Lift your elbows
2. Block the attacker from striking your head
3. Plant one foot on the ground

b

(continued)

Figure 8.1 *(continued)*

FOLLOW-THROUGH

1. Shout *NO!*
2. Perform an Eye Strike or a Heel Palm Strike
3. Scoot into Side Thrust Kick position

c

Misstep

Interlocking fingers behind your head.

Correction

Keep both hands in separate fists.

Avoiding Blows Drill 1. *Head Block*

Lie on your back and practice the Head Block several times at your own speed. Begin with your arms above your head. Practice moving swiftly from the blocking move to an Eye Strike or a Heel Palm Strike. When you feel comfortable with those two moves, add in a Scoot into Side Thrust Kick position and kick to the air. Practice 20 repetitions of the entire series of techniques, shouting *no* with each block, strike, and kick.

Success Check

- Fully protect your head.
- Execute a Heel Palm Strike or an Eye Strike to the air.

- Shout *no* with the strike.
- Sit up into the Side Thrust Kick position, with your hands on your side.

Score Your Success

Elbows over ears, hands clenched separately = 20 points

Explode from 0 to 100 percent with your *no* = 20 points

Get into proper Side Thrust Kick position after each series = 10 points

CHOKE HOLD FROM THE GROUND

This technique can help you escape from someone who is choking you on the ground. Just like escaping the standing Arm Bar Choke hold (step 5, Breaking Holds), your first priority is to secure your own airway. Bring your arms around

the outside of the attacker's arms and clamp your forearms down hard across his forearms (figure 8.2). You are not trying to pull his hands away from you or to push the attacker off you with brute force. All you have to do is clamp his forearms to your own chest and hold on. Next, pull up one leg and push your heel into the ground to roll you both over. Still holding on to the attacker, walk your legs up his body, using his hold on you to counterbalance. When your feet are at the attacker's face, you have at least two choices. If your legs are caught, you can use the Bunny Kick or the Cycle Kick and Scrape to free them. Or use the Scoot to move out into Side Thrust Kick position.

Figure 8.2　Choke Hold From the Ground

APPROACH

1. Choke hold, defender on back

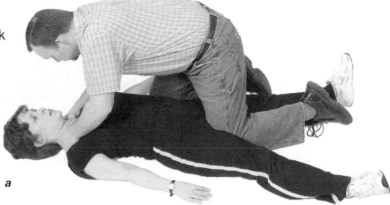

a

PLANT AND CLAMP

1. Bend your leg and plant your heel
2. Bring your arms around the outside of the attacker's arms
3. Shout *NO!* and clamp the attacker's forearms to your chest

b

FOLLOW-THROUGH

1. Push your heel into the ground and roll over
2. Hang on and walk up the attacker's body

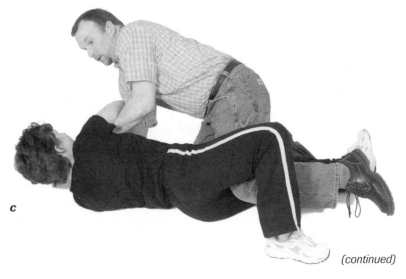

c

(continued)

Figure 8.2 (continued)

SIDE-THRUST KICK

1. Scoot into the Side Thrust Kick position

d

Misstep

Letting go or getting into a struggling match, trying to break his hold.

Correction

Clamping serves to secure even a tiny amount of airspace, which is enough to allow you to focus on the push-off and kick portion of this defense. Hang on and walk up the attacker's body.

Breaking Free

"I'm skeptical, I guess. My ex-husband used to choke me. I don't really buy it that the choke hold from the ground would work with him. But I guess another way to look at it is that I just had to do a lot more to break his hold on me. For me, I couldn't just, you know, stomp him or whatever. I think when I first signed up [for your class], I thought it would scare him so he'd stop, but things got worse, and I had to get a ton of help. I wound up having to leave him. I stayed at a shelter for three months, and I got a counselor and a new place to live. I had to accept a lot of free legal services and even food once, which really hurt my pride, but I left everything behind when I left him. I'm glad I did, but it was hard. It took a lot of work."

Yes, it does take an enormous amount of time, energy, and help to leave an abusive partner. Batterers generally are not changed by a victim's decision to take a self-defense class. In fact, sometimes learning self-defense can be a dangerous time for a battered partner. I'm so glad you did everything it took to break free. Congratulations! It's normal to have a lot of feelings come up when you're breaking free, and it's normal to need help. The fact that you were able to accept help is a mark of great courage.

Avoiding Blows Drill 2. *Choke Hold*

Lie on your back and practice breaking a Choke Hold on the ground. Practice moving swiftly from the clamping move to the leg push-off. When you feel comfortable with those two moves, add in the Scoot into Side Thrust Kick position and kicking to the air. Practice 20 repetitions of the entire series of techniques, shouting *no* with each clamp, pushoff, and kick.

Success Check

- Secure your own airway by clamping.
- Hold on securely to the attacker's forearms.

- Push off from the ground, and flip onto your side.
- Walk up the attacker's body into the Side Thrust Kick position.

Score Your Success

Secure clamp, hold on to arms = 20 points

Explode from 0 to 100 percent with strong *no* = 20 points

Get into proper Side Thrust Kick position with each attempt = 10 points

WARNING SIGNS OF ABUSIVE PARTNERS

Given that the majority of punchers are male partners and the majority of targets are their wives, girlfriends, and boyfriends, it's essential that you study the early warning signs of potential batterers. If you think that domestic violence will never happen to you, you have at least one thing in common with every battered partner I have ever worked with. Almost all batterers give signs early in the relationship of future abusive behavior. Why not avoid being punched by refusing a second date with an extremely jealous guy whose last girlfriend seems terrified of him? Or by choosing not to move in with your girlfriend who kicks her dog and broke the TV when she got fired? People who will hit you may also do the following:

- Call you names; ridicule your body, clothes, weight, or appearance
- Monitor your time; constantly call to check up on you; follow you
- Criticize you for little things, often in front of other people
- Accuse you of being unfaithful; be very jealous
- Treat you roughly—grabbing, pushing, pinching, shoving, pulling hair
- Refuse to take no for an answer; badger you until you say yes

- Prevent or discourage you from seeing friends or family or going to work or school
- Get angry with you when they are drinking or using drugs
- Blame alcohol or drug use for their behavior
- Control how you spend your money; refuse you access to money
- Threaten to hurt you, children, pets, or themselves in order to get their way
- Force you to have sex when you don't want to or to do sexual things you don't want to
- Hurt you during sex; ignore your feelings regarding sex
- Blame you for their anger and violence
- Apologize profusely after hurting you; promise never to do it again
- Damage property when angry (throw objects, punch walls, kick doors, tear photos)
- Scare you by driving recklessly
- View women as objects; insist that men are the "king of the castle" and get to make the rules and decisions
- Play mind games; insist that you're crazy or confused or overreacting
- Tell you that they are nothing without you
- Tell you that you are nothing without them

Someone who exhibits even one of these behaviors, even one time, is likely to hit you in the future. What kind of support might you need in order to avoid being hit? What might help you be safe now and in the future? To what lengths are you willing to go to protect yourself (and your property, your pets, and your kids) from violence?

Misstep

Thinking he'll change or that it will get better after he gets a job, leaves a job, gets a raise, the kids get older, he drinks less, or some other change of circumstance.

Correction

I don't know anyone who has been hit only once. Batterers rarely change, and, when they do, it's usually because of massive external consequences such as being sent to jail or assigned to court-ordered therapy.

Misstep

Thinking you caused it somehow.

Correction

You didn't cause the violence. If batterers hit because they were simply overcome with rage and unable to control themselves, they would also attack their bosses, waitresses, strangers in traffic, and police officers. Instead, they plan their assaults against the people they can control best—wives, girlfriends, partners, and children.

One Small Step

"My girlfriend fits all of these patterns. I've known for a while that she's abusive. But you don't know her. She would never, ever let me leave her. She's threatened to out me to my parents, she's threatened to kill me and herself, she can tell if I even think about leaving. It's like she's psychic or something. I just can't get away."

You are definitely in danger, and it will take time and help to get safe. Batterers use mental, emotional, and psychological torture to control their victims. Most battered women report feeling as though their partner is invincible, almost superhuman in strength. They aren't; they are simply cowards who prey on those they love. But it can take a while to unlearn all of these myths. In the meantime, what help are you willing to get? Is there just one action you can take? One safe person to tell? One other survivor you'd be willing to tell the truth to? Is your life worth one phone call to a shelter? When you're ready to leave, they can help you.

DOMESTIC OR DATING VIOLENCE SAFETY PLAN

If you are currently in a relationship with someone who has been abusive or may become abusive, it is essential that you get the support you need to complete this plan and find a secure place to keep it. Make a copy of figure 8.3 (page 116), complete it, and keep it in a safe place. Even if you are currently single or if you are married to the safest, sanest, most loving partner in the history of the world, completing the safety plan is still important. Having a plan in place before you are threatened or terrified increases your safety and can speed your escape.

You may answer the questions as they relate to your current partner, a future partner, or a stranger who has broken into your house. It will enhance your safety to think *before* an attack about how you will protect yourself and your children in case violence occurs in your home.

This particular plan has been written, amended, and shared by many and can be found at a variety of sites on the Internet, including those of the Nashville Police Department and various domestic violence shelters. There might be other questions you would like to add related to your particular situation.

Few current victims of abuse can complete a safety plan without help. Consider asking a trusted friend, a staff member of a domestic violence shelter, or a counselor to help you with it. You don't have to do anything you're not ready to do, and you don't have to do it alone.

Important Phone Numbers

It's worth taking the time to memorize all of these numbers. At least write them down in one place in case you ever need them quickly in an emergency. You may have to leave home quickly without your address book, your computer, or your cell phone.

Plan Basics

Completing the safety plan is a great first step, but you will need to go back and review it periodically to update phone numbers or resources and make sure you and your children know what to do.

You should also be ready to pack and leave quickly, if necessary. Helpful things to pack to take with you:

ID

Driver's license

Children's birth certificates

Your birth certificate

Money

Lease, rental agreement, house deed

Bankbooks

Checkbooks

Health insurance papers

Proof of car insurance

House and car keys

Medications

Address book

Photographs

Medical and immunization records for yourself and your kids

Social security card

Welfare ID

Green card

Work permit

Passport

Divorce papers

Protection orders

Jewelry

Small toys and comfort items for kids

Other _____

Getting Help

Have you heard the joke "He was born on third base, but he thinks he hit a triple"? It's used to describe someone who's had a lot of help in life from family, friends, money, luck, and connections but thinks it's only through hard work that he or she has succeeded. It's built on the false idea that some people don't need help, when in fact those who seem the most independent, in control, or powerful got a lot of help early in life. Every human needs help, regularly, to function. If you are abused, you need help to get to safety.

Increasing Independence

Batterers control their victims in many ways, not just through physical force. It is in the batterer's interest to keep a victim isolated and dependent on him. The batterer will try to enforce this by undercutting the victim's self-esteem and access to resources. Whether you are currently being abused or not, are there areas of your life in which you could be more independent? Where might an abusive person take advantage of your low self-esteem, fear, or lack of resources?

Home Security

It can take a while to make changes to your home to increase your safety. Start right away by getting the locks changed if an abusive person has ever had keys to your home. In some cities, renters can request that landlords pay for some of these changes. You may also be able to get

Domestic or Dating Violence Safety Plan

Important Phone Numbers

National Domestic Violence Hotline 1-800-799-SAFE (7233)

My local domestic violence shelter _____

Police _____

Counselor _____

Supportive family member _____

Supportive family member _____

Other support people (ministers, sponsors, mentors, teachers, friends) _____

Children's school/babysitter _____

Doctor _____

Work _____

Plan Basics

My safe place to keep this plan is _____.

I will review my safety plan every _____(time frame) in order to plan the safest route.

I will review the plan with _____ (friend, counselor, or advocate).

I will work on my safety plan _____ minutes a day until I have all of the information that I need.

Getting Help

Safe places to ask for help are _____.

Safe computer to use is _____. (may be friend's, public library, or your own if password protected)

Safe way to use the phone is _____. (may be a public phone, untraceable phone card, calling collect, using the phone at a shelter)

I can keep a bag ready and put it _____ so I can leave quickly.

I can tell _____ about the violence and have him or her call the police when violence erupts.

I can teach my children to use the telephone to call the police and the fire department.

I will use this code word _____ for my children, friends, or family to call for help.

If I have to leave my home, I will go _____.

I will leave money and an extra set of keys with _____.

I will keep important documents at _____. (these may include medical records, prescriptions, identification, checkbook or credit cards, phone numbers, etc.)

I will check with _____ and _____ to know who will let me stay with them or lend me money.

I can leave extra clothes with _____.

Increasing Independence

___ Getting my own cell phone   ___ Getting therapy

___ Borrowing money from _____   ___ Getting my own e-mail account

Figure 8.3 Domestic or Dating Violence Safety Plan

___ Getting a P.O. box

___ Learning to drive/practicing driving alone

___ Learning to balance a checkbook

___ Familiarizing myself with shared bank accounts, investments, resources

___ Getting access to my own paycheck

___ Buying my own car

___ Other

___ I will open a savings account by this date _____. (You can start even with very small amounts of money.)

Home Security

___ I will rehearse an escape plan and practice it with my children.

___ I can change the locks on my doors and windows as soon as possible.

___ I can replace wooden doors with steel doors.

___ I can install security systems—additional locks, window bars, poles to wedge against doors, electronic sensors, etc.

___ I can get help with researching, paying for, and organizing these changes from _____ and _____.

___ I can work on a home security plan for ____ minutes a day.

___ When an argument erupts, I will move to a safer room such as _____. (Note: Avoid rooms without exits, such as the bathroom, and rooms with weapons, such as the kitchen, or rooms where guns are stored.)

___ I can purchase rope ladders to be used for escape routes from the second floor.

___ I can install smoke detectors and buy fire extinguishers for each floor of my home.

___ I can install an outside lighting system that lights up when someone approaches my home.

I can tell the following people if my partner no longer lives with me and that they should call the police if they see him or her near my residence:

Neighbors _____

Church leaders _____

Friends _____

Others _____

Keeping Children Safe

I will teach my children how to use the phone to make collect calls to me and to _____ (friend, family, minister) if my partner tries to take them.

I will tell the people who care for my children who has permission to pick them up and who does not.

School _____

Day care _____

Babysitter _____

Sunday school _____

Coach _____

Others _____

I will tell the children not to intervene if he's beating me, but to call _____ and leave the house.

I will ask _____ to no longer take my children to see the abuser. If they break this boundary, I will _____.

Orders of Protection

___ I will call the police if _____.

___ I will get a protection order if _____.

(continued)

Figure 8.3 *(continued)*

___ I will give my protection order to police departments in the areas I go to visit my friends and family, where I live, and where I work.

___ If I visit other counties, I will register my protection order with those counties.

___ I can call the local domestic violence agency if I am not sure how to register my protection order with the police departments.

___ I will tell my employer, church leader, friends, family, and others that I have a protection order.

___ If my protection order gets destroyed, I know I can go to the county courthouse and get another.

___ If my partner violates the protection order, I will call the police and report it. I will call my lawyer, advocate, counselor, and tell the courts about the violation.

___ If the police do not help, I will call my advocate or attorney and I will file a complaint with the chief of the police department.

___ I can file a private criminal complaint with the district judge in the jurisdiction that the violation took place or with the district attorney. A domestic violence advocate will help me do this.

Work and Public Safety

___ I can tell my boss, security, and _____ at work about this situation. Consider giving them a picture and physical description of the batterer.

___ I can ask _____ to help screen my phone calls.

When leaving work, I can do the following:

When I am driving home from work and problems arise, I can _____.

If I use public transportation, I can _____.

I will shop at different stores and at different hours than I did when I was with my partner.

I will use a different bank and bank at different hours than I did when I was with my partner.

I can also do the following _____.

Drug and Alcohol Use

___ If I am going to use drugs or alcohol, I am going to do it in a safe place with people who understand the risk of violence and who are committed to my safety.

___ I will no longer use drugs or alcohol with anyone who is not safe, including _____.

___ If my partner is using drugs or alcohol, I will _____.

___ If I want to stop using drugs or alcohol, I will take this first, small action _____.

Emotional Health

___ If I feel depressed and ready to return to a potentially violent situation or partner, I can _____ _____.

___ When I have to talk to my partner in person or on the phone, I can _____.

___ I will use "I can . . ." statements and I will be assertive with people.

___ I can tell myself _____ when I feel people are trying to control or abuse me.

___ I will call three places to ask if they have support groups for survivors to get help and learn more about myself and my relationship.

___ I can call the following people or places for support _____.

___ Things I can do to make me feel stronger are _____.

financial help to pay for changes from crisis centers, supportive family members, or shelters.

Identify a neighbor who you can tell about the violence. Ask the neighbor to call the police if he or she hears any disturbance coming from your home. Your life is worth any possible shame this self-defense technique may trigger in you.

Keeping Children Safe

Batterers frequently use children to attempt to harm their partners. They may beat the children, threaten to beat them or take them away from you, lie to them about you, or attempt to turn them against you. They may use visitation as a time to harass, threaten, or harm you.

If you leave your home to escape, take your children with you. Be sure your children know the safety plan and what they are supposed to do in an emergency.

Orders of Protection

These are court orders that protect you from someone who has already hurt you. They are sometimes called restraining orders or personal protection orders. With the help of police and shelter advocates, you can get a court to issue a ruling that the abuser is no longer allowed to come near you. An abuser who violates that order can be arrested even if he has not harmed you again.

Continue completing this entire safety plan in case the police do not respond right away.

Work and Public Safety

A high percentage of workplace violence is attributed to abusive partners and ex-partners coming to work to attack their loved ones. It can feel embarrassing to reveal at work that you need help to be safe, but it's important to tell others what you need.

Drug and Alcohol Use

Drug and alcohol use by the batterer or the victim do not cause abuse. Many alcoholics and drug addicts do not threaten or beat their partners, but drug and alcohol use does increase the odds. Therefore preparing for the possibility is important.

Emotional Health

Because abusers use emotional violence and control techniques, getting support to become emotionally free from someone has a huge payoff in terms of your physical safety as well. How or where you get support for your emotional health is less important than your willingness to get help. Good help never blames you, supports you in making your own decisions, and honors your choices.

Anna's Story

I was in an abusive marriage for 16 years, and most of that time I had no idea. I really had no idea whatsoever. I mean, I knew that Harold was violent, and I knew that I was unhappy, but most of the time I believed him when he said I brought it on myself. All I thought about all day was how I was messing up, how I should try harder, work harder, earn more, weigh less, be more loving, be less judgmental.

The first thing that really got through to me was when a woman I worked with said, "How can you let him treat the kids like that?" I couldn't get upset about how he treated me, but when I realized the effect on the kids—that got me started. I joined a group at the shelter, and it helped a lot to hear how others got out. They would describe beatings and I'd get mad! I'd think, *She doesn't deserve that!* After a while, I started to feel that I didn't deserve it either.

I chose not to get a restraining order when I left him, but I was blessed with a lot of help. I stayed at a friend's place in another state, and my divorce lawyer volunteered a lot of his time. If I had to share one thing with other women being abused it would be this: You can do it! You can get out! Because all of those years I was certain that I wasn't strong enough or smart enough to get by without him, and I was wrong. It was just what he wanted me to think.

Avoiding Blows Drill 3. *Studying Success*

Answer the following questions in your Practice Journal. If you like, discuss Anna's Story and your answers with a friend or study partner.

1. When did Anna begin her self-defense?

2. How many kinds of self-defense did she use? List each one, including asking for help. Include the use of awareness and verbal, emotional, and psychological techniques, not just physical ones.

3. What might you have done differently in the same situation? Why?

4. What surprised you about Anna's experience?

5. What satisfied or empowered you most about this survivor's experience?

Want to read more success stories? Lots of survivors of domestic violence share their stories at www.wadv.org.

SUCCESS SUMMARY

Avoiding blows involves both simple and complicated techniques, including strategizing, increasing your awareness, planning, protecting your head, and dropping out of the range of blows. You now have practiced protecting your head on the ground and breaking free from a choke hold while in a prone position. You have looked deeply into your present safety and asked yourself who you can turn to for help. You've learned how to plan for a safe escape from an abusive partner. Two qualities can ensure successful self-defense: being willing to do whatever it takes and being willing to get help.

Before Taking the Next Step

Before moving on to step 9, Escaping Pins, take time to reflect on what you have learned to this point. Answer the following questions honestly.

1. Have you practiced blocking your head from blows from the ground position?

2. Have you drilled the Choke Hold from the ground position?

3. Have you studied the Warning Signs of Abusive Partners?

4. Have you completed the Personal Safety Plan?

5. If the entire plan is too overwhelming, can you complete just one section? Or can you get help to complete it?

If you answered yes to all five questions, you are ready to move on to step 9, Escaping Pins.

Taking the Step Further. *Homework Assignments*

Memorize the myth in this step and write about it in your Practice Journal. Share some of your thoughts and feelings about the myth and fact with at least one other person. Can you imagine ever loving someone despite a terrible failing on his or her part? Why do you think so many people get angry at the victims of domestic violence for not leaving? In what ways could physical self-defense techniques put a battered woman in danger? In what ways could they protect her?

Practice—Spend 5 to 20 minutes a day working on your Personal Safety Plan and practicing the moves from step 8, Avoiding Blows, until you begin step 9, Escaping Pins.

If you haven't yet completed the Personal Safety Plan, choose a date by which you will finish it and a safe person that you will share it with. Write down those plans in your Practice Journal.

If you're being abused, or wonder if you are, call the national domestic violence hotline or your local shelter and ask them what services they offer. Even if you're not ready to leave, it's good to find out what's available.

Escaping Pins

You have already learned a number of techniques to avoid being pinned to the ground, bed, or floor. Your best defense against a pin is to use your awareness and your ground fighting skills to avoid being pinned in the first place. These skills include keeping your feet between the attacker and your head, dropping to the ground, going from 0 to 100 percent, and using full force in all of your strikes. Step 9, Escaping Pins, presents some additional defenses, specifically for getting free from a pinned position as quickly as possible and into the Side Thrust Kick position to end the assault.

The techniques in step 9, Escaping Pins, apply primarily to defense against attempted violence with a sexual component. But please do not skip this chapter if you feel you are not at risk of sexual assault based on your gender, history, or relationships. There's a thinner dividing line between sexual assault and other attacks than you might think. Although muggers, burglars, and carjackers aren't primarily interested in trying to pin a victim to the ground (they're trying to get money, drugs, or property and then get away), even these attackers may include sexual taunting and humiliation as part of their violence.

Myth

The primary motive for sexual assault is sex. Perpetrators are sex-starved and driven out of their right minds by a sexually arousing thought or sight. Sexually aroused men cannot control themselves.

Fact   Studies show that the motive for sexual assault is aggression, not sex. Sexual assault is a crime of violence, committed by a person who uses sexual behavior as a weapon to control, humiliate, or dominate someone else.

Most rapists have consenting sexual partners and are ordinary, "normal" men. More proof of the fact that sexual assault is about power and control is the fact that the majority of men who sexually assault other men choose to identify themselves as heterosexual. Men as a category are *not* crazed animals. They can choose when to act out sexually and when not to. If someone poisoned food and force-fed it to you, you wouldn't call it "eating"—you'd call it assault. Rape is violence, not sex.

The first three techniques in step 9, Escaping Pins, all have one element in common—using weight transfer to get out from a pinned position. You will learn to use an attacker's own weight and momentum against him. This is very different than trying to lift someone's entire body weight or trying to force the attacker to move by overpowering him. If you have experience in martial arts, you may be familiar with the concept of weight transfer. One of the great benefits of this weight transfer, or Roll Off, technique is that it works the same whether you are large or small, weak or strong, short or tall. You just push off the ground and roll over.

Escaping Pins Drill 1. *Weight Transfer Basics*

Practice the Roll Off to get a physical sense of how it works. Begin by lying on your back. Pull up your right leg as far as you can and plant your right heel on the ground. Then push your heel into the ground and roll to the left, over onto your front (figure 9.1).

Now practice the Roll Off to the other side. Lie flat on your back, pull up your left leg, and plant your left heel into the ground. Now push your left foot into the ground and flip yourself over onto your front. Notice that at no time are you lifting up toward the ceiling.

Do the move again, but this time begin by lying on your front. Go slowly. Pull up one of your legs as far as you can and plant the toe of that foot on the ground. Slowly push that foot into the ground and flip over onto your back (figure 9.2). Practice on both sides at least a few times from your back and a few times from your front.

a

b

Figure 9.1 Roll Off from a face-up position: *(a)* incorrect, lifting hips up in the air; *(b)* correct, pushing with foot and rolling over.

Escaping Pins Drill 1. *(continued)*

Figure 9.2 Roll Off from a face-down position: *(a)* incorrect, lifting hips and shoulders up in the air; *(b)* correct, planting foot and rolling over.

Success Check

- Practice from four positions, face up and face down, left and right sides.
- Begin by planting your toe or heel in the ground.
- Roll over, not up.

Score Your Success

Securely plant foot = 20 points

Push off, roll over = 20 points

FRONT ROLL OFF

When you put the Roll Off together with other techniques you've already learned, you can successfully break out of a pin. If you are pinned on your back, face up, you can combine the Roll Off with an Eye Strike and Side Thrust Kick (figure 9.3).

Figure 9.3 | Roll Off, Front

APPROACH

1. Pinned on your back
2. Pull up your leg and plant your heel

a

EXECUTION

1. Push your heel into the ground
2. Attempt an Eye Strike while rolling over
3. Shout *NO!*

FOLLOW-THROUGH

1. Scramble into Side Thrust Kick position

b

c

It can be very freeing to know that you can fight back even if you have been pinned, even if an assault has begun. The key to making the Roll Off techniques work is to wait until you feel the weight of the attacker on your body. When the assailant has at least some of his weight resting on you, you can destabilize him by rolling him off. This technique asks you to use your 0 to 100 percent skills from previous steps to wait actively at zero. During that time, you are strategizing, breathing, pulling up your leg, planting

your toe or heel in the ground, and waiting for your opening.

Start by lying on your back and practice the front Roll Off, including the Eye Strike and ending in Side Thrust Kick position. Do this several times at your own speed. Practice on both sides. Use a mirror or ask a friend to check your alignment. Practice 20 repetitions, shouting *no* with each executed strike and following all the way through, to end in Side Thrust Kick position.

Misstep

Trying to lift the attacker up into the air.

Correction

Focus your attention instead on pushing into the ground and rolling over.

Misstep

Moving only the lower part of your body, thus twisting your back.

Correction

Include the Eye Strike. Even if one or both of your hands are pinned, the strike will help move your torso in the same direction as your hips and legs.

BACK ROLL OFF

The Roll Off when you're lying face down is very similar to the face-up technique. Instead of planting your heel in the ground, plant your toe (figure 9.4). Instead of attempting an Eye Strike, combine the Roll Off with a High Elbow

Strike to the attacker's face. One benefit to this move is that pulling up your leg to prepare for the Roll Off can lull the attacker into a false sense of security by mimicking compliance.

Figure 9.4 **Roll Off, Back**

APPROACH

1. Pinned face down
2. Pull up your leg and plant your toe

a

EXECUTION

1. Push your toe into the ground
2. Perform a High Elbow Strike while rolling over
3. Shout *NO!*

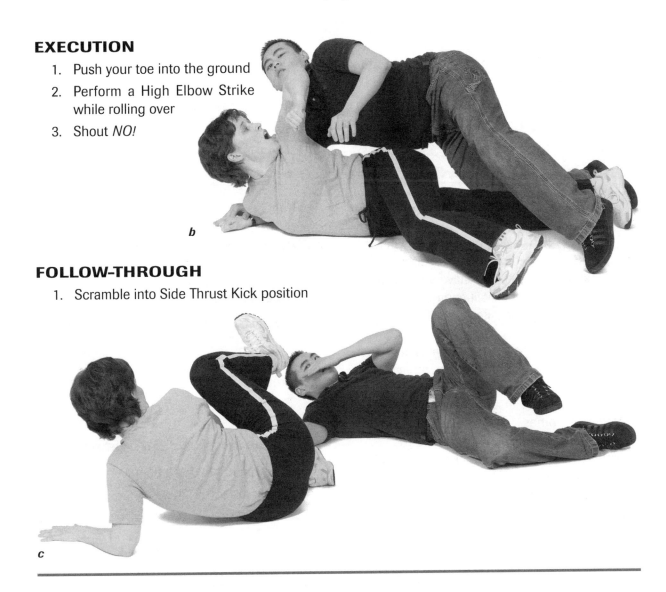

b

FOLLOW-THROUGH

1. Scramble into Side Thrust Kick position

c

Start by lying on your stomach and practice the back Roll Off series, including the High Elbow Strike and ending in Side Thrust Kick position. Do this several times at your own speed. Practice on both sides. Use a mirror or ask a friend to check your alignment. Practice 20 repetitions, shouting *no* with each executed strike and following all the way through, to end in the Side Thrust Kick position.

Misstep

Moving only your hips and legs and twisting your back.

Correction

Start slowly. Include the High Elbow Strike to assure that both halves of your body are working together.

Misstep

Trying to roll the attacker off of you before you feel his weight on you.

Correction

Stay at zero and breathe. You will be able to go to 100 percent as soon as you feel the attacker's weight.

Escaping Pins Drill 2. *Roll Offs*

This drill works best with two or three people, but you can also use your sofa cushions or a body bag if you like. It's best to practice on gym mats or good carpeting to protect yourself and your friends, and it's essential to have enough room for this drill. Your friends will end up 5 to 10 feet (1.5 to 3 m) away, opposite to the foot that you plant.

Start by choosing a defender to lie on her back, face up. Now have one, two, or even three friends lie on top of the defender. If you don't have people, use heavy cushions or even a large duffle bag stuffed with clothes.

The defender's job is to Roll Off the friends or the duffle bag. Although it will probably be obvious, remember that you don't have to lift them up into the air to get them off of you. No matter how much they weigh or you weigh, all you have to do is pull up your leg and push that heel into the ground. If you like, you can end the drill by getting quickly into Side Thrust Kick position. Practice both the front and the back Roll Off.

Success Check

- Talk two people into doing this drill with you.
- Begin by planting your toe or heel in the ground.
- Roll over, not up.

Score Your Success

Securely plant foot = 20 points

Push off, roll over = 20 points

Hurl friends some distance = 10 points

DOUBLE-LEG HOOK

You can also defend yourself against someone who attempts to pin you by sitting on your torso and shoulders. Although this position can be overwhelming or frightening, the Double-Leg Hook is actually one of the physically easiest techniques you've learned so far. First curl your arms up behind your attacker's legs and grab on. You can use the attacker's weight to counter-balance yourself just as having someone sit on your feet helps you to perform sit-ups. Your second move is to lift your legs and hook one or both feet around the attacker's shoulders (figure 9.5). All you have to do now is to sit up! What target is available to you at the end of the Double-Leg Hook?

Figure 9.5 **Double-Leg Hook**

APPROACH
1. Pinned on your back
2. Grab the attacker's thighs

EXECUTION
1. Double-Leg Hook
2. Sit up
3. Shout *NO!*

a

b

HAMMER FIST
1. Hammer Fist strike

c

SCOOT
1. Scoot out into the Side Thrust Kick position

d

You are now in the perfect position to do a Hammer Fist Strike to the groin or to use a Scoot to move out into the Side Thrust Kick position to kick the attacker's groin, knees, or head (in the unlikely event that the attacker sits up after a Hammer Fist Strike to the groin).

Start by lying on your back and practice the Double-Leg Hook several times at your own speed. Keep in mind that this technique is actually more difficult on your own than with someone's weight to counterbalance you. Begin by moving your hands into position to grab an attacker's legs, swing your legs up and slightly to the sides, and then sit up. Use a mirror or ask a friend to check your alignment. Practice 20 repetitions, shouting *no* with each executed Double-Leg Hook.

Escaping Pins Drill 3. *Double-Leg Hook*

Drill this technique on your own by adding all of the elements together in order. Begin on your back with the Double-Leg Hook. When you sit up, do a double Hammer Fist Strike to the ground between your legs where the attacker's groin would be. Remember not to link your fingers together and keep your thumbs on the outside. (Review Hammer Fist Strike, page 41, and the fist position for the Head Block on page 109.) After the Hammer Fist to the ground, use the Scoot to move backward a foot or so into the Side Thrust Kick position.

Remember to use your voice. Shouting *no* three times (during the Double-Leg Hook, the Hammer Fist, and when you get into position for the Side Thrust Kick) helps coordinate your body and mind, adds force to your physical techniques, and helps your body experience the drill more realistically.

To Increase Difficulty

- Increase your speed with each repetition.

- Perform the Leg Hook with just one leg (it works just the same).
- Add a Side Thrust Kick to the air at the end of the drill.

Success Check

- Grab onto the attacker's legs to stabilize yourself.
- Hook one or both legs over the attacker's shoulders.
- Sit up.
- Perform a Hammer Fist Strike to the ground.

Score Your Success

Securely plant foot = 20 points
Push off, roll over = 20 points

BITE AND PUNCH

The Double-Leg Hook is a good technique to use if someone has pinned your head, arms, and shoulders and is sitting up straight or leaning back toward your feet (so that you can see the ceiling when you look up). If an attacker is holding you down with his groin near your face such that you can't see the ceiling, use the Bite And Punch technique.

Bend your knees and plant both feet solidly in order to ground yourself. Your next task is to create some space between you and the attacker's groin by biting him (figure 9.6). A defender can bite an attacker's leg, hand, or groin from this position.

Figure 9.6   Bite and Punch

APPROACH

1. Pinned on your back
2. Plant both of your heels

a

BITE

1. Bite the inside of the attacker's thigh

b

PUNCH

1. Punch to the groin
2. Shout *NO!*

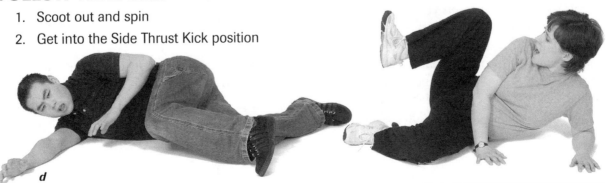

c

FOLLOW-THROUGH

1. Scoot out and spin
2. Get into the Side Thrust Kick position

d

When I get to this point in my classes, I often hear, "That's disgusting, I can't do that!" I agree; this type of sexual assault is disgusting. Unfortunately, it's also quite common, and so it's important to learn defenses against it. One student stated her disgust quite passionately: "The 'bite' idea is totally gross. I hate that. I can't see myself actually doing that! What about diseases? I just don't want that anywhere near my mouth." One choice you have that could better protect you from some sexually transmitted diseases is turning to bite the rapist's inner thigh or hand, although this still exposes you to blood. Unfortunately, choosing not to defend yourself physically against sexual assault also carries a risk of contracting an STD. Many students find this section triggering because it's such a common type of assault. If someone has orally assaulted you, know that it wasn't your fault. Now might be the time to find someone safe to talk to about your experience. You don't have to keep it a secret or struggle through this alone. If it's too triggering, skip this technique and move on to step 10, Delivering Knockout Blows.

After being bitten, the attacker will move. Like an Eye Strike, a bite will get a reaction from an attacker even if you do it wrong, miss, or don't do it very hard. It's an attention grabber. This gives you exactly what you need—enough free space to enact your next move, a swift punch to the testicles. Make the Hammer Fist (both hands separately clenched) and punch quickly up toward the top of your head. There's no need to lift the assailant's weight with your fists. You are not shoving the attacker off of you. You can count on a quick punch to provide all of the motivation necessary for the attacker to move of his own accord. (From this position, he will most likely fling himself over your head.) All that's left to do is to spin around, get your feet in the place where your head used to be, and do a Side Thrust Kick.

Misstep

Shoving instead of punching.

Correction

Practice the punch while you are standing. Your doubled fists should go straight up past your nose and end straight up in the air over your head.

Misstep

Trying to do a Double-Leg Hook when you can't see the ceiling.

Correction

Don't worry. If you notice that your legs can't reach far enough to hook around the attacker's shoulders, that is your cue to Bite and Punch instead.

Escaping Pins Drill 4. *Bite and Punch*

Start by lying on your back. Practice this series of moves several times on your own. Mime the bite to the air. Punch up toward your head. Your fists should move just past your own nose, not up toward the ceiling. Include your voice by shouting *no* after the bite, during the punch, and during the spin. Use a mirror or ask a friend to check your alignment. Practice 20 repetitions, shouting *no* with each repetition.

Success Check

- Plant both of your feet on the ground.
- Bite.
- Punch upward, targeting the attacker's testicles.
- Spin. Move your head to where your feet begin.

- Get into the Side Thrust Kick position, with both of your hands on the side.

Bite = 10 points

Spin 180 degrees = 10 points

End in the Side Thrust Kick position = 20 points

Score Your Success

Securely plant feet = 20 points

Answering Common Questions

1. What if I roll him off but he doesn't let go of my arms?

That's actually great for a defender. Walk up his body with your feet and kick him in the head. When the attacker holds on to the defender, he ensures that he's still in range of your kicks. This technique works in the same way as when you broke free from a choke hold on the ground in step 8, Avoiding Blows (page 110).

2. What if I try to fight back and roll him off and everything but then he pins me again? I know you said it's a myth that fighting back means we'll be hurt worse, but wouldn't that be really dangerous?

If you get repinned, you can still defend yourself. Return to 0 percent and lie ("I'm so sorry. I won't do it again. I was just scared."), or use the time to regroup and catch your breath. You will get another opening. And remember, if you're getting tired, the assailant probably is too.

3. What if he tells me not to fight back? What if he says, 'You won't get hurt if you do what I tell you'?

He's lying. Being sexually assaulted is hurtful. Some survivors would say that the psychological and emotional harm that a rape victim experiences are worse than the physical injuries. Assailants use threats such as "don't you bite me" and "if you try anything, I'll kill you" to get what they want, not to help protect their victims. Although you always have the choice not to fight back physically, you do not have to choose it because an attacker threatens you. In an IMPACT class, you can practice hearing threats and verbal abuse but not responding. Stay at zero, watch for your opening, breathe as slowly and regularly as you can, and focus on your own body, not the attacker's words.

ADDITIONAL PINS

There are at least two situations in which you should make an opening without waiting until you can find a particular technique to use: 1) when someone is trying to get you to get into a car or 2) when someone is trying to tie your hands or feet. Go immediately to 100 percent using your voice and make your own opening. Going to 100 percent in these scenarios may include stomping, shouting, kicking, performing the Knee To Groin Strike, biting, or any number of techniques you've already mastered.

If someone is trying to get you into a car, he is planning to take you to a location where he can hurt you worse than where you are now. Even if threatened with harm or promised future safety if you get in, even if you don't feel safe in your current location, *do not get into the vehicle*. Anytime someone is trying to tie you up, you lose access to some of your best weapons. Make an opening by going to 100 percent with your voice and spirit to avoid being tied up.

Nita's Story

Nita was at a large party with friends and agreed to go to the room of one of the guys who lived there. They were making out when she started to feel uncomfortable. She noticed at first that she was feeling ashamed, as though she had maybe made a bad decision. She'd been drinking that night, and her first thoughts were about how she could get out of the room without anyone downstairs noticing her.

When she tried to stop and distract the guy by talking to him, he ignored her and told her she was too uptight and should just relax. Soon after that, he pushed her down on the bed and pinned both her hands over her head. She kept trying to dissuade him verbally, but he held both of her wrists with one hand and started pulling her pants down.

At that point, for the first time, she got really, really angry. She yelled, "Stop It!" as loudly as she could and scrambled around on the bed until she knocked him off balance. This freed one of her hands, and she dug her fingers into his eyes. She tried to kick him in the groin twice but missed both times.

At some point in their struggle, Nita managed to stand and was heading for the door when he grabbed her from behind. She bit his forearm hard and ran. She saw a friend outside the bathroom and they left the party together. She chose not to prosecute him for attempted sexual assault, but the next week and after that every year on the anniversary of the assault, she and her friends would paint the large rock on campus with his name and the words: "He tried to rape me. Don't go out with him!"

Escaping Pins Drill 5. *Studying Success*

Answer the following questions in your Practice Journal. If you like, discuss the success story and your answers with a friend or study partner.

1. How many kinds of self-defense did Nita use? List each one. Include the use of awareness and verbal, emotional, and psychological techniques, not just physical ones.

2. What might you have done differently in the same situation? Why?

3. What surprised you about Nita's experience?

4. What satisfied or empowered you most in this success story?

SUCCESS SUMMARY

Avoiding pins, or breaking free after you have been pinned, requires the use of physical, emotional, and psychological techniques. In addition to the basics of weight transfer, you can use the Eye Strike, the High and Low Elbow Strikes, the Bite and Punch, the Double-Leg Hook, the Side Thrust Kick, and the Hammer Fist Strike. Strategies include turning in, going from 0 to 100 percent, and waiting for an opening. For many students of self-defense, the prospect of being pinned and needing to stay both alert and passive is a terrifying one. But you've now heard many success stories, including those from men and women who weren't sure they could do it, didn't know if they were strong enough, and even "made mistakes" during their defense. You can do it too!

Before Taking the Next Step

Before moving on to step 10, Delivering Knockout Blows, take time to reflect on what you have learned to this point. Answer the following questions honestly.

1. Have you practiced the weight transfer techniques from all four positions (face up and down, left and right sides)?

2. Have you combined the weight transfer with your other ground techniques and drilled the Roll Off techniques?

3. Have you drilled the Double-Leg Hook?

4. Have you drilled the Bite And Punch technique?

5. Have you memorized the two situations in which you should "make an opening"?

If you answered yes to all five questions, you are ready to move on to step 10, Delivering Knockout Blows.

Taking the Step Further. *Homework Assignments*

Memorize the myth in this step and write about it in your Practice Journal. Share some of your thoughts and feelings about the myth and fact with at least one other person. Have you ever been told that men can't help themselves or can't stop sex after a certain point? By whom? How old were you? Out of all the steps so far, which felt the easiest to you? Do you know why? Which felt the hardest? Do you know why?

Physical practice—Spend 5 to 20 minutes a day practicing the moves from step 9, Escaping Pins, until you begin step 10, Delivering Knockout Blows. It's generally more helpful to practice for 5 minutes every day than 35 minutes once a week. Remember to incorporate your voice with each technique!

Treat yourself! You've been working very hard physically and emotionally to study a disturbing topic. It's time for a break. Decide how many days or weeks off make sense for your schedule and make a specific plan to do something nice for yourself that you would not normally do—go to the circus, spend an entire day at the park with a dog, get a massage, let yourself lie on the sofa and watch the game all afternoon, make cookies with your kids, or ask your partner to take the kids to the movies so you can lie in the tub for 2 hours. If you find it difficult to treat yourself, remember that perpetrators often target people who cannot take good care of themselves. Do it as a part of your self-defense training!

Delivering Knockout Blows

Because most assailants are looking for a victim and not a fighting partner, an assault rarely progresses to the point at which you have to knock the attacker unconscious. In fact, students of realistic self-defense classes report in large numbers that using their skills outside of class is much easier than in class. I've lost track of the number of times I've heard feedback like this, "I only did an Eye Strike, and I did it wrong, but he left me alone" or "I was all ready to do the Knee to Groin strike, but he was already lying on the ground" or—my favorite—"I put my hands up in protective stance and opened my mouth to yell and they apologized and ran away." Sometimes students even sound *disappointed* that they didn't get a chance to use all of their skills!

Although, hopefully, you'll never need to deliver a knockout blow, it's important to study knockout blows for several reasons. There may be a situation in which a knockout blow is your best choice, perhaps if you are attacked when camping and have a long hike in front of you before you can get to safety, or perhaps if an assailant breaks into your home late at night and you need time to alert your children and get to safety. It's also an important element of psychological self-defense. Knowing that you can knock someone out *if you have to* will be evident in your self-confidence and your willingness to defend your boundaries verbally, emotionally, and physically.

Myth, part I   It's easy to knock somebody out. I've seen it in the movies a thousand times. Just punch someone in the head, and he's out cold.

Myth, part II   It's almost impossible to knock somebody out. Only boxers, marines, or professional bodyguards are strong enough. Unless you know all of the right pressure points and have fists of steel, you could never do it.

Fact   The truth is somewhere in between. It's definitely harder than it looks in the movies; for example, it might take ten blows instead of one. But it's also easier than the average person might imagine. You can do it with some of the techniques you've already mastered!

There are two basic types of knockouts. One happens when the body is feeling so much pain that it shuts down as a protective mechanism and the attacker passes out. The other type of knockout occurs when someone is hit in the head with sufficient force that the brain knocks against the skull once or twice and she or he loses consciousness. In step 10, Delivering Knockout Blows, you'll study some refinements to the techniques you've already learned (Side Thrust Kick, Knee to Groin) and learn two new techniques that target the attacker's head. You'll also learn the skills you need to end a fight by assessing the perpetrator's consciousness and getting to safety.

KNEE TO HEAD

Whether you know it or not, you've already practiced the Knee to Head many times in *Self-Defense: Steps to Survival*. It is almost exactly the same move as the Knee to Groin (step 4, Kicking With Feet and Legs). Once again, hit with the top of your upper thigh, not actually your knee (figure 10.1). This gives you a weapon with more surface area, which simplifies targeting and provides increased force to your strike, incorporating the muscles of your back and butt, not just your leg. This is a good move to use when an attacker is kneeling or bent over and you are standing. You might have a chance to deliver a Knee to Head after a successful Knee to Groin or High Elbow Strike. Begin by reviewing the physical stance for the Knee to Groin in step 4, Kicking With Feet and Legs (page 51).

| Figure 10.1 | **Knee to Head** |

APPROACH

1. Protective stance
2. Assess distance to target

a

(continued)

Figure 10.1 *(continued)*

EXECUTION

1. Knee to the head
2. Shout *NO!*

b

FOLLOW-THROUGH

1. Step through the strike
2. Remain in protective stance
3. Assess and repeat if another strike is needed

c

Starting in protective stance, practice the Knee to Head Strike several times at your own speed. Practice with both legs, and use a mirror or ask a friend or instructor to check your alignment. Practice 20 repetitions, shouting *no* with each executed knee. Don't forget to step *through* rather than stand in place and pull your leg back after you strike. If you are practicing correctly, 10 repetitions of Knee to Head should walk you clear across the room.

Misstep

Holding onto your target by grabbing the attacker's head.

Correction

This move, although popular in movies, could unbalance you or leave you vulnerable to the attacker grabbing your hands or pulling you down. Keep your hands up in protective stance for balance and to protect your face and head if you go down to the ground quickly.

Misstep

Doing the Knee to Head from too far away. Making contact with your shin or toe.

Correction

Move in (figure 10.2). Proper range is extremely close, just as with the Knee to Groin.

Figure 10.2 Defender in proper range to deliver Knee to Head.

Knockout Blows Drill 1. *Knee to Head*

This drill enables you to practice two important elements of the Knee to Head: actually making contact with a target and assessing the proper striking distance. Ask a practice partner to hold a target for you, ideally, a weighted medicine ball of approximately 20 pounds (9 kg), but you can also use a soccer ball in a pinch. (See the Resources section in Self-Defense Today (page xxii) for information on sources.)

Have your friend hold the target loosely at his or her hip or slightly lower, as if the target is the head of an attacker who is kneeling or bent over at the waist. Get into protective stance at least 6 feet (1.8 m) away from your partner. Practice kneeing the target firmly, walking through the target each time. When you make contact with the target, the holder should let go.

If three people can practice the drill together, your second friend can stand 10 to 20 feet (3 to 6 m) behind the target holder and act as a goalie. (You can also use an actual soccer net for that function.) Give each person a chance to practice the Knee to Head, and do at least 20 repetitions. Your goal is to get some good air on that ball.

To Decrease Difficulty

- Do fewer repetitions and give yourself adequate time.

- Begin the drill in a static position very close to the target. Gradually progress until you begin from farther away.

To Increase Difficulty

- After two repetitions, change your angle and distance from the target.

- Ask the target holder to move the target very slowly while you set up.

- Begin on the ground in the Side Thrust Kick position. On the count of 3, stand, get into protective stance, assess your distance, and then perform the Knee to Head Strike.

Success Check

- Begin in protective stance.
- Set up an accurate distance to the "head."
- Make forceful contact with the target.
- Walk through the strike.

Score Your Success

Knee the "head" out of the holder's hands = 20 points

Walk through each strike = 20 points

Shout *no* with each strike = 20 points

SIDE THRUST KICK

As you've no doubt gathered by now, the Side Thrust Kick is probably your most powerful technique and can also serve as a knockout blow if you target the face, head, groin, or knee. Review the essential elements of the Side Thrust Kick position and alignment (figure 10.3).

Figure 10.3   Side Thrust Kick

APPROACH

1. Side Thrust Kick position
2. Knee and toe point up
3. Both hands on one side in front of you

a

EXECUTION

1. Kick out
2. Roll your hip over
3. Keep both hands on your side
4. Shout *NO!*

b

FOLLOW-THROUGH

1. Extend your body in a straight line
2. Facing away, look over your shoulder at the target
3. Return to the Side Thrust Kick position

c

As a refresher, practice a few Side Thrust Kicks to the air. Use a mirror or ask a friend to check the following points of alignment:

Are both of your hands on your side?

Is your bottom leg tucked in close?

Are you resting on the elbow, forearm, and hand of one side? (neither your wrist nor your upper arm should be in contact with the ground)

Are your toe and knee pointed toward the ceiling at the beginning of the kick?

When your leg is fully extended kicking, are your top hip and shoulder rotated and pointed toward the ground?

Do you return fully to the Side Thrust Kick position at the completion of each kick?

Side Thrust Kick Targeting and Distance

To use the Side Thrust Kick fully as a knockout blow, correct targeting is essential. Find a target you can use for practice. You won't actually kick it, so it can be a chair, a wall, or even a friend's head. Get down on the ground into the Side Thrust Kick position. Remaining on your side, use your top arm to point to the exact place where you intend to make contact. Practice this now.

Most likely, here's what you discovered when you pointed. Your pointing arm should be *behind* your kicking leg (figure 10.4). When you kick with maximum striking power, your foot kicks out slightly behind you at an angle, not in the direction that your hands are pointing on the ground.

Figure 10.4 Side Thrust Kick targeting: *(a)* incorrect, pointing at target in front; *(b)* correct, pointing at target with arm behind kicking leg.

In addition, your bottom leg should be either resting against the bottom of the target or no more than 6 inches (15.2 cm) away from it (figure 10.5). Your target is not the front of the target, but *behind* it. In order to deliver a knockout blow, you need to kick through it, not just kick the surface of it.

Figure 10.5 Side Thrust Kick distance: *(a)* incorrect, several feet away; *(b)* correct, 6 inches away.

Misstep

Toeing, pushing, or shoving the target instead of powerfully kicking through it.

Correction

Get closer. Take the time to set up your kick, use the Scoot to get into position, and take a deep breath before you kick.

Side Thrust Kick Power

In addition to correct targeting, your ability to get into correct Side Thrust Kick position quickly and to return to that position fully afterward greatly enhances the power and effectiveness of each kick. A Side Thrust Kick delivered from the proper position, with full extension and full recoil afterward, can make all of the difference between knocking someone out in one or two kicks versus having to deliver five or ten kicks to get the job done. Maximizing your recoil increases your force, is less likely to tire you out, and protects you from having your extended leg grabbed by the attacker.

Misstep

Leaving your leg partially or fully extended after kicking.

Correction

Recoil quickly. Return your knee as close as possible to your face. Stay on your side, with your torso slightly curled or coiled, prepared for the next kick.

Knockout Blows Drill 2.   Side Thrust Kick— Putting It All Together

This drill requires a person to read to you while you practice all of the elements of the Side Thrust Kick, but your reader does not have to be trained in the kicks themselves. This is another drill that older kids may enjoy helping you with. You will need at least 20 feet (6 m) in which to maneuver. Begin on the ground in the Side Thrust Kick position. Your reader, or drill sergeant, is going to shout out the following commands in random order:

Kick! (Side Thrust Kick)

Switch! (switch kicking sides)

Scoot in! (remain coiled in the Side Thrust Kick position while scooting forward or in a circle; continue to use the Scoot until the next direction is shouted)

Your sergeant should vary his or her delivery and may include up to five kicks or switches in a row. You shout *no* with each Side Thrust Kick and each time you switch. Feel free to do the Scoot silently. Do this for several minutes or until you're ready to tell your drill sergeant he or she is grounded.

To Decrease Difficulty

- Practice for shorter periods and give yourself adequate time to recover after a technique.
- Ask your drill sergeant to slow down and allow more time between commands.
- Eliminate the switch and use your dominant leg only.
- Decrease repetitions.

To Increase Difficulty

- Ask your drill sergeant to speed up and read the commands more quickly.
- Ask her or him to shout out a wider variety of commands with fewer repetitions.
- Increase the repetitions or the total length of the drill.

Success Check

- Recoil! Pull your kicking leg back forcefully and immediately.
- Remain in the Side Thrust Kick position at all times—with your knee and toe pointed up, both legs tucked in close, and both hands on your side.
- Use your *no* with every kick and switch.
- Maintain your force, energy, and commitment, even if you're getting tired.

Score Your Success

Shout *no* with each technique = 1 point per *no*

Survive 1 minute with your drill sergeant = 25 points

Survive 2 minutes with your drill sergeant = 50 points

Survive 3 minutes with your drill sergeant = 75 points

AX KICK

The ax kick is an excellent knockout blow. Used against the attacker's head or face, it packs an enormous punch. You can also Ax Kick the groin or knee. Depending on weight and distance, most of you can easily knock out an assailant with an Ax Kick. This kick is best used at close range against a target that is very low to the ground (figure 10.6). In fact, it's possible to injure your own knee by trying to Ax Kick a target that is too high or too far away from you, so please follow the alignment instructions carefully.

Figure 10.6 Targets for the Ax Kick: *(a)* incorrect, target too high; *(b)* incorrect, target too far away; *(c)* correct, low and close target.

The Ax Kick begins from the same position as the Side Thrust Kick, but instead of rotating your leg to kick out, raise your foot up toward the ceiling, and then drop your heel directly down in front of your bottom leg (figure 10.7). It is essential that your bottom leg be tucked as closely as possible to your body in order to protect you from axing your own shin. In fact, I once sported a bruise the size of a baseball for almost a month after demonstrating to a class the wrong way to Ax Kick; fortunately, I wasn't using anywhere near full force.

Figure 10.7   Ax Kick

APPROACH

1. Side Thrust Kick position

EXECUTION

1. Raise your foot to the ceiling
2. Drop your heel to the target
3. Shout *NO!*

b

FOLLOW-THROUGH

1. Keep your entire leg bent
2. Recoil immediately to the Side Thrust Kick position

c

Using the proper alignment protects your knee. Don't extend your leg; your knee should be bent before, during, and after the Ax Kick. Target the area directly in front of your bottom leg, not out in front or to the side.

Starting in the Side Thrust Kick position, practice the Ax Kick several times at your own speed. Begin slowly, making sure that the floor is adequately padded, and keep your bottom shin tucked in close to your body. Practice with both legs. Use a mirror or ask a friend to check your alignment. Gradually build up speed and force, practice 20 kicks, shouting *no* with each one.

Misstep

Attempting to Ax Kick a target that is too high or too far away.

Correction

Your target must be at ground level and less than 6 inches (15.2 cm) from your foot.

Knockout Blows Drill 3.   Ax Kick— Putting It All Together

Did you fire your drill sergeant from the last exercise? You might want to rehire her because the Ax Kick drill requires that you continue the same drill, this time with the addition of the command *Ax*. Once again, begin on the ground in the Side Thrust Kick position. Your assistant should shout out these commands in random order:

Kick!

Switch!

Scoot in!

Ax!

Make sure that you have enough padding or carpeting on your practice area so that you won't hurt your heel when you do the Ax Kick.

To Decrease Difficulty

- Ask your drill sergeant to slow down and allow more time between commands.
- Eliminate the switch and use your dominant leg only.
- Decrease repetitions.

To Increase Difficulty

- Ask your drill sergeant to speed up and read the commands more quickly.
- Ask her or him to shout out a wider variety of commands with fewer repetitions.

- Increase the repetitions or the total length of the drill.

Success Check

- Recoil! Pull your kicking leg back forcefully and immediately.
- Remain in the Side Thrust Kick position at all times—with your knee and toe pointed up, both legs tucked in close, and both hands on your side.
- Use your *no* with every kick, switch, and ax.
- Maintain your force, energy, and commitment, even if you're getting tired.
- Keep your kicking knee bent before, during, and after the kick.

Score Your Success

Shout *no* with each technique = 1 point per *no*

Survive 1 minute with your drill sergeant = 25 points

Survive 2 minutes with your drill sergeant = 50 points

Survive 3 minutes with your drill sergeant = 75 points

ENDING THE ATTEMPTED ASSAULT

Your goal is to end the attack as quickly as possible and to get yourself and anyone with you to safety. Should you choose to knock out an attacker, your most important asset is not your bicep size or your weight, but your commitment. Interestingly enough, commitment often requires that you slow down. When you are adrenalized, it's easy to speed up and become inefficient. You might begin to kick and miss, deliver blows too far from your target, or hold your breath and stop shouting, thus robbing yourself of some of the energy you need to end the assault. Slow down and make each strike count. You have more time than you think you do. Your attacker is startled, unprepared, and, possibly, injured and flailing as well. You have enough time to set up, target, and fully commit to your techniques.

Keep in mind that any serious assault that you survive is a success. No points are awarded for speed, style, or finesse. You may have to deliver 20 Side Thrust Kicks before you are able to focus and line up the perfect knockout blow. You may completely miss your target five times in a row, twist your ankle, and experience a fleeting moment of panic before you take a breath, assess your attacker's position, and knock him or her out with a Knee to Head. That's normal, and your moves will still work!

In addition to accessing your commitment, there are several other elements to ending an attempted assault. If you believe you have successfully knocked out the perpetrator, get up, and walk around to his or her head from at least

an arm's length away in your protective stance (figure 10.8). This helps protect you from being grabbed by your feet if the attacker is not fully unconscious or from falling if you are shaky or going into shock.

1. **Look around you.** Are you safe? Does the attacker have any friends coming toward you? Are you in the way of traffic? Does anyone else need help?

2. **Assess the attacker.** Is the attacker fully unconscious? If not, and you are far from help, consider getting back down on the ground to kick again. You're not well protected legally or physically if you try to deliver another blow while you are standing in this position.

3. **Stomp.** Shout *no* and stomp the ground near the attacker's head. This helps bring you fully into your body if you are going into shock or hyperventilating. It will also cause the attacker to flinch if he or she is faking it.

Figure 10.8 **End It**

APPROACH

1. Maintain Side Thrust Kick position after the knockout strike

2. Stand and move to the attacker's head

a

EXECUTION

1. Look while still in protective stance
2. Assess the attacker

b

FOLLOW-THROUGH

1. Shout *NO!* and stomp
2. Get down and repeat kicks, if necessary
3. Get to safety

c

Misstep

Trying to avoid ending the fight, turning away, or trying to run before the attacker is effectively dissuaded or unconscious.

Correction

Don't be afraid to knock the attacker out. Turn in. Slow down. Take a breath. Set up. If the attacker is giving up, he will run away from you. If the attacker is still in target range, you are still in danger.

The Power to End the Assault

In IMPACT padded attacker self-defense classes, students have the opportunity to practice delivering knockout blows in safe and realistic scenarios that model actual assaults. The padded instructors are professionally trained to assess speed, force, and targeting accurately and to communicate to students when they've delivered a kick that would knock out an assailant in a real-life assault. This type of specialized training enables students to experience, directly and physically, their own power and to determine realistically what it takes to knock out an assailant. The experience is life changing for most students. Here are some comments from IMPACT students:

- "I have never experienced such a feeling of personal power before in my entire life."

- "Knowing that I could physically stop someone from hurting me changed every aspect of my life. After my IMPACT class, I took a job as the sole caretaker of 100 acres of wilderness, on land next to a prison. My relationships with men improved. I said no to an abusive partner and went back to school. All of this flowed from our class. After years of trying to recover from the sexual abuse in my childhood, I feel safe for the first time ever."

- "This course was the scariest thing I've ever done. I thought about bailing a hundred times but I'm glad I stuck it out. The hardest part for me was the extended fights where the instructor played someone on PCP or having a psychotic break. I got pinned in mine, but I just went to zero and waited for an opening. To know that I could even knock out that guy was absolutely incredible."

- "When I came to my sister's graduation [from an IMPACT class], it just looked really violent to me. Even the first few days of our class, I kept wondering if I could really knock someone out. I didn't think I even wanted to. I'm a pacifist. I hate all kinds of violence. But it really helped me to picture having to defend my daughter. I still don't know if I'd actually do this if someone came after me, but, if anyone tried to hurt my girl, I know that I would do anything necessary to keep her safe. And now I know I can!"

- "I think this course should be mandatory and in all of the schools. I wish I could have learned this when I was 16. No one ever really told me how to defend myself before. I mean, I'd been to sort of one-day workshops on personal safety, but I never really felt safer after them. Usually, I just felt worse. But, with IMPACT, we actually did all of the moves instead of just talking about them. I got really mad when he grabbed me, but then it was like it triggered my instincts and I just knew I could do it. The first time my mugger went down in the knocked out position, I wanted to cheer!"

LEGAL CONCERNS

"Is it legal to knock someone out to defend myself?"

Sometimes, students have concerns about the legality of self-defense. Imagining such a powerful action as knocking someone unconscious in your own defense can be a new and frightening idea for those of you who have never had to do it before. The short answer is yes, it is legal to defend yourself. Although the law varies somewhat from state to state and country to country, most communities agree that using physical force when someone has harmed or is threatening to harm you is legal, appropriate, and wise. You have a right to defend yourself physically, forcefully, and to the point that you are safe.

It's also true that, in the United States, you are free to sue almost anyone for almost any reason. For myself, I would not allow that thought to stop me if I or someone I loved were being attacked. I would rather avoid being raped and explain my actions in a courtroom than submit to being raped based on the fear that someone might get angry if I defended myself. Survivors of domestic violence have been prosecuted for defending themselves from their batterers, usually for trying to disable the batterer before or after an attack. Luckily, more and more judges around the country are beginning to understand battered women's syndrome and post-traumatic stress disorder and are allowing evidence into the courtroom about the survivor's experience.

The choice is yours to make. Most actual opportunities to defend yourself do not require knocking someone out. Many times, you can use one technique and then run, but there may also be times when you cannot. If your child were trapped in the assailant's car, if the attacker was determined to chase and injure you, if one of your legs were hurt and you could not run away, delivering a knockout blow would be an excellent choice. Self-defense is a *response* to unprovoked violence. You have a right to defend yourself.

I Just Got Mad

In Louisville, Kentucky, 69-year-old Rosetta Smith successfully defended herself against an assailant at least 40 years younger than she. Smith is a double amputee. During the assault, Smith's attacker removed her prosthetic legs and attempted to choke, rape, and rob her. Her triumph over him speaks to the truth that our will to resist and to defend ourselves can overcome seemingly impossible odds.

When the assailant first came into her home, Smith screamed. She tried to reason with him, told him to leave her alone, and refused to help him when he demanded she remove her dress. When he demanded money, she says, "I just got mad and I said . . . I need money, too, we all need money!" At one point, he ran into another room searching for cash and Smith hid behind a door. She even found the presence of mind to take $50 from her purse and hide it under her mattress. When he returned and jumped on her again, Smith says, "I just grabbed him by his privates and told him to leave me alone, and then he vomited all over the place and fell asleep on top of me."

Even with her attacker unconscious, Smith was not yet safe. She realized she was trapped under his body and too weak to move. She prayed for help and strength and says at that exact moment her fear was removed and she was given the power to escape. She pulled herself out from under him, dragged herself to the phone, and called the police. When the police arrived, Smith's attacker was still unconscious. He was arrested and imprisoned. Knowing now that she can defend herself, Smith told an interviewer, "I think I can handle it, if he comes back after me."

Adapted from *Her Wits About Her*, edited by D. Caignon and G. Groves, 1987. New York: Perennial Library. Pages 106–108.

Knockout Blows Drill 4. *Studying Success*

Answer the following questions in your Practice Journal. If you like, discuss the I Just Got Mad success story and your answers with a friend or study partner.

1. When did Rosetta Smith begin her self-defense?

2. How many kinds of self-defense did she use? List each one. Include the use of awareness and verbal, emotional, and psychological techniques, not just physical ones.

3. What might you have done differently in the same situation? Why?

4. What surprised you about her experience?

5. What satisfied or empowered you most about Smith's experience?

Knockout Blows Drill 5. **Match the Photo to the Technique**

Study the series of photos. Each shows a different defender and attacker position. Decide for yourself which techniques you could use in each situation, and then check your answers against the answer key (page 154). Note that each defender has more than one choice available. (Hint: Each defender will have at least five choices for each scenario). Include both techniques and targets and give as many choices as possible, not just physical strikes. You may choose any technique from the first 10 steps.

1. Defender pinned on back, choking

2. Defender sitting on couch, attacker facing and trapping one of defender's hands

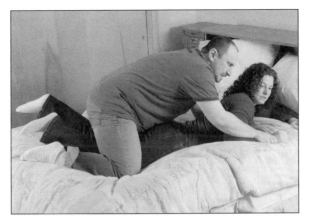

3. Defender lying in bed, attacker lying behind

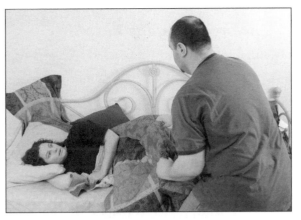

4. Defender lying on bed, attacker standing by side of bed

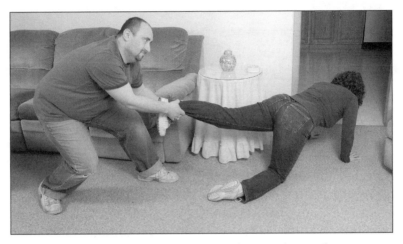

5. Defender on knees, trying to get away, attacker grasping one foot

Score Your Success

4 or 5 correct answers for one figure = 10 points each

2 or 3 correct answers for one figure = 5 points each

SUCCESS SUMMARY

Defenders rarely need to knock an attacker unconscious. If you do, remember the importance of your physical and emotional commitment, correct targeting and distance, and maximizing power by perfecting your physical alignment. Legal and ethical issues about knocking someone out are personal, and the choice is yours. Studying knockout blows gives you the choice to use these techniques should you ever have to. No points are awarded for style or finesse. Any attack that you survive and walk away from is a success.

Before Taking the Next Step

Before moving on to step 11, Dealing With Weapon Attacks, take time to reflect on what you have learned to this point. Answer the following questions honestly.

1. Have you drilled the Knee to Head both with and without a target?
2. Have you completed the Side Thrust Kick alignment checks?
3. Have you drilled the Side Thrust Kick for targeting and distance?
4. Have you drilled the Ax Kick?
5. Have you learned and practiced the three parts of ending an attack (look, assess, stomp)? Do you know what each is for?

If you answered yes to all five questions, you are ready to move on to step 11, Dealing With Weapon Attacks.

Taking the Step Further. *Homework Assignments*

Memorize both parts of the myth in this step and write about them in your Practice Journal. Share some of your thoughts and feelings about the myths and fact with at least one other person. Have you ever seen anyone get knocked unconscious in real life? What was it like? How was it similar to or different than knockouts you've seen on television? If not, what do you imagine it might be like? When might *you* choose to knock out an assailant?

Physical practice—Spend 5 to 20 minutes a day practicing the moves from step 10, Delivering Knockout Blows, including the Side Thrust Kick, Knee to Groin and Knee to Head, and Ax Kick until you begin step 11, Dealing With Weapon Attacks. Incorporate your voice with each technique. Your family and neighbors should be well acquainted by now with your *no* shouts!

Answer Key

Answers for Knockout Blows Drill 5. Match the Photo to the Technique (page 152)

1. Defender pinned on back, choking—Break Choke Hold, do Roll Off, Knee to Groin, Side Thrust Kick to face or groin, Ax Kick to head or groin

2. Defender sitting on couch, attacker facing and trapping one of defender's hands—Bite, Knee to Groin, Eye Strike, Heel Palm, Roll Off, drop to ground, Side Thrust Kick to knees, groin, face

3. Defender lying in bed, attacker lying behind—Bite, Roll Off, Scoot into Side Thrust Kick position on bed or drop to ground, Side Thrust Kick to knees, groin, head, Ax Kick

4. Defender lying on bed, attacker standing by side of bed—shout, get into Side Thrust Kick position, Side Thrust Kick to groin, knees, or head

5. Defender on knees, trying to get away, attacker grasping one foot—Turn in, Scoot in, Side Thrust Kick to face or groin, Switch, sit up to deliver Eye Strike or Heel Palm

Dealing With Weapon Attacks

For many people, being attacked with a gun is a worst case scenario. You only have to watch a handful of American movies or television shows to witness the enormous presence of guns in our culture, in our subconscious, and in our fears and fantasies. One recent evening, I flipped channels for an hour at 7:00 in the evening and saw 13 shootings and 46 threats with a weapon or recovery from a weapon attack. And I wasn't counting the news.

Any attack with any weapon is, of course, a very serious assault. It requires all of your attention, commitment, and willingness to stay in the moment. If you choose to fight physically, going from 0 to 100 percent will never be more important than in these assaults. But you might be encouraged to learn that, even in the United States, where it is relatively easy to purchase a gun, weapon attacks are by far the minority of assaults. According to the U.S. Department of Justice Criminal Victimization Survey of 2004, out of 5.2 million reported violent crimes, 78 percent were committed by unarmed offenders, 16 percent by someone with a weapon other than a gun, and only 6 percent by an offender with a firearm (U.S. Department of Justice, 2005). Given the underreporting of some of the most common types of violence (sexual assault, assault by an acquaintance or family member, and domestic violence), the actual percentage of weapons attacks may not be known. But, no doubt, it is far less common than other assaults and far less common than you'd imagine after an evening in front of the television. Even in the case of murders, only 68 percent of murders by strangers and 50 percent of murders by family members involve a firearm (Durose and Harlow et al., 2005).

Just as in any other type of assault, the choice of whether or not to defend yourself physically is always yours to make. There are no single right or wrong answers in any self-defense instruction, and choosing not to fight back if you believe you will be hurt worse is a valid and courageous choice. Step 11, Dealing With Weapon Attacks, incorporates written drills and real-life success stories that invite you to consider your own choices. Because of the severity of a weapon assault, step 11 also includes a drill that, for some students, may be the most difficult drill in the entire book.

One study compared 24 studies of the effectiveness of various self-defense strategies against sexual assault. Although fewer women resisted when the perpetrator used a weapon, when they did fight back, that resistance often effectively helped them avoid rape. Another study that looked solely at assaults by strangers with weapons found that "resisting was associated with a 52 percent greater chance of avoiding rape than not resisting. Seventy percent of those who did not resist were raped, while a much smaller number, 18 percent, of those who resisted were raped" (Fein, 1993).

> *Myth*   If the assailant has a gun, or you think that he might, you have to give up and do anything you're told so that you won't be killed.
>
> *Fact*   Firearms, although serious and dangerous, are not a sign that there is nothing you can do. Most people do not know how to aim and shoot a gun properly, and most gunshots are not fatal. No matter what the movies show you, it is extremely difficult to shoot a moving target accurately.

It's actually quite difficult to use a gun. Even police officers with years of training regularly miss their shots. Many who attempt suicide with a gun fail on their first attempt. Few people understand the kickback of a firearm and miss even at point-blank range. Most perpetrators who use weapons are relying on the victim's conditioned fear response to the intimidation of implied violence. If an attacker is using a weapon, he or she does not feel strong enough or brave enough to face you without one. The attacker is frightened of you and dependent on the weapon. Although, of course, you will react to the presence of a weapon with fear and adrenaline, unlearning some of these myths can help you decide what strategies are available to you.

ESCAPE

Escape is an excellent choice for defense against a weapon. The first element to escaping a weapon attack is to get out of the range of the weapon. The range of a knife attack is the length of the attacker's arm. An attacker with a bat can reach slightly farther. With a firearm, the attacker's range is, of course, even farther away. Should you choose to escape from someone with a gun, run in a zigzag pattern rather than a straight line (figure 11.1). It's very difficult to hit a moving target and even more difficult to hit a target moving in an unpredictable pattern.

Figure 11.1   Escape

APPROACH

1. Protective stance
2. Trust your intuition

a

EXECUTION

1. At first sign of weapon, run and shout *NO!*
2. Zigzag

b

FOLLOW-THROUGH

1. Zigzag—use cars, houses, trees, etc. as barriers
2. Stop only if assured of safety

c

Even if you are wearing heels, you can escape by running. Remember, you can always kick off your shoes. In an adrenalized state, it's unlikely you would even notice what shoes you were wearing.

The timing of the escape defense is important. Ideally, bolt in the other direction at the very first sign of a weapon. You hope to avoid getting cornered and to maximize your distance from the attacker. Even if you are shot at while running away, you are safer than being shot at while in close range, and you are safer than if you are forced into a car with the attacker. If attacked by a stranger whose goal is property or money, you can buy yourself some time by dropping your purse, backpack, wallet, or car keys as you run.

To complete your escape, you need to get to safety. This could mean getting to a police station, enlisting the help of several people on a crowded city corner, getting to your car and driving away, or requesting an escort to a domestic violence shelter. Victims of domestic violence in particular tend to have difficulty accurately assessing safety. If your drunken partner threatens you with a knife and then wakes up repentant and promises to never do it again, you have not yet gotten to safety. It may be very tempting to relax. It's exhausting to live in a state of terror, to know your life is in danger. People in refugee camps, prisons, and abusive relationships feel the effects of that hypervigilance for many years. You can use the help of professionals—such as police, therapists, and other survivors who have escaped—to help you assess whether you've gotten to safety yet.

Misstep

The most common and natural misstep is freezing.

Correction

Breathe. Go from 0 to 100 percent. Even if your head is saying "This can't be happening," run.

Have you ever heard an alarm go off in your school or office building and done nothing? I have on several occasions. The first thing I did was look around me, and, when no one else leapt to their feet and rushed out the door screaming, I figured everything was probably OK. The problem was that those people were looking at me and basing their choices on *my* lack of reaction as well. So far, I've been lucky enough to have been a part of several false alarms instead of several fires to which I failed to react. This inability to react affects many victims of assaults. Denial, fear, and the fight-flight-freeze response all work together to keep a victim standing in front of a perpetrator, even in broad daylight with adequate help nearby.

Defending Against Weapons Drill 1. *Escape*

For some, this could be the most difficult drill in the book. For this drill, you walk on a street with other people present whom you do not know. Scream for no reason whatsoever, change directions from the way you had been walking, and run away as fast as you can in a zigzag pattern. You must be seen by strangers for this to count. If you happen to be a large, male martial artist or football player, point to a beagle, shriek in pretend terror, and run away as fast as you can. Obviously, you should not run into traffic for this drill. And be prepared for some serious stares.

To Decrease Difficulty

- Do it with a friend who screams and runs with you.

- Photocopy this page and take it along as evidence to prove your sanity.
- Go back afterward and explain to the beagle walker why you did this.

To Increase Difficulty

- Drop an empty wallet, bag, or purse behind you as you escape.
- Choose a very crowded street or neighborhood.

Success Check

- Shout *no*.
- Change directions. Don't just move from a walk to a run in the same direction.

- Be seen by strangers who don't understand what you're doing.
- Run at least a block or around a corner. Going 5 feet (1.5 m) and then laughing doesn't count.

Score Your Success

Completing the drill = 100 points

Completing the drill without screaming = 50 points

In February of 2004, an 11-year-old girl was kidnapped, raped, and murdered in Florida. The story made the national news for a week, perhaps because she'd been abducted outside of a car wash with a security camera. The soundless camera footage was extremely disturbing. It showed an adult male talking to the girl for a few moments and then grasping her forearm and leading her away. The girl was unable to run away from him, not because she lacked the size, weight, or strength, but because she appeared terrified, adrenalized, frozen, and unsure. Your willingness and ability to throw caution to the wind, make a scene, scream your head off, and run away as fast as you can may save your life. And it requires practice.

ASSESS LETHALITY

Another self-defense skill to deal with weapon attacks is to assess the particular attack for lethality. How likely is it that this person is willing and able to kill you? Unfortunately, we frequently get vastly differing recommendations about responding to lethal attacks, such as "never fight back," "always fight back," "don't make him angry," or "go ballistic." This is partially because there are many types of assailants with weapons, and each has a different motivation, skill level, and likelihood of delivering on a threat to kill.

One of the international experts in assessing lethality is Gavin De Becker, best-selling author of *The Gift of Fear and Other Survival Signals That Protect Us From Violence.* This book is an excellent resource for any individual who wants to learn more about predicting and preventing violence. In his book, De Becker reveals four important categories to consider when you have received a threat of violence, whether from an abusive ex-husband, disgruntled former co-worker, or international terrorist. He suggests asking the following questions about the perpetrator's perceptions (De Becker, 1997):

- Perceived justification—Does the person feel justified in using violence?
- Perceived alternatives—Does the person perceive that he has available alternatives to violence that will move him toward the outcome he wants?
- Perceived consequences—How does the person view the consequences associated with using violence?
- Perceived ability—Does the person believe he can successfully deliver the blows or bullet or bomb?

The perpetrator who is most likely to shoot you is not merely "the one with a gun." It is the one who believes he is justified and has no acceptable alternatives to get what he wants. This attacker believes there are no consequences to violence (or only acceptable consequences) and that he or she has the means and the ability to commit violence.

Misstep

Ignoring your gut feeling that a threat or a person is serious and that you are in danger.

Correction

Trust your instincts and get help. If you sense something is wrong and you are not taken seriously, go somewhere else for help. Keep asking until you get good help. This can take a while.

Defending Against Weapons Drill 2. *Assessing Lethality*

Read the following three scenarios. Answer the questions for each perpetrator in your Practice Journal. Ask yourself whether you think this individual is likely to follow through on his threat and use violence. Although there may be many answers and shades of gray, focus on the evidence you have available to you in order to assess the perpetrator's future possible actions. After you've completed all three scenarios in the drill, check your answers in the answer key (page 167).

Coworker

Sam and Cathy had worked together for 2 years. They had little contact but were friendly and had spoken on the phone a few times over the weekend. Sam began calling and e-mailing frequently with long stories about his recent break-up, abusive childhood, and the troubles he was having at their office (he'd been written up twice for poor performance). She told him to back off, but he continued to write, frequently asking to meet Cathy after work. She went once, felt very uncomfortable, and later wrote Sam, telling him to cease contact entirely or else she would report him to human resources for harassment. Sam wrote twice more, including the sentence, "I can't believe you'd do this to me. Don't you care about what happens to me at all?" Cathy sensed that he was deeply depressed and wondered if he might try to harm himself or her. In his last e-mail to her, Sam said, "If you don't meet me after work today, I'm over you. One more talk. That's all I'm asking. Don't you think you owe me that?"

What is Sam threatening to do?

Justification: Does Sam think he is justified in using violence? How do you know?

Alternatives: Does Sam think he can get what he wants without violence? How do you know?

Consequence: What does he think the consequences of violence would be? How do you know?

Ability: Does he believe he can successfully deliver on his threat? How do you know?

Do you think Sam is likely to use violence? Why or why not?

Separated Husband

Dave and Jenny were married for 13 years. For the last 10, he was increasingly violent and abusive to her and their children. Twice, Jenny was hospitalized after Dave beat her, and there were many other trips to the emergency room. Although he threatened to kill her if she ever left him, Jenny initiated divorce proceedings and filed a restraining order against him. She hasn't seen him in over a month, although he has been mailing love letters and pleas to change her mind to both the house and to her lawyer's office. About 2 weeks after she began attending a self-defense class at a karate studio, she got an envelope at the house regarding Dave's recent application for a firearm license.

What is Dave threatening to do?

Justification: Does Dave think he is justified in using violence? How do you know?

Alternatives: Does Dave think he can get what he wants without violence? How do you know?

Consequence: What does he think the consequences of violence would be? How do you know?

Ability: Does he believe he can successfully deliver on his threat? How do you know?

Do you think Dave is likely to use violence? Why or why not?

Teenager on the Street

You've seen this young man on the street outside your office building several times in the past year. You assume that he's homeless. You've given him a dollar or two before when he asks you, even though you wonder uncomfortably if he's going to spend it on drugs. After working late one night, he approaches you outside the building with his hands in his jacket pockets. He seems unusually sweaty, anxious, and jumpy. He begins by asking, "How was work? Do you remember me?" Then he says, "Look, I need your wallet and your PIN number. Don't act surprised and don't be a jerk. I need it. If you don't, I can shoot you, you know." He gestures toward your chest with his pocket, and you wonder if he really has a gun.

What is the young man threatening to do?

Justification: Does the young man think he is justified in using violence? How do you know?

Alternatives: Does he think he can get what he wants without violence? How do you know?

Consequence: What does he think the consequences of violence would be? How do you know?

Ability: Does he believe he can successfully deliver on his threat? How do you know?

Do you think the teen is likely to use violence? Why or why not?

To Decrease Difficulty

Do this drill with others and discuss your thoughts and answers.

Success Check

- Answer all questions.

- Read and compare your answers to those in the answer key.

- If anything confuses you, discuss it with someone else and compare your thoughts and feelings.

Score Your Success

3 out of 3 correct answers to all three final questions = 60 points

2 out of 3 correct answers to final questions = 40 points

1 out of 3 correct answers to final questions = 20 points

No correct answers to final questions = 0 points

In addition to De Becker's assessment questions, also consider the following when attempting to assess the lethality of any particular attack or attacker:

- **Do you know this person?** Perpetrators of violence, with or without weapons, are more likely to know their victims than not.

- **Has he or she threatened you before?** Most violence is planned, not a sudden, uncontrollable outburst. Previous threats may indicate that this person has been planning an assault. Gavin De Becker refers to the choices of men who kills their wives and partners as "America's most predictable murders."

- **Has he hurt you or others before (others may include ex-partners, children, and ani-**mals)? If yes, he has already indicated a willingness to use violence as a tool to get what he wants. And he may have come to believe that the consequences of that violence (or the lack of consequences) were worth it.

- **Are you willing to hurt this person in your own defense?** If you are not willing to hurt this person (and many victims are not), then you are in much more danger than the victim who is willing to injure an attacker. Knowing that you are not willing to hurt the attacker is an extremely important piece of information. The attacker may be able to assess this as well. What can you do to escape instead?

Overcoming Fear of Weapon Attacks

Fear of weapons is real and powerful. My students have a lot of emotions when we discuss this topic.

"Well, this is totally my worst fear," one student confessed. "I've always had nightmares about being shot, even when I was really little. And ever since 9/11, when they crashed those planes with box-cutters! I mean, I would've definitely been frozen in my seat if I was on those planes!" If you share this sentiment, you are not alone; many people are terrified of weapons, and not just guns. You might want to review some of the statistics in this step to remember the relative rarity of these assaults. It may also be helpful to remember that most people who are shot do not die from their wound. But if intellectual knowledge doesn't help with this fear, consider taking a full contact self-defense class such as the one mentioned below. You will also benefit by doing the visualizing success drill on page 165.

From another student: "I'm so glad I took my IMPACT weapons class last year. Basics [the Introductory IMPACT class] was great; I felt safer after I graduated. But, at the same time, I was aware that in my neighborhood there are a lot of addicts, a lot of desperate people with guns, a lot of nuts really. I needed to demystify weapons, to be able to hold them and see how they look and feel. I learned that I could handle even a gang-banger if I ever had to. I hope I never have to! But I love knowing that I could, that I'd still have choices even if they have a gun." That's great news! Anyone interested in an advanced IMPACT class can contact a chapter in their area to register for a weapons defense class. Having the experience of physically practicing defenses against weapons and getting to handle them can take away the paralysis of fear.

BARGAIN AND LIE

Bargaining with someone who is holding a weapon calls on many skills. You need to stay at 0 percent, as discussed in step 7 Fighting From the Ground (page 96). You also can rely on your verbal self-defense skills from step 2, Defining Your Space. You want to give the perpetrator the feeling that he is about to get what he wants. Some lies might include, "I'll do anything you want if you just put the gun down," "If you move the knife away, I can get up and show you where my purse is," "I promise not to scream," "Yes, my roommate's asleep upstairs," "I'm sorry I shouted, you frightened me," or "Can I just go to the bathroom first?"

Your goal is to get the attacker to put down or let go of the weapon long enough for you to get an opening and go to 100 percent. You may have an opportunity to escape or to kick the weapon out of range while you focus your counterattack on the perpetrator. It is to your benefit that the attacker will probably in that moment be more focused on the weapon than on you. You may

take this opportunity to focus entirely on disabling him or escaping from him.

Here's an ingenious suggestion from Dr. Judith Fein, from her book *Exploding the Myth of Self-Defense*. When you are faced with an armed assailant who is trying to force you into a vehicle, she suggests a combination of lying, waiting at 0 percent, and physical strikes. "I suggest feigning a faint. You simply pretend to pass out. If you have ever observed the police trying to carry off a protestor, you would notice that it takes several police officers to carry off a single limp demonstrator. If the rapist still wants to cart you off, he will have great difficulty trying to do so with one hand. Therefore, when you feel two hands on you, the gun isn't in his hands any longer and you will have your opportunity to immediately physically incapacitate him" (Fein, 1993).

I must admit, I don't know if I could make myself close my eyes in this scenario. But her suggestion has a lot of merit. And how empowering to realize that, even if you accidentally faint in reaction to an adrenaline rush, it could work to your advantage!

GRAB AND KICK

You may wind up fighting back physically against an attacker with a weapon. Perhaps you will choose to attack fast and early at the first sight of the weapon. Perhaps you do not have an escape route, or you see an opening when the weapon is dropped or laid aside. Grab the attacker's hand, the one holding the gun, knife, or bat, with both of yours and hang on (figure 11.2). Keep your arms locked and straight and thrust the weapon away from your head.

Figure 11.2 | Grab and Kick

APPROACH

1. Protective stance
2. See the weapon

EXECUTION

1. Grab the weapon hand
2. Shout *NO!*
3. Move in swiftly to kick knees, groin, or head

a

b

(continued)

Figure 11.2 (continued)

FOLLOW-THROUGH

1. Continue to knockout blow

2. Look, assess, shout *NO!*

3. Maintain control of the weapon, pointing it away from yourself and the attacker

c

Misstep

Focusing on the weapon instead of the attacker.

Correction

Keep your eyes on your target. Your assailant will probably be focused on and distracted by the weapon, which is of benefit to you.

Misstep

Going from 0 to 25 percent. That is, struggling before you have an opening or attempting a strike silently or halfheartedly.

Correction

Once you have an opening, use the full force of your vocal and physical techniques to fight until you have fully knocked out or disabled the attacker and gained control of the weapon.

This is not the time to bargain or lie or attempt to escape. Just as you learned in step 5, Breaking Holds, turn in toward the attacker with all of your energy and commitment and use your feet and legs to disable or knock him out. Techniques that you might use in this position include the Front Snap Kick, Knee to Head, Knee to Groin, Ax Kick to the head or groin, or standing Side Thrust Kicks to the attacker's knees. It is essential that you move quickly and that you go from 0 to 100 percent with full commitment and full voice.

Your hands or arms could quite possibly be cut using this technique against an assailant with a knife. During a life-or-death struggle, cuts are unlikely to affect your ability to defend yourself. Py Bateman survived an extremely violent attack by a heroin addict with a knife, and she required surgery afterward. She writes that, at the time of the assault, "I never felt any pain while I was fighting. Not even when I cut my hand grabbing the knife by the blade. My consciousness was dominated by the determination to come out alive and my plans for how to do that" (Caignon and Groves, 1987).

Defending Against Weapons Drill 3.   *Visualizing Success*

Spend 5 to 20 minutes a day visualizing the four strategies for successfully defending against weapons. For each strategy (escape, bargain, assess, grab and kick), visualize an armed attack from beginning to end. Each ending should include an image of you free from all harm in a safe location. If you find that your visualizations tend to get out of control and you inadvertently see yourself being harmed, go back to the beginning and slowly visualize each successful move you make until you can see a positive outcome.

To Decrease Difficulty

Some students will find this drill easier if they write about it instead of visualizing. Write a short scenario (a page or so) in which you successfully use each of the four techniques. Use powerful and positive language about your success.

Success Check

- Visualize (or write about) each strategy at least once.
- If anything confuses you, discuss it with someone else and compare your thoughts and feelings.

Score Your Success

Earn 50 points per technique

SHOULD YOU CARRY A WEAPON?

I choose not to carry a weapon of any kind—guns, mace, pepper spray, brass knuckles, baseball bats, etc. There are several liabilities to carrying a weapon that I'm not willing to risk. First, any weapon can be taken away from you and used against you. I am particularly aware of this when it comes to firearms. Those of us who have not previously shot someone may find ourselves unable or unwilling to do so. And even a momentary freeze response on the part of the victim could result in the attacker's gaining control of the weapon.

In addition, most of us are unwilling or unable to keep weapons at hand. You cannot safely open a heavy door, grocery shop, pick up your son at daycare, parallel park, or walk a dog with pepper spray open, aimed, and ready in your hand, at least not without attracting a lot of attention! If you are about to be assaulted, the last thing you need to be doing is rustling through your purse or glove compartment looking for a weapon. This only distracts you from presenting a confident and aggressive front, watching for signs of the attacker's intention, and preparing your own defense. You need that time to get ready to strike.

And firearms are extremely dangerous to kids and others in your home. Emergency room physicians reported in *The New England Journal of Medicine* that "a gun in the home is 43 times more likely to kill a family member or acquaintance in an accident or suicide than it is to kill an intruder" (Kellermann et al., 1993). You may think that *you* are smart enough or skilled enough to prevent such an accident in your own home, but so did all of those people who lost a loved one.

If you do choose to own and carry a weapon, it is essential that you get professional training in its care and use. Take shooting lessons regularly to retain the skills you need. Learn the expiration date of any chemical weapons that you carry. Because using pepper spray or mace on a windy day could easily result in getting sprayed yourself, I recommend that you purposely spray yourself before you begin to carry these weapons. You should know what the results are, how it feels, and what medical help you will require if you are accidentally sprayed. You don't need to discover that information for the first time when you are actually fighting for your life.

Misstep

Allowing the possession of a weapon to give you false confidence.

Correction

Continue all of the awareness elements of self-defense and continue to practice all of the physical elements of self-defense, rather than relying solely on the psychological comfort of a weapon.

Marilyn's Story

Nine years ago, my ex-boyfriend pistol-whipped me with a gun. I knew he'd kill me, so I gave up. I promised him that the kids and I would move back in, and I let him rape me. I did everything he wanted, but the whole time I was thinking, thinking I had just about had it. I snuck out the side door after he passed out. Luckily, the kids were at his sister's place, so I went and got them and we all went straight to the shelter. It was the third time we'd stayed at the shelter, but hopefully the last.

It took me a long time afterward to get my self-respect back. I remember this one session with my therapist. She kept saying, "He raped you. You didn't 'let him rape you.' He had a gun. That's rape. He raped you." I did the right thing. It didn't feel like the right thing; it felt like just another lousy choice of mine. But now, when I work with other battered women, I can see that the choice comes when we leave. I didn't have a choice that last night he raped me, but I chose to run away and to do everything it took to stay away. Now I know that what I did was self-defense too. I got away. I got my kids. We lived, and I tell the girls at the shelter now that's what success is—staying alive.

Defending Against Weapons Drill 4.   *Studying Success*

Answer the following questions in your Practice Journal. If you like, discuss Marilyn's Story and your answers with a friend or study partner.

1. When did Marilyn begin her self-defense?

2. How many kinds of self-defense did she use? List each one. Include the use of awareness and verbal, emotional, and psychological techniques, not just physical ones.

3. What might you have done differently in the same situation? Why?

4. What surprised you about Marilyn's experience?

5. What satisfied or empowered you most about her experience?

SUCCESS SUMMARY

These types of attacks bring together all of the self-defense skills you have practiced in previous chapters, from awareness and verbal techniques, to kicking and tracking skills, to the emotional skills of commitment and being willing and able to go from 0 to 100 percent. Practicing these skills full force, without apology, prior to the onset of a weapon assault gives you the physical, verbal, and emotional preparation you need to draw on these skills in the future.

Before Taking the Next Step

Before moving on to step 12, Defending Against Multiple Assailants, take time to reflect on what you have learned to this point. Answer the following questions honestly.

1. Have you completed the escape drill?
2. If you answered no, are you willing to complete it this week?
3. Have you completed the assessing lethality questions in your Practice Journal?
4. Have you completed the visualizing success drill?
5. Did your visualization include all four strategies?

If you answered yes to all five questions, you are ready to move on to step 12, Defending Against Multiple Assailants.

Taking the Step Further. *Homework Assignments*

Memorize the myth in this step and write about it in your Practice Journal. Share some of your thoughts and feelings about the myth and fact with at least one other person. Have you ever seen a gun or had someone point one at you? How did you react? Are there other actions you would like to take to address your concerns about weapons?

Answer Key

Answers for Defending Against Weapons Drill 2. Assessing Lethality (page 160)

Coworker

What is Sam threatening to do? Sam is threatening to continue harassing Cathy or to stop contacting her.

Justification: Does Sam think he is justified in using violence? How do you know? It's unclear. He has not specifically threatened violence to her, although he has indicated that he believes she "owes him" something.

Alternatives: Does Sam think he can get what he wants without violence? How do you know? The answer is probably not. He seems to want Cathy's time and attention, and he felt that outcome was threatened when he increased contact and she responded assertively.

(continued)

Consequence: What does he think the consequences of violence would be? How do you know? Cathy has told him she will report him to his employer, and, since he's already been written up twice, he may understand the consequences to be getting fired.

Ability: Does he believe he can successfully deliver on his threat? How do you know? He has the ability to continue contacting Cathy.

Do you think Sam is likely to use violence? Why or why not? The answer is probably not, although that does not mean his behavior is not a problem. Cathy might be best protected by keeping detailed records of his behavior and logging a formal complaint with her employer, particularly if the company has a sexual harassment policy and a history of responding appropriately to such complaints.

Separated Husband

What is Dave threatening to do? Dave is threatening to kill Jenny and possibly their children.

Justification: Does Dave think he is justified in using violence? How do you know? The answer is probably. He informed Jenny during their marriage of his plans to kill her if she left, and now she has left.

Alternatives: Does Dave think he can get what he wants without violence? How do you know? The answer is probably not. Because of the divorce, the restraining order, and Jenny's refusal to see him, Dave probably feels that violence is now his only option to control her.

Consequence: What does he think the consequences of violence would be? How do you know? It's unclear. He may feel that consequences are of no importance now that he has lost control of the victim.

Ability: Does he believe he can successfully deliver on his threat? How do you know? Yes, he has purchased a weapon and knows where Jenny lives and where her divorce lawyer works.

Do you think Dave is likely to use violence? Why or why not? Yes, he seems to have the justification and to see no alternatives or serious consequences, and he definitely has the ability to use violence.

Teenager on the Street

What is the young man threatening to do? He is threatening to rob you or shoot you, or both.

Justification: Does the young man think he is justified in using violence? How do you know? He may feel that he is justified in taking money because of his intense need, particularly if he is addicted to drugs.

Alternatives: Does he think he can get what he wants without violence? How do you know? Yes, he has asked you indirectly to comply without violence and seems to hope that violence will not be necessary to get your money.

Consequence: What does he think the consequences of violence would be? How do you know? It's unclear, but he is either aware of the consequences of showing the weapon (increased jail time) or worried enough about consequences that he does not have a weapon.

Ability: Does he believe he can successfully deliver on his threat? How do you know? The answer is perhaps yes, perhaps no. His stating "I can shoot you" might be a sign that he's trying to convince himself.

Do you think the teen is likely to use violence? Why or why not? It's unclear. His primary motive seems to be cash rather than violence, but, if he is not able to get the money without violence, he may resort to it.

Defending Against Multiple Assailants

There's a lot of good news in step 12, Defending Against Multiple Assailants! First, assailants who attack a victim in pairs or groups are cowardly. They do not feel strong or confident enough to face you alone. This is of enormous psychological benefit to you from the outset. There are no new physical techniques in step 12 because you have already spent weeks practicing the exact body skills you can use to defend yourself successfully against attack by multiple assailants. Instead, you'll focus on successful strategies for confronting multiple assailants and ending these assaults as quickly as possible.

Just as discussed in step 11, Dealing With Weapon Attacks, know that you have more time and more options than you think you do. For example, most attacks by multiple assailants are planned, even more so than assaults by a single perpetrator. These pairs or groups are relying on a script in their heads about how the attack is supposed to progress, and that script does not include "The victim is going to fight back and I might get hurt." Giving even one small indication that you're going to be a danger to them disrupts their script and serves to make them instantly reconsider. It's not unusual for groups of assailants to flee after the defender delivers one strike against one attacker.

Myth   I'd have to study martial arts for 20 years to even begin to defend myself successfully against multiple assailants, like in that movie where that guy fights off 20 ninjas, doing the splits and kicking two of them in the face at once while he's punching another one! That's so cool!

Fact   Normal people without martial arts training, visual effects editors, or flying wires have successfully defended themselves against multiple assailants. Strategy is more important than speed or flexibility, and you only have to hit one perpetrator at a time.

FIRST STRATEGY: TARGET THE LEADER

There is always a leader. Someone in the group of aggressors thought this attack up and suggested it to the others. She or he may be the leader of a gang, the class bully, or the fraternity brother that everyone looks up to. The others are generally going along with the leader's plan and are not motivated enough to begin the assault without him or her. Every member of a group of assailants, including the leader, has less motivation to hurt you than you have motivation to protect yourself. And your motivation is a huge part of your success.

The ring leader may be the one talking, the one out front giving directions, the biggest, or the smallest. Trust your instincts to pick the leader. If in doubt, focus on the person who comes toward you first. Stay focused. Groups may try to distract you by touching you lightly from different directions or by trying to engage you verbally or visually. Keep your eyes on the leader and move fast, early, and powerfully to disable him or her.

Misstep

Hoping they'll change their minds or waiting until an attack has progressed to physical contact before you strike.

Correction

Trust your instinctual sense of danger if threatened by a pair or group. You are best protected if you hit first with full commitment. You do not have to wait until you have been hit or hurt.

SECOND STRATEGY: LINE THEM UP

Remember the skill of tracking that you practiced in step 2, Defining Your Space? If you skipped step 2 and jumped ahead to more difficult topics, go back and practice the tracking drill with a friend (page 21). Your goal in tracking is to stay in protective stance and remain facing the assailant even if she or he tries to circle around behind you. Lining up multiple attackers is advanced tracking. You move to keep the assailants lined up in front of you. The one closest to you should be blocking the second one behind him or her.

You may need to move faster and more often when tracking multiple assailants than when tracking a single assailant. Don't be afraid to circle them swiftly, at each moment keeping only one of them directly in front of you. If the second assailant is blocked by the first, you only have to fight one at a time. You have more time than you think you do. Increasing the length of time it takes an attacker to reach you, even by a second or two, works to protect you. See figure 12.1.

a

Figure 12.1 Defending against multiple attackers: *(a)* incorrect, defender between assailants.

Figure 12.1 *(continued)* *(b)* correct, assailants lined up.

Multiple Assailants Drill 1. *Lining Them Up*

Practice advanced tracking with at least three people. Make sure that each participant takes a turn as an attacker and as a defender. Begin with one defender and two attackers. Once you feel comfortable, add more attackers to the drill. You'll need a large enough area to move around in. Begin slowly at first and gradually increase in speed. The goal of the two attackers is to get the defender between them. The defender's goal is to keep both assailants lined up so that one is always directly behind the other.

To Decrease Difficulty

Begin more slowly and designate one of the two attackers as the leader.

To Increase Difficulty

- Use a smaller space or more people.

Success Check

- Remain in protective stance.
- Keep the attackers lined up in front of you approximately 80 percent of the time.

Score Your Success

Remain in protective stance = 50 points

Keep the attackers lined up = 50 points

THIRD STRATEGY: STANDING KICKS

Review the standing techniques from step 4, Kicking With Feet and Legs, and from step 10, Delivering Knockout Blows, including Knee To Groin, Knee to Head, and Front Snap Kick. An additional target to consider is the kneecap. If the attacker is in front of or to the side of you, you can deliver what is basically a standing Side Thrust Kick to the kneecap (figure 12.2).

Figure 12.2   Standing Side Thrust Kick to the kneecap.

Misstep

Doing too much at once, attempting several techniques but not fully committing to any.

Correction

One strike delivered at 100 percent power is worth much more than six strikes at only 50 percent power.

FOURTH STRATEGY: CHOOSE WHEN TO FIGHT AND WHEN NOT TO FIGHT

In any self-defense scenario, the decision to fight back is always up to you. There is no shame or disgrace in making the choice not to fight physically. Not only is this choice intensely personal, because of the wide variety of attacks and attackers, there is no "one size fits all" rule that I can give you about whether, when, or how to fight. Victims who choose to submit physically in order to survive an assault are doing the right thing for themselves and are to be honored.

In the first self-defense workshop I ever took, the teacher told us that she'd once successfully stopped a mugger from trying to steal her purse, but that she broke her toe in the process. She later came to feel that her purse wasn't worth it. It took her toe months to heal, and, although the pain wasn't terrible, it was enough of a bother that she later wished she'd let go of the purse. I was inspired by her story to realize that not every situation is worth fighting for.

Choosing not to fight physically does not rule out the other active and essential elements of self-defense. As nonviolent activists can attest, nonviolent responses to unprovoked violence can be profoundly healing and can even change the world around us. Survivors who choose not to fight physically are still defending themselves by strategizing, using verbal techniques, planning, waiting for an opening, staying in the present moment, and preparing for escape.

Some nonphysical methods of fighting back include the following:

Memorize the physical descriptions of the attackers.

Lie in a fetal position, with your arms in a Head Block and your back to a wall to protect your kidneys.

Instruct an ally to run for help while you distract the attackers.

Survive and connect with other survivors.

Become a self-defense instructor.

Learn karate with your sons and daughters.

Hire an excellent therapist and move from surviving to thriving.

Press charges and work to see that the perpetrators cannot hurt others.

Support other survivors as a counselor, volunteer, lawyer, doctor, or family member.

Write about your experience and donate some of the earnings to organizations for survivors.

Post flyers all over your neighborhood with pictures of the perpetrators.

Warn other women and girls about a rapist on campus.

Become a youth advocate offering safe and fun programs for young people after school.

Refuse to give up on your life.

Found a women's center, crisis line, or walk-along program on your campus.

Tell your story at a public speak-out for survivors during Sexual Assault Awareness month.

Transform your survival into art—paint, act, sing, or write about your experience.

Multiple Assailants Drill 2. *It's Your Choice*

What each of us is willing to fight for is an extremely personal decision. It is important to think deeply about your choices before you are confronted by danger. Considering ahead of time your risk factors, options, and priorities enhances your ability to respond quickly and clearly if you are threatened in the future.

Take some time to ponder the following circumstances and whether you would choose to fight back physically in each of them. Consider your own history, background, priorities, comfort level, and feelings. Score each question personally on a scale of 1 to 10 as follows:

1 = I would definitely defend myself/fight back any time this scenario was presented

3 = I would probably defend myself/fight back most times this scenario was presented

5 = I might defend myself, I might not, depending on the details of this circumstance

7 = I would probably not defend myself/fight back most times this scenario was presented

10 = I would definitely not defend myself/fight back and would attempt to comply with whatever the other person wanted

____ 1. A mugger in a ski mask with a gun demands that you give him your wallet or purse.

____ 2. A group of four young men demand that you give them your wallet or purse.

____ 3. A group of four young men at a party laughingly demand that you pull down your pants. They have you surrounded and seem quite drunk.

____ 4. Someone you can't see runs up behind you in a dark parking lot and knocks you to the ground.

____ 5. An assailant who has just thrown a punch at you grabs your own pepper spray out of your hand and attempts to use it against you.

____ 6. A man with a knife tells you to get into the back seat of his car and not to make a scene.

____ 7. You see a man and woman arguing in a crowded street and he begins to punch her in the head and stomach. When you ask her if she needs help, he starts cursing angrily at you.

(continued)

173

Multiple Assailants Drill 2. *(continued)*

___ 8. After a long and uncomfortable first date which you are very grateful is coming to an end, your date playfully locks all the car doors and then says she or he won't let you out of the car until you give her or him a kiss.

___ 9. Your spouse asks you to do something sexually that is far outside your own comfort zone. It is very important to your partner, who is thinking about leaving you if you say no.

___ 10. Shouting crazily, a man takes a swing at your partner in a crowded street.

___ 11. You catch the most respected member of your extended family with his hand inside a neighbor's child's pants.

___ 12. Over the past year, a coworker repeatedly walks up behind you and rubs your shoulders and back, winks at you, and wonders aloud if she or he can "do more for you."

___ 13. You're driving in an unfamiliar neighborhood with your kids (or someone else's) when a teenager with a gun points the weapon at you through the window and demands that you give him the vehicle.

___ 14. One of your least favorite coworkers or classmates offers to help you with some difficult work if you go out to dinner with him this weekend.

___ 15. One of your least favorite coworkers or classmates offers to help you with some difficult work if you go out to dinner with her this weekend.

___ 16. You're the only person at an ATM machine at night. You're approached by an agitated woman with her hand in her pocket. She tells you she has a gun and demands that you withdraw all of your money and give it to her.

___ 17. Someone breaks into your home and demands to know where you keep valu-ables, promising that no harm will come to you if you do not make any noise.

___ 18. Someone breaks into your home and threatens you with sexual assault, promising that no harm will come to you if you do not make any noise.

___ 19. A respected member of your school, workplace, or religious community hugs you every time he sees you. You dread this moment and wish it would stop happening.

___ 20. You are repeatedly told to work late for no extra pay. Your boss seems unstable and angry and not the kind of person to take no for an answer. It happens again on a night when you had been looking forward all week to going out with friends.

Were there any scenarios for which you weren't sure if you would be willing to defend yourself or fight back? Any that surprised you? Did the gender of the perpetrator make any difference to you? Or the presence of a weapon? Remember, there are no incorrect answers here.

I have worked with students who feel they would be willing to defend themselves in every situation a perpetrator could devise, and I have worked with students who would choose *not* to defend themselves physically in any of the previously described situations but who wanted to have the ability to do so if their children were similarly threatened. My students have varied reactions to this exercise. Here are some of their responses:

• "When I filled out the sheet about what I'd fight back for, I realized I would do anything to protect myself from rape or assault, and other people too, but I don't think I'd get physical just for money or my car or anything. How hard could it be to cancel my credit cards or file an insurance claim if my car is stolen? It's just not worth it." *I feel the same way. My bank card, my pin number, my car, my purse—the aggravation of losing and replacing these items might be great, but the risk to me of even a minor injury would not outweigh the benefits. But, for each scenario in which the perpe-*

trator threatened or implied harm to me or another person, I would be prepared to fight. For me, the defining factor is not whether there are multiple assailants or weapons present, but whether there is danger to myself or any other human being.

• "I was raped by two men when I was 13 and I didn't do anything right. I got into a car with them, I didn't scream, I didn't run, I didn't fight back. It's like I just froze up. There were all these people on the street and I didn't ask any of them for help. I can't stop remembering it and feeling like a failure. Why didn't I fight? What if it happened again?" *You did exactly the right thing, and I am so glad that you are alive. There are many reasons why you didn't fight—instinct, training, terror, a feeling that you might be hurt worse if you fought them. I suspect no one ever taught you as a child how to fight or even that you might someday need to fight. You did not fail. If it were to happen again you would have choices available to you now as an adult studying self-defense that weren't available to you as a 13-year-old. Surviving a trauma of this magnitude is a lifelong journey. Don't stop until you get the help you need to let go of blaming yourself. Experiment to find the help that works best for you. In my own life, letting go required many years of therapy, a safe spiritual practice, working with and listening to other survivors, confronting one of my*

perpetrators, and taking a padded attacker self-defense class. You can do it. It's worth it. You did the right thing.

• "I would fight if there were no weapons, but, if there were weapons, I'd do what they want. It's too scary. My stepdad always had guns in the house and I just know they terrify me. I freeze up sometimes just seeing someone with a gun on television." *I honor your choice. There are no right or wrong choices. You are already much further along in your training than most people because you are aware of your feelings, have thought deeply about your history and your willingness, and have thoughtfully considered your options. You're doing the right thing.*

Consider discussing your answers with friends or classmates. Notice if anyone has a very different response than yours. Notice if any of your responses are different today than when you were younger. Do you see any patterns? Is it easier or harder to imagine fighting back in those scenarios with individuals known to you?

Score Your Success

Complete It's Your Choice = 100 points

Discuss your answers with another person = 50 points

EXTREME GROUP VIOLENCE: GANGS, POLICE, MILITARY, PRISON

This book focuses primarily on defense against the most common types of violence in the United States outside of the prison system—attacks by a single, unarmed rapist or mugger. But there are some extreme types of attack by multiple assailants that deserve mention here in case you ever have to face them. Attacks by urban gangs, particularly those involved in the drug trade, attacks by police officers or militia or military groups, and group assaults against prisoners by guards or other prisoners do occur and require additional defense techniques.

If you have to live in a neighborhood ruled by gangs, in a city under militia rule, or in prison, your situation has much in common with the victims of batterers who hold them hostage. Your safety strategy, escape plan, and ultimate survival obviously require more than an Eye Strike. Some important questions to consider are the following: What are you willing to fight for? Who are your allies? If you have no allies, how can you find or make allies? What danger is imminent, and which dangers are still in the future? How might you minimize the severity of the violence directed at you? Has anyone ever escaped from your situation before? What did they do? How can you find out more about those who escaped and survived? What specific non-self-defense actions can help keep up your spirits while you survive? Who can help you?

Barbara Richmond survived an attack by an angry mob in another country and then an intended beating and torture by local police (Caignon and Groves, 1987). She was able to escape from the mob and she chose to submit to the police. Eventually, she successfully used verbal techniques to secure her release from the police.

Stephen Donaldson was raped by multiple assailants in prison and went on to create meaning out of this devastating experience by surviving and publishing "Hooking Up: Protective Pairing for Punks" (Donaldson, 2006). He went on to become the president of Stop Prisoner Rape, an organization founded by other survivors of rape behind bars. They offer prisoner resource guides and other advice from prisoners and survivors at www.spr.org/en/ppadvice.asp. His suggestions and information about prison culture in general could be helpful to anyone facing imprisonment.

12-Year-Old Hero

"My daughter, who is now 12, took the KidPower workshop 3 years ago. Recently, we moved to a smaller town to get away from the violence in the city. My daughter was very excited about going to her first formal dress-up dance at her new school. It must have been poorly supervised, because a group of about 15 ninth-grade boys started playing a game in which they captured girls by linking arms in a circle around them.

"The first time my daughter and her seventh-grade friends were surrounded, they just moved away. They felt awkward about this game, but this was their first time at a school dance and they didn't know what to think. My daughter saw that three other girls who got captured later were disheveled and crying. She saw the boys pawing at the girls and making sexual remarks.

"Then she and her friends were surrounded again. This time, one boy grabbed our daughter from behind and tried to put his hand up her shirt. She stomped on his foot and elbowed him in the groin.

"This action broke the circle and my daughter and her friends were able to escape. It also stopped the behavior of the boys, and they left all the girls alone for the rest of the dance. The story went through the school that my gentle seventh-grade daughter had beaten up a ninth-grade boy! She was a hero! A number of girls have come up to her to tell her how glad they were that she did what she did and to ask her for advice on what they might do.

"My husband and I have written a letter to the school, describing the incident and demanding that preventative action be taken through better supervision of school events and training for both the boys and the girls. We believe that our daughter's KidPower training, even after 3 years, helped her handle an awful experience in a way which left her feeling empowered instead of helpless."

Used by permission of Kidpower Teenpower Fullpower International, a nonprofit agency dedicated to bringing self-protection and confidence skills to people of all ages and abilities. Kidpower was founded in 1989 by a mother who defended her children from a man who was threatening to kidnap them. www.kidpower.org

Multiple Assailants Drill 3. *Studying Success*

Answer the following questions in your Practice Journal. If you like, discuss 12-Year-Old Hero and your answers with a friend or study partner.

1. When did the girl begin her self-defense? When did her parents?

2. How many kinds of self-defense did they use? List each one. Include the use of awareness and verbal, emotional, and psychological techniques, not just physical ones.

3. What might you have done differently in the same situation? Why?

4. What surprised you about this girl's experience?

5. What satisfied or empowered you most about this survivor's experience?

SUCCESS SUMMARY

Step 12, Defending Against Multiple Assailants, gathers together all of the techniques of previous steps and adds some new strategies, including targeting the leader, lining up the group members, using standing kicks, and choosing when to fight. You've analyzed in depth your own personal values and choices about what you are willing to fight for, and you've gotten some resources for scenarios of extreme group violence.

Before Taking the Next Step

Before moving on to step 13, Continuing Your Training, take time to reflect on what you have learned to this point. Answer the following questions honestly.

1. Have you learned the four strategies for defending against multiple assailants?

2. Have you drilled the technique of lining up the group members?

3. Have you assessed which of the techniques learned in previous steps could be used for standing kicks?

4. Have you completed the questions in It's Your Choice and asked yourself if there's anyone you'd like to talk with about your answers?

If you answered yes to all four questions, you are ready to move on to step 13, Continuing Your Training.

Taking the Step Further. *Homework Assignments*

Memorize the myth in this step and write about it in your Practice Journal. Share some of your thoughts and feelings about the myth and fact with at least one other person. What looks unrealistic to you in the movies about fights against multiple assailants?

Set a date by which you'd like to complete the final chapter, step 13, Continuing Your Training.

Congratulations! You have completed all of the action chapters in *Self-Defense: Steps to Survival!* What will you do to celebrate yourself? I think you deserve a gift—dinner out with friends, some item you've always wanted, a quiet afternoon at home with a good book, season tickets. You deserve it; you've worked hard!

Continuing Your Training

Congratulations! You did it! I hope you're feeling confident, strong, and safe. Working through *Self-Defense: Steps to Survival* has taken time, courage, willingness, and a great deal of effort.

You have a lot to be proud of! This final step now invites you to consider your future choices for continuing to build on the training you've begun.

Myth   There's nothing I can do to end violence in our lifetime. That's just the way it is in the 21st century. Rape will always happen, criminals will always exist, the best we can hope for is to lock our doors, stay inside, and get lucky.

Fact   It's not so. The combined efforts of everyone working to end sexual violence has resulted in a reported decrease in rapes of 64 percent in the year 2005 (Bureau of Justice Statistics, 2005). In the past 20 years alone, enormous strides have been made in legislation, awareness, and access to support services for survivors. Yes, violence is still common, but there are many things we can do to make ourselves, our families, and our communities safer.

Change is happening, and it's happening faster than you might believe. I've noticed it even in my own lifetime. When I watch popular movies from the 1970s depicting "love" relationships between men and women, I notice instantly a level of disrespect and verbal and physical violence against women that is no longer considered generally normal and acceptable in the U.S. media. Yes, we have a long way to go. But progress is evident all around us. By studying *Self-Defense: Steps to Survival*, you have become a part of that progress. You have made the world a safer place by learning how to defend yourself from violence.

The Canadian men who founded the White Ribbon Campaign (www.whiteribbon.ca) are a great example of everyday community members seeing an intolerable situation and choosing to make a difference. On December 6, 1989, a gunman in Montreal murdered 14 young women engineers. Many people responded. Some worked to change and enforce laws governing the sale of automatic weapons in Canada, some worked to draw attention to the murderer's hatred of women and feminists, some chose to double their efforts to end domestic violence and bring batterers who murder to justice.

One group of men responded by forming the White Ribbon Campaign. In their words, "In 1991, a handful of men in Canada decided we had a responsibility to urge men to speak out against violence against women. We decided that wearing a white ribbon would be a symbol of men's opposition to men's violence against women. . . Wearing a white ribbon is a personal pledge never to commit, condone, or remain silent about violence against women." They now publish education and action kits and provide curriculum materials to secondary schools in Ontario, encouraging boys and men to refuse to be violent and to speak out against violence.

We don't have to give up, and we don't have to live our lives in fear. I have a friend who never walks in the woods because she's afraid of assault. I know her ex-husband, and I can tell you she's safer in the woods than she is dropping off her kids for weekend visitation. We don't have to let the assailants steal the world from us. One of my favorite success stories in *Her Wits About Her* is Joan Joesting's. She sums up many experiences of harassment and successful defense with this truth: "I have bicycled over 13,000 miles in three countries in all types of areas. Using these [techniques], I have avoided rape while on the roads and have had much more fun than I ever dreamed possible. If I had listened to all the people who had warned me about rape, I would have missed the experience of a lifetime" (Caignon and Groves, 1987).

Choices for Continuing Your Training

Place a check mark next to any items that interest you or might interest you in the future.

_____ Tell someone else about this book and your experience with it.

_____ Meet weekly, monthly, or quarterly to review this book with your study partners.

_____ If you studied alone, start a group to study it together. The others will thank you!

_____ Physical practice—spend 5 to 20 minutes each day or each week practicing your moves. Remember to incorporate your voice with each technique.

_____ Go to KatyMattingly.com to read more self-defense success stories and share your own!

_____ Go to an IMPACT class graduation to witness full force techniques in action.

_____ Go to an IMPACT Web site and watch a video of a class in action.

_____ Take an IMPACT class or contact a chapter to host a class in your city.

_____ Take a realistic padded attacker course.

_____ Buy and read *Her Wits About Her* for inspiration and heroines.

_____ Buy and read *The Gift of Fear.*

_____ Continue to say *no* weekly to something you'd normally go along with.

_____ Watch movies for self-defense opportunities: search for openings, techniques, and strategies you'd use and point out to others what the victims could do to defend themselves.

_____ Continue to use your Practice Journal to review techniques, to complete boundary setting homework, and to note challenges and successes.

_____ Find a skilled therapist with whom you feel comfortable. It's normal to need help.

_____ Go back to your Personal Safety Assessment and look for any further changes you'd like to make in your relationships at work, at home, or in your community.

_____ Read the success stories of domestic violence survivors at wadv.org/Survivors.htm.

_____ Sign up for a martial arts class.

_____ Take a course in meditation to practice staying in the present moment.

_____ Outline a physical security plan (changing keys, locks, learning to change a tire, etc.).

_____ Take up a sport, join a local team, or look for lessons.

_____ Attend a 12-step meeting for people affected by alcohol, adult children of alcoholics, survivors of incest, or others to meet other survivors and ask how they did it.

_____ Contact your local domestic violence shelter for help filling out your safety plan.

_____ Join a support group for survivors of violence.

_____ Run for public office on an anti-violence platform.

_____ Volunteer at your local women's shelter, crisis line, or support agency.

_____ Make a donation to an organization that helps victims to regain control of their lives.

_____ Ask your school, college, or university to offer for-credit coursework in self-defense.

_____ Other

Pick one item you checked off in the list and set a timeline for when you'd like to achieve it.

Self-defense and personal safety are a lifetime project. Here are examples of how some previous students have chosen to continue their training.

• "I've always wanted to learn karate. Studying self-defense just makes me even more interested. I feel more confident now that I could learn something hard, even spar with men. And I like the idea of continuing to build up my balance and body awareness. I'm definitely rereading that list [see NCASA guidelines under Resources in Self-Defense Today, page xxiii] before I interview the karate school next week. Now that I'm not so scared, I want a chance to practice physically with other people!"

• "I found an IMPACT [padded attacker] class and took the four-day Basics program. It was totally amazing. I knew a lot of the moves, but the chance to do them on the instructor in the suit made it so real! Now I know that I can do it. I know it in my body, not just in my mind's eye. Feeling that kind of power in my legs and my arms, seeing that mugger go down when I knocked him out, it's just incredible. I think everyone should take this class!"

• "I decided after your class to tell my husband that I was raped in college. That was hard; he's still really upset. But I actually feel better. I had no idea it was so common, so many people [in our class] said it happened to them too. I didn't realize how hard it was to carry that around as a secret in my head. I feel free now, more than I have in a long time."

• "The best part of this class for me was sharing it. Every handout you gave I'd make copies and give them to my wife and kids. I signed up my teenage daughters last summer and talked to their friends' parents too. I just think we have to get this information to as many kids as possible. This fall, I'm bringing somebody in to talk to the high school health class about safety. In fact, I think even the girls would tell you that it's making me a better dad. I used to be so anxious when they'd go out; now I know that they can handle themselves in most situations, and they know that they can ask me for help. Thank you."

Success Story

Even one person can make a huge difference in the world. In the following success story, a woman in Little Rock, Arkansas, went to incredible lengths on behalf of a young neighbor who was being brutally attacked. Not only did she save that woman's life, she went on to share her story and inspire thousands of us with her courage and her refusal to give up. Just knowing about her success has made me a more courageous human. The headline in the *San Francisco Chronicle* read: "65-Year-Old With a Cane—Disabled Editor Routs Rapist."

"I don't have courage. My heart was in my throat, but you can't stand by and watch while someone gets hurt, and he was killing her." Ms. Babcock, a disabled World War II veteran who wore a brace on her leg, had recently been released from the hospital after having open heart surgery. When she heard her neighbor screaming, she ran down a flight of stairs and attacked the perpetrator with her cane. She cursed him and attracted other helpers with her shouting. At one point during the fight, the attacker fell to his knees in front of a car, and Ms. Babcock opened the door and slammed it repeatedly against his head and leg. She helped the victim escape, assisted her with pressing charges against the assailant, and went onto a daytime talk show to spread the word about women's safety.

SUCCESS SUMMARY

You have now completed an intensive and realistic self-defense training program. You have learned the truth about the perpetrators and victims of violence and unlearned some of the most common and pervasive myths about why violence occurs and how to avoid it. You have studied and practiced both basic and advanced awareness skills—ones to use on the street, at home, and in your personal relationships. You've learned skills for setting boundaries, for deterring potential attackers with your words and your body language, and for sending a firm message to perpetrators out to "interview" potential victims. You have learned and physically practiced techniques for striking with your hands, arms, feet, and legs and studied how to apply those techniques whether standing, sitting, or lying down. You have learned specific self-defense strategies for success, such as turning in, going from 0 to 100 percent, staying in the present moment, choosing to fight from the ground, and assessing and responding to early warning signs from assailants.

You have learned to avoid blows and escape from pins and how to knock out an attacker from a variety of positions using a variety of targets. You've analyzed strategies for responding to attacks from multiple assailants and assailants with weapons, and you have made an honest assessment of your fears, priorities, and plans given a number of self-defense scenarios. You are safer. You are stronger. You have choices.

Taking the Step Further. *Homework Assignments*

Memorize the myth in this step and write about it in your Practice Journal. Share some of your thoughts and feelings about the myth and fact with at least one other person. Do you have a hero who achieved something when no one else believed she or he could? Have you ever accomplished something in your personal life that you thought was impossible?

Do you know anyone who might benefit from feeling safer? Nobel Prize-winning author Toni Morrison wrote, "The function of freedom is to free someone else." Is there one person you'd like to tell about your journey through *Self-Defense: Steps to Survival?*

◨ **References**

Anonymous in Los Angeles. 1998. *Clothes and size are not destiny.* www.prepareinc.com.

Bass, E., and Davis, L. 1994. *The courage to heal: A guide for women survivors of child sexual abuse.* New York: HarperCollins Publishers.

Bureau of Justice Statistics. 1994. *Violence against women.* Rockville, MD: U.S. Department of Justice.

Bureau of Justice Statistics. June 2005. *Family violence statistics, including statistics on strangers and acquaintances.* U.S. Department of Justice, Office of Justice Programs. NCJ 207846. www.ojp.usdoj.gov/bjs.

Caignon, D., and Groves, G., eds. 1987. *Her wits about her: Self-defense success stories by women,* pp. 106–108, 111, 153–156, 164, 182-184, 212-213, 235, 245–253. New York: Perennial Library.

Catalano, S. M. 2004. *Criminal victimization.* U.S. Department of Justice, Bureau of Justice Statistics. NCJ 210674.

Danylewich, P. H. 2001. *Fearless: The complete personal safety guide for women,* p. 46. Toronto, Ontario, Canada: University of Toronto Press.

De Becker, G. 1997. *The gift of fear: survival signals that protect us from violence,* pp. 32, 33, 69, 97–98. Boston, MA: Little, Brown.

Donaldson, S. 2006. *Hooking up: Protective pairing for punks.* www.spr.org/en/ppadvice.asp

Durose, M., Harlow, C. W. et al. 2005. *Family violence statistics.* U.S. Department of Justice, Bureau of Justice Statistics. NCJ 207846.

Federal Bureau of Investigation (FBI). 2005. *Uniform crime reports: Preliminary annual uniform crime report, 2005.* www.fbi.gov/ucr/05cius

Fein, J. 1993. *Exploding the myth of self-defense: A survival guide for every woman,* pp. 53, 69, 71–72. Duncan Mills, CA: Durrance Publishers.

Kellermann, A.L. et al. 1993. Gun ownership as a risk factor for homicide in the home. *New England Journal of Medicine.* 329(15):1084–1091.

KidPower. No year. *From a mother.* www.kidpower.org/Success-stories.html

National Organization for Women (NOW). No year. *Violence against women in the United States.* www.now.org/issues/violence/stats.html.

Rape, Abuse, and Incest National Network (RAINN). No year. *Key facts.* www.rainn.org/statistics/index.html.

San Francisco Chronicle. 1987. *65-year-old with a cane—Disabled editor routs rapist.* July 31, 1987.

Tjaden, P., and Thoennes, N. November 1998. *Prevalence, incidence, and consequences of violence against women: Findings from the national violence against women survey.* National Institute of Justice, Centers for Disease Control and Prevention. www.ncjrs.gov/pdffiles/172837.pdf.

Ullman, S. E., and Knight, R. A. 1993. The efficacy of women's resistance strategies in rape situations. *Psychology of Women Quarterly.* 17(11):23–38.

United Nations Department of Public Information. No year. *Women and violence.* www.un.org/rights/dpi1772e.htm.

United States Department of Justice. No year. *Crime characteristics.* Bureau of Justice Statistics. www.ojp.usdoj.gov/bjs/cvict_c.htm.

United States Department of Justice. 1985. *The crime of rape.* Bureau of Justice Statistics bulletin.

United States Department of Justice. September 2005. *Criminal victimization 2004.* Bureau of Justice Statistics. NCJ 210674.

Warshaw, R. 1994. *I never called it rape.* New York: HarperCollins Publishers.

Zawitz, M. W. et al. 1993. *Highlights from 20 years of surveying crime victims: The National Crime Victimization Survey, 1973–92.* U.S. Department of Justice, Bureau of Justice Statistics.